GENERAL TEACHING METHODS IN COLLEGES

GENERAL TEACHING METHODS IN COLLEGES

Ed
Dr. Sita Ram Sharma

SHUBHI PUBLICATIONS
DELHI

ISBN 81-87226-73-0

First Indian Edition - 2002

With the blessings of LORD SHIVA.

Published by **SUBHI PUBLICATIONS,** F K 30, Shastri Nagar, Delhi-52 and distributed by **A.P.H. Publishing Corp.,** 5, Ansari Road, New Delhi, and printed at *Efficient Offset Printers*, 215, Shahzada Bagh, Industrial Comples, Ph-II, Delhi - 35.

PREFACE

The editor gratefully expresses its deep sense of gratitude to the university grants commission India, the British Council and the American Studies Research Center Hyderabad, for their kind permission to use their material extensively while preparing the book. Thanks are due to Sh. Sanjay of Shubhi Publicatione New Delhi for having thought to get a book on college teaching prepared for publication in India.

Dr. Sita Ram Sharma
Editor

CONTENTS

1(I)

TEACHING IN THE UNIVERSITY

THE practitioner of any vocation, be never so skilful, needs to pause, every now and then, to reflect upon the aims of his personal contribution to his chosen profession. Those who are beginning their careers as university teachers take them up as a rule after a period spent in research and at the point when they add teaching to research. They need to think about their teaching aims in order that their work may be directed to new ends. Those who have been teaching for a period of years may have fallen into a routine that has hardened too early and can, perhaps, recover elasticity by reflecting for a second time on the general aims of university teaching. And there are a few whose service has been so long that they have forgotten their original aims, so that these have become, as the poet Stephen Vincent Benet wrote, 'words used, kept in the pocket, rubbed shiny with use and forgotten'.

You could approach this question of the aims of university teaching by asking what are the expectations of students and how they should be met. Bruce Truscot, who wrote a number of controversial books about university life in the 1940s, did exactly this. His book *The first year at University* begins with a rhetorical question to an imaginary student, 'Well, here you are and what do you think of it all?' Whilst myself pursuing this attempt to link aims with expectations I discovered that a sharp contrast existed between my own expectations of university life and the expectations of my children, all of whom went up to the university a generation later. My own expectations were very high, even idealistic; but they were not disappointed. I supposed that I should meet at the university, in my chosen subject, professors whose reputations were international and I expected much more from such contacts than from my previous sixth form teachers. I hoped that I should quickly find myself at the research front of my subject. I expected that I should find in the university library a rich mine of literature that three years would be all too short a time to explore. I hoped to find an intellectually exciting life in the company of others like-minded which was disciplined, yet free from the immature restraints of a country grammar school. The realisation was actually better than my expectations. My professor's work was known from California to Tokyo; and even in my first year I not only listened to many of his lectures but spoke to him often and went more than once to see him at work in his research laboratory. The more spacious individual work of the laboratories was much more congenial than the crowded rooms at my school and I met there demonstrators who were generally working at the same time for a higher degree and these also, in time, took me into their confidence about their own researches.

The verdict of my children was different. In a generation universities had doubled in size at the same time as the research front in most subjects had receded beyond the vision even of the better graduates. Research itself was much more highly organised and promoted by large teams working in postgraduate departments now separated by a long gap from undergraduate work. In their first year at the university my children rarely saw a professor and never spoke to one. They thought that most of the teaching was less good than that given in their own sixth forms. Looking back at the end of their undergraduate course they expressed the view that their first year at the university was largely wasted. This verdict may be typical of a critical generation that has had to struggle less hard for a university education than an earlier generation but it certainly forces all university teachers to look closely at the aims of higher education and to see how far powerful social and economic forces are altering them.

A quite different approach to the question of aim was taken by the Committee appointed by the Prime Minister in 1961 under the chairmanship of Lord Robbins 'to review the pattern of full-time higher education in Great Britain'. It was, in fact, the approach of considering how universities had responded to the changes that had come over higher education in the course of a century. It selected three changes as of paramount significance. The first was the very remarkable change in the financial position of universities, including the steady growth of dependence upon government aid. The second was the rise of higher education in institutions other than universities; and the third was the very quickening of the desire for higher education on the part of the rising generation.

The Committee began its work by defining the four aims of higher education as follows.

(1) 'Higher education should give instruction in skills suitable to play a part in the general division of labour.' This is the economic aim; the need for higher education to meet national requirements and increase material prosperity.

(2) 'What is taught should be taught in such a way as to promote the general power of the mind.' This is an extension of the economic aim since at a time of technological change a nation will need leaders, particularly in administration and politics, who may be specialists but whose higher education has imparted to them practical techniques on the plane of generality that makes it possible for them to be applied to all problems of national life.

(3) The third aim is 'the advancement of learning'. This is the research aim, and the recognition that the search for truth as an essential function of higher education includes the belief that teaching in universities will be most vital whin it partakes itself of the nature of discovery.

(4) The fourth aim is the provision 'in partnership with the family, that background of culture and social habit upon which a healthy society depends'.

These four aims are all what I should describe as 'extrinsic' aims in higher education; they are very sound as far as they go but when they omit the basic 'intrinsic' aim, which is more important than any of them, their incompleteness can be seen. This is particularly the case in relation to the third, the research aim. Modern research, particularly in the sciences, develops at an immense pace. For example, the Gmelin *Handbook of Inorganic Chemistry* which records research activities, appeared in 1924 and not again until 1958 when it noted that in the interim there had been a production of 25,000 research works on zinc alone. Scientific research has solved many problems that seemed quite obscure in the middle of the century. But every solution of a problem has revealed new problems and new horizons. The riches of nature seem inexhaustible. The further the frontier of ignorance is pushed back by research the wider the field for further research is seen to be. Research pursued for the sake of research could therefore be simply an infinite regress. But if it were just this it would be a disappointing pursuit. The pursuit of truth is exciting but if it led to nothing but further pursuit it would be most unsatisfactory. Happily it does nothing of the kind. Every research reveals the created world as a world of pattern and order which can inspire genuine and enduring intellectual passion. The four extrinsic aims must be accompanied by a love of knowledge that is the central and 'intrinsic' aim of higher education. The university teacher must be a researcher but he must also love knowledge for no other reason than that it is lovable if his teaching is not to be dulled by extrinsic utilitarian aims.

If research is pursued for its own sake and not as a means to the end of knowledge, it can lead to the production of such a quantity of second-rate research that this clutters the ground and gets in the way of the researchers of genius. This has already happened in America. Higher education has expanded there faster than in most other countries of the world and the demand for teachers in higher education is always for individuals with a research degree. At almost any cost a graduate must find a research degree. At almost any cost a graduate must find a subject for research and write a research thesis in a year or two. As a result a flood of spurious or at best second-rate research literature fills the shelves of university libraries and gets in the way of first-rate research.

A different kind of imbalance between the demands of teaching and research can distort the undergraduate programme of study. A teacher who gives research a much higher priority than teaching may be more concerned to ensure that students learn the latest developments in his speciality than to use his subject as a means of developing the students' powers of thought. But a merely factual knowledge of the latest developments in a growing subject may be a wasting asset. What is more important is the development of mind and its training as this is defined in the second aim of the Robbins' Report.

In a different way, the emphasis in the first aim defined by the Robbins Committee can fall too heavily on the side of teaching and lead to the failure to produce research-minded students. The pursuit of this aim combined with the fact of the rapid expansion of knowledge has too often been the production of first degree courses that are overloaded with facts. The student then spends so much of his time memorising facts that he has insufficient time to master the principles underlying his subject and to develop his powers of conceptual thought. The only sure remedy for this evil is to keep the nature and content of courses under constant review in order to eliminate all unessential and obsolete material. And this may not be simply a matter of detailed pruning. There will also be occasions when the development of a subject makes it desirable to re-examine the whole approach to it in undergraduate courses.

An acceptance of the intrinsic aim of higher education is also necessary if the fourth aim of the Robbins Committee is to be realised. Universities will not contribute to the health of society unless they see their task as broader than that of only teaching and research. University teachers are bound to work in the field of abstraction if they are to give something better than merely short-term answers to politicians who are generally themselves looking too much for short-term solutions. Sociologists, anthropologists and political scientists must build up models of society that are in one sense artificial but which are nevertheless necessary if long-term social policies are to be formulated. Because so much of its teaching is in the realm of the conceptual, the university must always remind the society of which it is part that although the world is material yet mind is pre-eminent.

University teaching has necessarily to begin with what is tentative and it operates best in an atmosphere of criticism. The best research worker needs to consider even the naive and immature criticisms of undergraduates and that is why he should meet them as a teacher in both the lecture theatre and the tutorial group. The researcher who considers teaching to be a bore because it interrupts research will soon be replaced by undergraduates abler than he is whose criticisms he has failed to evaluate. Beginning with what is tentative and sceptical, university teachers always go on from research to the formulation of universal laws pronounced and taught with conviction. Only as they do this with a sense of social needs are the five aims of university teaching realised. When these aims are realised, the university then becomes a place where ideas powerful enough to transform the world are elicited, developed, tested and diffused.

1(II)

OBJECTIVES OF COLLEGE TEACHING

Since discussion of the college teacher's activities requires a frame of reference, the logical way to begin is with a statement of the goals of instruction. Actually few matters pertaining to college teaching are more difficult to state. Professional experience may qualify a teacher to speak with authority on specific aspects of instruction, but what gives him the same right to determine goals? What *are* the right goals of teaching? Few questions produce a greater diversity of answers, and originality here is not a criterion of worth. Yet if education is to be conducted with any measure of consistency there should be common effort at understanding and agreeing upon objectives.

The goals of college teaching proposed here are not presumed to be the sole, true, or "right" goals. All that is claimed on their behalf is that they are reasonable and that they could be right, and even this the reader must judge for himself. The following criteria may assist in making such judgment:

1. Are the proposed goals important and feasible? Do they seem justified by the arguments offered in their support?
2. Are they mutually consistent and do they contribute to an organized conception of college teaching?
3. Are they sufficiently clear and definite to serve as a practical guide to teaching and learning?

There is no feeling of assurance that the goals will be accepted as offered nor any wish that they should be. Educational progress results not from ready concurrence but from giving hard thought to important issues. Independent exploration and assent are necessary conditions of consensus regardless of how we may strain for the latter. If the proposed goals are unacceptable to the reader, it is hoped that he will formulate or review his own, subjecting them to equally strict examination.

Lack of Clarity Regarding Ulterior Goals. Most college teachers would agree that instruction has aims broader than the simple mastery of subject matter. The test of successful teaching is in how the student has learned to live. Every teacher of liberal or applied studies sees in his subject a contribution to an educated way of living; unless a subject of study holds such promise it is not an educational discipline. Education deals with human growth—in mind, spirit, character, and effective behaviour—and every subject of instruction is a tool employable toward this end. Important as is the student's immediate mastery of a subject, advancement toward the less patent ulterior goals of instruction is of greater moment. A portion of what is learned today is forgotten tomorrow. What remains and becomes the base for further growth is that which enters into a person's make-up, changes his habits and attitudes, reconstitutes his ideals, and enlarges his interests. Every teacher knows this and shapes his teaching accordingly. Which science teacher is not aware that through biology, chemistry, geology, or physics he is seeking to instil not inert information but insights into laws and processes of nature, ways of acquiring knowledge and truth about the material world, appreciation of how others have worked and learned, and interests that will challenge the students' imagination and effort?

In varying extent teachers understand what they hope ultimately to accomplish. But this understanding is not sufficiently defined and commonly shared to assure the best results in teaching. Teaching is not an individualistic process in which teachers may proceed in separate directions. Indefiniteness of purpose, conflict or inconsistency, duplication, or collective neglect or omission operate to the disadvantage of students. Not even a believer in *laissez faire* would maintain that liberal education can be accomplished without some common recognition of aims and some coordinated effort. Current shortcomings of college teaching need not be accentuated in order to drive home the point. It is not true that we drift in seas of learning without chart, compass, or rudder; it is probably true that outcomes and conduct of instruction could be improved were we inspired with clearer mutual realization of purposes.

To say that we aim at "liberal" or "general" education is not enough.

The term "general education" [writes Clarence H.Faust] like the term "liberty" and "equality" has acquired a wide range of meanings, including some irreconcilable ones. It cannot be defined by the simple expedient of pointing to examples.... Almost every college in the country, if presidents, deans, and catalogues are to be believed, provides a general or liberal education for its undergraduates, but it is impossible to discover any substantial common element in the educational program of our colleges.

Not that college programs should necessarily have a large common element: as instruments of education they may vary widely. But the ends for which they are being used should have strong elements of identity, else we are not educating for the same purposes or do not clearly know what we are educating for.

It is not for want of effort that the goals of college teaching have not been clearly established. A sizeable literature on the subject exists, but for various reasons much of it has not been practically influential. Sometimes the language of discourse, though literate and urbane, is not readily translatable into teaching and learning experience. What sounds uplifting in a commencement address or witty and wise in an informal essay may not be usable in planning a course of instruction. Some of the literature has been too forensic, bent on cut-arguing the other fellow rather than stating the case fairly for both sides, thus diminishing its effect on many in the profession who have remained open-minded and accessible to reasonable argument. We spend much of our substance driving out "demons" who aren't there or who are possibly, after all, not demons-the elective system, specialization, emphasis on science, vocationalism, progressivism, and the like. Added to the inherent difficulty of dealing with a subject so abstract, these tendencies may help to explain why we have fallen short of clarifying instructional objectives.

We need an affirmative statement of teaching goals almost as definite as the Ten Commandments, almost as compelling in their conviction. This we shall never get, and even as an ideal it is too remote. What we can have is clarification of what we are attempting in our effort to further the student's education. The goals should be sound in terms of society's needs and the learning behaviour of the student; clear and definite so that they can be understood and their acceptability determined; formulated in terms which make evaluation of outcomes possible; and applicable in such a way as to stimulate creative effort in teaching. This is a tall order.

Misconceptions Concerning the Goals of College Teaching.

1. *That they are universal and absolute.* There is a tendency to assume that the goals of higher education are universal in range and immutable in character. If only they could be identified! It is true that some of our stated ideals have not changed much through the ages: love of God, the brotherhood of man, ideals of truth, integrity, courage, and justice are part of a universal tradition transcending the limits of time, place, and order of society. But all ideals, however, are of equal universality and permanence. The values of religion are not conceived by us precisely as they were in the Middle Ages, and the concept of justice has changed by historical evolution. No civilization can evade the task of examining universal values and translating them into working principles consistent with the demands of its own age. For education to base its goals on universal ideals as abstractions would be to attempt to build a sound structure of human character on a foundation of words: the result might be ornamental but is sure to be substantively defective.

Even granting the existence of truly universal ideals, the goals of teaching cannot be limited to such. Other values claiming the allegiance not of the whole but of only a fraction of mankind may have equal or greater significance, viz., Christianity, democracy, the Anglo-Saxon concept of jurisprudence. The Christian religion is not universal in the sense that it is not accepted by a majority of the world's population; the ideal of democracy is alien to some of the world's largest nations; democratic England and democratic France follow different systems of legal justice. Yet it would be unthinkable to fail to include among goals of instruction the ideals of Christianity, democracy, and our inherited legal tradition. Furthermore, new ideals are constantly in the making: in their emergent stages they may be understood by and acceptable to a relative few. Yet they cannot be neglected in college teaching.

In formulating goals of instruction it is not sufficient to assume that we can adopt without reservation ready-made ideals culturally transmitted to us. We must fashion our own goals by analyzing both our traditional inheritance and the more recent and emerging principles by which our way of life is being ordered. Each generation has an obligation to do this for itself.

2. *That they are epitomized in the term "training the mind."* For many teachers a statement of goals in such terms as "clear and disciplined thinking, sound reasoning, knowledge and intellectual power" carries conviction. These are important goals, but two things must be considered with reference to them. First, they are not as attainable as their facile expression might lead us to believe. It takes more than a daily diet of grammar, rhetoric, logic, mathematics, or any prescribed study successfully to train the mind. We have long experimented with this sort of training in one form or another, and though we have succeeded in educating some students, we have failed lamentably with others. It is not intelligent to propose, as some have, to keep this method of training and discard the unsuccessful students. We need other forms of training as well, concerning some of which our knowledge may still be scanty. Possibly the ends of formal discipline are more attainable indirectly, by nourishing the mind with a variety of studies rich in substantive experience rather than through a few specified formal subjects. Intellectual discipline is a creditable goal but its difficulty of attainment should not be underestimated nor experimentation with more productive ways of achieving it abated.

Second, training the mind is not enough. Man is not all mind: he has feelings, emotions, physical needs, and a corporeal existence. Mind itself needs to be not only trained but also equipped with ideals to guide its reasoning, interests to challenge its imagination, and something "to think about." A moral character and an exemplary way of life are not inevitably the outgrowth of good mental processes. The effective thinker may be a scoundrel or a decent person, an atheist or a devout believer, a democratic person or an authoritarian, a demagogue or a statesman. Without a rich substance of knowledge a disciplined thinker may be an arid person; without positive faith and ideals, a lost and unhappy one.

To an extent the intelligent person creates his own world of knowledge and belief, and so forms his own character and way of life. But not entirely; and in any event he must have a foundation from which to proceed. The creative intellectual life is mainly that of reconstructing one's ideas and beliefs, not of building them *de novo*. The resultant philosophy of life must to a degree be common with that held by others in the same cultural setting. It is given to few gifted individuals to formulate a unique philosophy of life and hold it against the onslaughts of shared experience. Education is not a game of chance played with the lives of individual youth, but an organized attempt by society to perpetuate and improve itself by influencing young people to follow in its footsteps, adopting what is best around them and carrying it toward higher levels of achievement.

3. That there is inherent conflict between liberal and practical values. It would be good for education if the ghost of this ancient argument were finally laid to rest. On this issue practice has outdistanced theory: while the historic debate is continued, there are few liberal colleges which do not include among their offerings preprofessional or utilitarian courses, and almost half the youth in higher education are enrolled in colleges of agriculture, business, education, engineering, journalism, technology and other applied arts and sciences. Is it right to conclude that colleges have become illiberal to the extent that they have admitted courses in business administration, personnel management, labor economics, industrial psychology, and social work, or that youth in specialized colleges are being largely denied a liberal education? A fairer conclusion would be that a redefinition of liberal education is taking place which, avoiding the old dichotomy between liberal and practical learning, seeks to synthesize elements of both into a new compound serving practical as will as cultural needs.

There might have been a time when utilitarian demands on living did not exact so heavy a tribute on intelligence. One could earn a livelihood, attend to family and social wants, and use his leisure time for intellectual and creative pursuits challenging his talent and imagination. (It is doubtful that the time ever existed when problems of economic survival, statecraft, social organization, and achievement in higher occupations did not drain off a large portion of human intellectual energy: the difference between formerly and now may be one of degree.) Contemporary living, however, commands all the intelligence of which one is capable. Well-trained minds are engaged not only in cultivating the arts of scholarship but also in directing business and industrial enterprises, solving engineering problems, inventing machines and ways of using them, developing mass media of communication, administering public affairs, and other tasks both difficult and critically important. Many of these tasks call not only for a staunch mind in an almost indestructible body, but for a great deal of specialized "know-how" which cannot be gained without specific training. The self-made engineer is virtually nonexistent and the self-trained industrialist is becoming increasingly rare. Yet these people most require the values which liberal education can afford.

The majority of college graduates will not be captains of industry or leaders in public affairs. They will be men and women engaged in a middle-income occupation who aspire to be effective citizens, parents, friends and neighbours, and private individuals. They also require an education which goes beyond the abstractions of the historic disciplines and comes to grips with the real problems of living. Their education should be liberal enough to encompass those personal, social, political, economic, and even vocational problems with which they need help. An education so general that it lacks the capacity to explore these problems is not adequate.

There is small danger that, in affording such education, colleges will be diverted from their mission of liberalizing students into one of providing narrow forms of training. That could happen if the colleges were not alert to their task of using the substance of studies not as an end in itself but as a means of fostering breadth and depth of understanding, the power to use knowledge, and the character to use it properly. Things have not come to such a pass. The problem before us is to establish and maintain for each student the appropriate balance of cultural and functional learning experience which will fit him for the pursuits of living.

The same argument applies to specialized colleges which have emphasized training for specific occupational endeavours. An exclusive training of this sort does not prepare a person for comprehensive living, and may not even be the best sort of vocational preparation. It is men of creative imagination and disciplined thought who make advances in professional discovery or invention. A trained specialist in business, engineering, or medicine may be nonetheless a poor citizen and inadequate human being. These institutions need to liberalize their goals, reducing but not be to imitate liberal institutions of learning but to widen students' educational horizon so that they gain in effectiveness as cultivated persons and members of society.

Elements of Permanence in College Education. Much in college instruction is in continuation of a tradition extending from the beginning of civilization. In the course of its history mankind has accumulated learnings essential to survival, social stability and development, and individual growth; tempered and refined by experience, these learnings have becomes embodied in the tradition transmitted from one generation to the next. The continuing refinement of tradition and its perpetuation are an important function of college teaching.

Conflict has developed concerning the role of tradition in education. Actually traditional learnings are an indispensable tool in human development, and we could use more of them than we possess. Only a fraction of the knowledge that mankind has acquired has been preserved and transmitted. A person in his lifetime learns more than he can convey to another; a culture remote from us in time or place may have mastered the art of peaceful living to an extent unknown to us today, but we are dependent for knowledge of that culture upon the piecemeal and partial discoveries of the research worker. Each generation makes some contribution to living which it never can transmit in full to its successors. All the more reason for cherishing what we have, and trying to recover more. But it is wrong to assume that the essence of traditional learnings has been carefully distilled and placed within convenient reach—that it is available, for example, in certain books, disciplines, or religious or secular institutions. Our tradition is in unorganized as well as organized learnings discoverable wherever men gather and in whatever they do. Not being neatly classified, they must be dug out, sorted, and evaluated. Reliance upon tradition calls for discrimination selection and use of learnings. To affirm that education must be rooted in tradition is not to waive responsibility for identifying the traditional elements valid for present purposes.

The most enduring traditional elements in a world of material change are ethical and moral concepts governing relations of people, and esthetic standards guiding their tastes. A teacher can impart few things of greater worth than the inherited ideals, beliefs, attitudes, and principles of right and graceful living and their application to contemporary experience. But even fundamental ethical, moral, and esthetic learnings do not always come forward and identify themselves, and they do not teach themselves. Responsibility for presenting them to students must be assumed by every teacher on all educational levels, and teaching them calls for subtle skill.

To this portion of the traditional heritage should be added the intellectual: tools of thought and of expression, ways of learning and of assessing knowledge, and a large storehouse of ideas and information on almost every conceivable subject. It is manifestly impossible to convey all or most of the intellectual heritage; it is essential to convey that portion of it which has close relevance to present and future living. A college education which chose to turn its back on the intellectual tradition would be no education at all, while one which sought mainly to recapitulate past learning would be equally misguided. The problem is to choose carefully from the past that which can light the way toward the future. Study of Aristotelian philosophy is justifiable even in a crowded college curriculum, but as much cannot be said of Aristotelian science or psychology. Wholesome respect for the intellectual tradition need not blend us to its limitations: it constitutes a foundation for education, not the whole structure.

Some of the most important intellectual learnings are in the form of ideals to the development of which mankind, past and present, has collectively contributed: intellectual honesty, objectivity in assessment of knowledge and in forming conclusions, the practice of thinking logically, brushing away irrelevancies, of organizing ideas clearly, validating sources of information, checking references, questioning authority, thinking experimentally, and pursuing the truth wherever it leads. It is on this element of our tradition, rather than on obsolete theories or information, that emphasis in instruction should be placed. The danger is that we may take these outcomes for granted, without assuming explicit obligation for them. Ideals and values are formed only as opportunity is afforded for using them in meaningful experience.

Tradition has given us the ideal of the balanced person—balanced in qualities of mind, character, and body, with respect to personal aims and social obligations, between a yearning for freedom and a respect for order, between individuality and conformity. We should not abandon this ideal through improper emphasis on the intellectual or the materialistic. Liberal education is itself a great historic concept which though re-examined and adapted to a changed world, should remain our steady objective.

—And of Change. There are aspects of college teaching for which no precedents exist. It is unnecessary here to review the major developments in our time which have created unique problems in education. Mention of a few patent facts should suffice. One is the size and constituency of the college population. There has never been a time when so large and varied a student body was engaged in pursuit of higher education. The consequence has been not only an increase and enlargement of institutions of learning, but a fundamental change in the meaning of college education. To the new problems confronting us the old familiar answers do not apply. Educating two and a half million students is a different task from educating one quarter of a million. Basic matters must be reconsidered including goals of instruction, courses of study, teaching methods, and even educational standards. To a growing extent changes along these lines are being effected. One may not like the changes, but realistically one has to admit the need for new thinking on the intent and method of higher education.

Another factor of educational standards changes lies in the increased complexities of living in the modern world. With due respect to past ages, there was never a time when "life, liberty, and the pursuit of happiness" presented so much of a challenge to the capacities of the human intellect. The need for understanding and living intelligently in the world is matched only by the difficulty of so doing: only the simple-minded nowadays feel confident that they know what is happening. In a relatively short time our social world has undergone revolutionary changes, and the revolution still proceeds. In a material sense fundamental ways of life have probably ben altered more within the last century than in all the previous period since Europe's emergence from the Dark Ages. Social scientists have been kept busy cataloguing the changes and noting their effects, but even they tend to be left behind by the sweep of events.

Not every aspect of living has been thus affected, nor has it been equally difficult to accommodate to all changes. Many problems of material existence have been simplified. Though the extent of knowledge is greater, our access to it is easier, and there is no reason to assume that in time even the most perplexing of our social problems cannot be understood and resolved with hard and patient work. But we should not underestimate the task of education students in an understanding of society and the art of good citizenship. It is improper to assume that because in the past persons with general liberal training acquitted themselves creditably in the exercise of social and civic responsibilities without specific directive instruction, students can be relied upon to continue to do so in the future. It is safer to take steps to assure that a college education, in addition to its scholastic values, should also help young people to become alert, sensitive, and contributing members of society.

The college teacher is faced with a task which, though not novel, is more difficult than formerly—the making of citizens. How this is to be done constitutes a problem, considering the size and diversity of the student population and the number and potency of conditioning influences outside the school. It cannot be done through any one prescribed course of study, specific allotment of course credits, or examination. Training in citizenship is a function shared by teachers in all courses of instruction, and by the program of informally guided extracurricular experience. How the student is directed in use of social and leisure-time campus activity may have as much bearing on training in citizenship as any courses of formal instruction.

The size and composition of the student population and the greater challenge in educating for citizenship are two factors contributing toward change in higher education. There are others, each involving instructional obligations differing in degree and kind from those of the past: more general need for systematic occupational orientation, for fostering mental and emotional well-being in times characterized by hurry and tension, for productive use of leisure in an urbanized environment featured by mechanical "labor-saving" devices, for spiritual stability and a humanistic sense of values in a world adrift. In sum, as college teaching looks toward preserving what is best in our past, so should it address itself, less confidently perhaps, toward meeting the new demands of the present and the future.

Goals of Instruction

By indirection some important goals of college teaching have already been suggested. The following summary offers not a comprehensive listing of all major goals of instruction but rather a selection of those toward which common instructional effort should be directed. If any slight has been incurred, it is with respect to special values which may accrue from the study of a specific subject. Such neglect is tantamount to admission that in imparting to able and interested students the distinctive values of its respective disciplines, college teaching does well. Instruction in mathematics succeeds in turning out able young mathematicians, and the study of history fine future historians. College teachers should continue to emphasize their specialized aims in instruction but pursue also the common general goals involving all students.

1. *Physical and mental health*. Higher education cannot be occupied with cultivation of the intellect to the neglect of other forms of

development. Its business is the cultivation of the whole person in all the respects essential for competent living. While its responsibilities do not extend to such learnings as the student can attain for himself or as other educative agencies can provide better, it has an obligation to assess progress toward balanced attainment and furnish help whenever needed. The development of physical and mental health falls partly in this category.

Modern living places great strain on the human biological system. Medicine has performed wonders in conquering disease, setting up health safeguards, and extending the span of life but has not been notably successful in reducing disabling nervous and mental disorders. To reach old age is not unusual, but to live one's life with serenity and mental composure seems more difficult. A person's constitution is part of his native endowment and there is a limit to what environmental influences and formal training agencies can do toward fortifying it. But to the extent that education can foster good health through instillation of knowledge, habits, attitudes, and interests, it has an obligation to do so.

By the time the student reaches college his basic patterns of healthful living have been formed. It is the college's function to induce intelligent self-examination of these patterns, their reconstruction where necessary, and the cultivation of additional heathful pursuits and interests designed to carry a person successfully through a lifetime. A fact deserving of greater attention than it receives is that college graduates in the main lead an existence requiring less than average muscular activity and greater "wear and tear" of the vascular and nervous systems. More appropriate propaedeutic health programs could be devised than are now in use.

Health and physical education are important, but the goal of healthful living requires more than this. Physical well-being is not enough to insure mental health unless a person is fortified with strength and breadth of spirit to which liberal-arts study contributes more than calisthenics. In a sense the entire college course is a program in health education, and every teacher a contributor to health development to the extent that his instruction promotes a sense of values and a constructive philosophy of life.

2. Ethical and moral quality. The college has wonderful material to work with, and exceptional opportunity to train outstanding men and women. Without reflection on the college-trained product, it is questionable whether this is achieved to the extent possible. We tend to honor in the abstract the principle of ethical and moral education, but to practice it incidentally, only as occasions offer cause for commendation or reproach. That we are successful is more of a tribute to the quality of our students than the result of conscious, persistent effort to make character training a central goal of instruction. If teachers undertook to cultivate ethical and moral ideals as resolutely as they cultivate knowledge, society would profit greatly. There are never enough men and women of outstanding integrity, moral courage, and independence of spirit to discharge to exacting responsibilities of leadership and to stimulate others by their example.

In a sense befitting the college, the aim of character education is to produce responsible people who "stand on their own feet"; who apply with sensitive and honest discrimination standards of right and wrong and do not fear to stand by their judgment; whose pattern of conforming or nonconforming behaviour is dictated by decency, good sense, and regard for truth, not by convention, expediency, laziness, or desire to be "different."

Character [writes Tead] is manifested in a certain personal resolution and determination to adhere persistently to the best the person knows and can discover in his choices of activity and commitment. Character denotes a capacity to stand and having done all to stand with courage and perseverance, with willingness and with ability to face up to and pay the price of consequences of decisions personally arrived at as wise or sound... Fidelity to rational and defensible standards is a hallmark of the person of character. The care which the individual exercises in establishing, evaluating, and revising the standards used to shape his decisions is itself a further index to his fidelity. Ability to criticize, revalue, and bring into a more comprehensive system of values one's always extending body of experience is a character attribute no less than intellectual one.

Considering the diversity of forces at play, college education is not among the most formative influences in character development. The student's character has been shaped by heredity, family training, environmental associations, the church, and earlier school experience. What the college can do is to serve as an intellectualizing, coordinating, and when necessary corrective influence, helping the student to transform precepts into principles and to organize principles into a personal philosophy, to know and improve himself as a person, and to be more resolute in the exercise of rationally justified conviction.

3. Intellectual independence. There is no adequate substitute for the old disciplinary ideal of the trained mind. Knowledge is unavailing without the power to use it, and ethical values need intelligence to guide their application. Disagreement with the theory of formal discipline does not imply rejection of its ideal; such disagreement centers on the exclusiveness of the ideal, and the narrow and questionable means used in furthering it. Modern educational thought is more inclined to the assumption that any intellectual pursuit rich in substance and comprehensible in terms of the student's experience can be an instrument of mental training, provided the mind is exercised thereby. Mastery of content is important, but a more permanent goal should be that of developing the powers and habits of mind requisite to independent acquisition of knowledge, evaluation, and application in use. Intellectual independence is at a premium in both individual or collective pursuits. "Our goal in education is to help students to help themselves, each with his own set of qualities, his own background of family and neighbourhood, his own inherited and acquired philosophy, and whatever particular future may be his."

The problem is how to do it. If sampled observation may be trusted, much of current teaching practice reflects the assumption that by engaging in study of a powerful subject the student is concomitantly learning to think well. Creditable independent achievement is recognized and rewarded, but not nearly enough is done to stimulate and train the student in the exercise of independent effort reaching toward progressively higher levels of achievement. We tend to forget that only to a limited degree is growth in independent power automatic. Instructional emphasis on factual attainment will produce the informed person, emphasis on techniques the technician. To foster creative and critical thought instruction must elicit a quality of learning which stimulates initiative, imagination, and the exercise of mind in rigorous and productive operation.

The nub of the problem is in the conception of what constitutes teaching and learning. If teaching means imparting subject matter and learning a process by which the student assimilates his own respectable share, this is one thing; if teaching is conceived as enhancing the student's realization of the values of a subject, helping him to bring to bear his own resources in formulating and pursuing a method of attack, and guiding him in the process, that is another. The college curriculum is not perfect, but with the exception of disputable fringe courses, offerings as currently constituted are potential disciplinary tools. There is enough in the college program to provide every student with a lasting intellectually-formative experience without returning to older discarded studies. It remains to teach them as they should be taught.

4. Deep intellectual interests. It is not possible to encompass within the years of schooling all the education a person needs to carry him through life. When the compulsions of formal study have ceased, a person assumes his own obligation to continued self-education. While the urgency of practical need provides incentive for some self-education, self-impelling intellectual interests must account for the rest. A person continues to grow as his interests inspire him to sustained quest for knowledge and its improved use.

Continuance of self-education in adulthood is too important to be left to chance opportunity and experience. Our accomplishment on this score is not good. Too many college-trained people, once they leave college, slough off serious intellectual pursuits other than those related to professional and economic demands, settling down to a routine of social and a vocational living offering little exercise to talent and imagination. Tastes become conventionalized and distinctive capacities stunted through disuse. Able people "relax" in their evenings reading detective stories or picture magazines and watching television shows. In time such habitual relaxation draws them away from the main streams of intellectual and artistic life in which they are competent to participate, leaving them subject to the common inanities of leisure-time "enjoyment." Strong interests may not assure a flourishing intellectual existence but they are a potent force in this direction.

Instruction in any subject should include among its goals the cultivation of interests looking beyond the immediate requirements of study. No great problem presents itself with those students who early reveal a special inclination for the subject; it takes poor teaching to discourage students with, for example, a strong bent for mathematics or art or literature. The problem is greater with students who show no special preference for a field of study. The situation then provides a test of teaching skill, and though it may be unrealistic to expect to engage every student's interest, some students should be reached. There is room form differences in intellectual tastes, and students should be free to choose as their special interest subjects toward which they feel most congenial. A person need not distribute his interests widely over the cultural landscape, but each should cultivate some beyond those serving immediate utilitarian needs. Interests productive of growth through a vocational activity should be particularly encouraged.

In the final analysis each teacher must determine for himself how this may be accomplished. Some general principles hold true: interests are generated through challenging but satisfying learning experience, when students become convinced that they can make a contribution to a subject which they hold in high esteem, when they are so deeply drawn into the subject that they become captive to its inherent demand for mastery. The approach to instruction cannot be lackadaisical or impersonal ("those who can will learn") or from the viewpoint "for specialists only." The teacher must present his subject so as to make it appealing to students, try to involve each student personally, elicit from him an ever-increasing contribution of effort, and help him to realize as much as possible from his intellectual investment.

5. Enlightened citizenship. While the obligation to educate for citizenship requires no justification, it may be necessary to explain why it is incumbent upon the college, following twelve years of earlier schooling, to assume this as a specific function. All organized instruction concerns itself with the training of citizens, and to the extent that the learner's capacity permits, instils understanding, ideals, attitudes, and habits of approved civic conduct. The secondary school does an earnest and, on the whole, effective job with teen-age students representing an intellectual cross section of the American public. But its effort is accommodated to the lower intellectual level and lesser maturity of its students. Large as the college population has grown, it is still relatively select, intellectually and socially: out of it will come not only the leadership of society but also a large private citizenry capable of molding its opinion and influencing its action. Such a citizenry needs training in social and civic responsibility far beyond the limits attainable through earlier schooling.

Citizenship training in the college is of a different order from that offered on lower educational levels. Without discrediting the ideals and principles cherished by society, instruction in the college must submit them to the students' critical examination. How were they achieved, what alternatives to them exist, what are their relative merits and shortcomings, what strengths and weaknesses are displayed by our social principles in action, how may social improvement be effected without sacrifice of basic ideals? What, then, are the civic responsibilities of educated men and women, and how are they discharged? The college postulates no single answer, but helps students arrive at a rational affirmation of their faith in the ends and processes of democracy and affords them opportunity for testing these beliefs in practice. In the final analysis the student decides for himself; the college can help him toward critical assessment of beliefs and more responsible use of the civic franchise.

The process of general education is itself conducive to the training of citizens: whatever aids in building mind and character contributes toward citizenship. Instruction in the social studies is an important contribution factor. Every classroom is a citizenship center, and every discipline a medium of training. The teacher needs to alert himself to opportunities which exist or can be created for the development of civic ideals, attitudes, and habits later to be exercised in a larger social sphere. In its organized life the college should constitute a citizenship laboratory, offering the chance not only to practice established principles of democratic behaviour but also to experiment with new ways of implementing democratic ideals. Outcomes should be assessed, and resultant learnings clarified for the student. Terminating his college course a student should feel that he has had an experience in civic living which will benefit him in the future.

6. Economic competence. It is not an assault on the ideal of liberal education to suggest that college instruction has a special responsibility to prepare the student for his economic role in society as worker or producer, consumer, planner, and social critic. The economic phase of existence is critical in its influence on general well-being, and most people either require or strongly benefit from direct educational preparation for difficult economic responsibilities. To argue that the business of the college is general education and that a person's economic future is his private concern is a refusal to face reality.

There is more to economic competence than ability to earn a livelihood. A person must be prepared to take his place in the economic partnership of society and address himself to the solution of its problems as well as his own. He is not only a consumer of goods and services, investor, property owner, and tax payer but may be called upon to direct or participate in public undertakings as councilman, school board member, or arbitrator in labor disputes. He needs training in the conduct of larger social responsibilities and of his own economic affairs. This training the college willingly provides through its general educational process, including courses specifically pointed toward growth in economic understanding. Where the profession commonly balks is in admitting that vocational orientation is an essential element in preparation for the economic needs of living. This is considered outside the sphere of general education, obtainable by the person in his own way or through other training facilities.

Orienting a student toward a vocation does not necessarily involve specialized vocational training. The college program cannot reasonably be fractured into the hundreds of vocational splinters leading off into students' later pursuits. Responsible leaders of industry agree with educators that a liberal training fostering moral and intellectual development and acquisition of important knowledge is fundamental to success in the type of occupations in which college graduates commonly engage; and that specialized occupational skills can be acquired later through formal study or in the course of job experience. Acting on this belief, specialized colleges have been for some years broadening their base of general education, seeking to establish a proper balance with technical studies. The liberal college has a different problem: most of its graduates do not enter the technical occupations but those placing greater premium on intelligence, initiative, industry, leadership, and ability to get along with people than on preparatory specialized skill. The solution of this problem lies not so much in balancing general and vocational studies—although some representation of the latter is necessary—as in using the resources of general education to help the student explore career possibilities, ascertain his interests and aptitudes in relation to possible vocational choice, make an intelligent selection, and develop a suitable plan of preparation.

The scope of the existing program of general education is adequate to afford many students at least a good start toward preparation for a career. By definition liberal studies embody and in turn show the way to many fields of human endeavour. The student needs to be guided toward what is for him the right fields. Sometimes, in recognition of widespread interests or needs among students, the college will expand its offerings to admit additional professionally oriented courses, shaping them so as to enhance their liberal values. Often the student will have to decide that, in the interests of a career, he must continue specialized study in an institution beyond the graduate level. The point is that a college graduate should not be taken by surprise at the need to establish himself in a proper calling but should be ready for it. Such readiness may consist of knowing what he wants to do and being prepared with general knowledge and understanding of the job. Approaching the point of entry, the student will discover for himself whether he needs specialized preparation and how it may be obtained. After all we are educating the student further to educate himself.

The career values inherent in general college studies should be pointed up and extended. The value of an instrument of liberal learning is not impaired when its vocational possibilities are made explicit and opportunities afforded for student self-exploration. The limit in scope and diversity of liberal offerings has not been reached; more courses will be admitted, even under vocational pressure, which will be found to possess liberal value. Some of the most respected current offerings were professional in origin; perhaps some day courses now on the vocational fringe may be regarded as bulwarks of liberal learning.

The Educated Person. The foregoing suggests a conception of the educated person different in some respects from that which has traditionally guided the college. The conception may be unacceptable to some: it is not primarily one of a humanist or scholar. Yet the attributes are there, although their emphasis is on producing not the studious, contemplative man but the effective one. Some of our graduates become scholars, teachers, research workers, men of letters and of the arts. But not all or most. How shall these be certified? Do we call them near-scholars or near-men-of-letters, like the young man whose calling-card was inscribed "Failed A.B."? These are young men and women whose education was not meant to fit them for a life of study but for less dedicated but equally useful pursuits. Are they not entitled to be called educated or, conversely, should not education seek to make them better, more enlightened, and more effective in the things they are called upon to do? The college must continue to produce scholars, but should not mold its pattern of education on the scholarly life alone.

Society needs educated people— highminded, thoughtful, informed, and competent, the qualities which bring distinction in the world of the arts and science are much the same as those needed in the conduct of prosaic life activities. Business and politics, industry and domestic pursuits require high levels of intellectual honesty respect for truth and accuracy, quest for knowledge, bold and imaginative thinking, and patient persistence. The moral and intellectual virtues which once distinguished the rare, cultivated person need to be extended to as many people as possible.

The educated person today needs powers surpassing those of any previous age. There is more to be learned, yet to be a learned person is not enough: one must be right thinking, right feeling, right doing. If our educated person lacks the erudition of the Renaissance scholar or the urbanity of the Victorian gentleman, that is no cause for discouragement. He is probably better balanced, and balance is what we urgently require. We are educating so many that among them are bound to be distinguished artists, scholars, and spiritual leaders who will advance mankind's highest achievement. The potential "remakers of mankind" should not be neglected, but education should not be conceived in their terms alone. They are also educated who with kindness and intelligent skill fulfill their obligations to themselves and to society as citizens, workers, neighbours, family men and women, and human beings.

SELECTED BIBLIOGRAPHY

Carmichael, Oliver C., *The Changing Role of Higher Education.* New York: The Macmillan Company, 1949. 102 pp.

Cole, Stewart G., *Liberal Education in a Democracy.* New York: Harper & Brothers, 1940. 309 pp.

Conant, James B., *Education in a Divided World.* Cambridge: Harvard University Press, 1948. 249 pp.

Donham, Wallace B., *Education for Responsible Living.* Cambridge: Harvard University Press, 1944. 309 pp.

General Education in a Free Society, Report of the Harvard Committee. Cambridge: Harvard University Press, 1945. 267 pp.

Gideonse, Harry D., "On Re-Thinking Liberal Education," pp.30-52 in *Strengthening Education at All Levels,* Report of the Eighteenth Educational Conference Hekd under the Auspices of the Educational Records Bureau and American Council on Education. Washington: American Council on Education, 1953.

Greene, Theodore M., *Liberal Education Reconsidered.* Cambridge: Harvard University Press, 1953. 46 pp.

Henderson, Algo D., *Vitalizing Liberal Education.* New York: Harper & Brothers, 1944. 202 pp.

Jones, Howard Mumford, *Education and World Tragedy.* Cambridge: Harvard University Press, 1946. 178 pp.

Kallen, Horace M., *The Education of Free Men.* New York: Farrar, Straus and Company, 1949. 332 pp.

Livingstone, Sir Richard W., *On Education.* New York: The Macmillan Company, 1944. 290 pp.

Russell, Bertrand, *Education and the Good Life.* New York: Boni and Liveright, 1926. 319 pp.

Smith, Huston, *The Purposes of Higher Education.* New York: Harper & Brothers, 1955. 218 pp.

Taylor, Harold, ed., *Essays in Teaching,* Chapter I, "The Idea of a College." New York: Harper & Brother, 1950. 239 pp.

Tead, Ordway, *Character Building and Higher Education.* New York: The Macmillan Company, 1953. 129 pp.

Ward, F. Champion, Faust, Clarence H, et al., *The Idea and Practice of General Education,* Chapter I, "The Problem of General Education." Chicago: University of Chicago Press, 1950. 333 pp.

Whitehead, Alfred N., *Aims of Education And Other Essays.* New York: The Macmillan Company, 1929. 247 pp.

Woody, Thomas, *Liberal Education of Free Men.* Philadelphia: University of Pennsylvania Press, 1951. 296 pp.

2

GROWTH OF THE COLLEGE TEACHER

The Ideal of Professional Growth. Professional excellence is not entirely a function of experience, nor is assiduous pursuit of one's duties a guarantee of distinction. The road to professional mastery lies in utilizing one's intelligence, energy, and opportunities of experience in a steady, deliberate effort to foster growth. It is self-training on the job which converts a promising but half-prepared beginner into a passable teacher and impels him toward continuously higher attainment.

Growth in a desired direction is not fortuitous. It needs to be planned and guided. Rudimentary proficiency may result from normal involvement in teaching experience, but this is only a small part of total possible growth. The possibilities and range of growth are as extensive as the teacher's own capacities within the limits of a spacious profession. The goals may lead into realms of creative scholarship, educational philosophy, theories of learning, experimental teaching practice, government of the college community, and other useful professional activity.

The agent of growth is the teacher himself. In a profession not dominated by competition from within or pressure for immediate results from without, the teacher is the keeper of his own conscience. His resolution must be strong enough to enable him at times to compensate for shortage of time, energy, or resources, or even for indifferent support by institutional superiors. Other useful activities compete for his time and attention, tempting absorption in immediate routine to the neglect of less obvious but more urgent needs. It is not easy, after a busy day of college activity, to resume in the evening one's interrupted thought on a research paper or monograph in preparation. Yet this often has to be done is the teacher would be fair with himself and the profession. The best people in an institution are frequently the most overworked, and unless careful to reserve some energy for creative activity are likely to expend themselves in work which is useful but nonproductive of growth.

All professional activity does not have equal potentiality for growth. The person who has reduced his teaching to practiced routine and fails to set for himself new goals of endeavor ceases after a time to develop. Professional enrichment results from reinvestment of intelligence and energy in new learning experience, refreshment with new knowledge, acceptance of new challenges, or new ways of approaching familiar tasks. A teacher need not change jobs frequently in order to sustain growth; he needs only to enlarge and improve his conception of his job and strive for better ways to do it.

Individual Differences in Growth. Like others, college teachers differ in capacities, interests, and inclinations for various aspects of their work. Some prefer classroom contact with students and shun administration, others find an absorbing interest in administrative assignments. In general a person's promise of growth is more through development of his relative strength than correction of weakness. While an effort should be made to remedy shortcomings in competency and maintain balance in positive accomplishment, the greater proportion of one's energy should go toward cultivating his best talents. Narrow and one-sided concentration is undesirable; on the other hand, an attempt to distribute one's resources impartially among all teaching functions is not likely to be most productive.

In the light of the requirements of his job and his known qualifications the teacher should reach for a high level of general competency, yet pursue with greatest zeal the tasks toward which he is most inclined. It is important for a scholar to be a good course instructor, to associate with students in extracurricular activity, to contribute his scholarly insights to extra-instructional institutional undertakings, but he can learn to do these things well without sacrifice of scholarly proclivities. The gifted extrovert can cultivate his specialities in human relations without neglecting the demands of scholarship. There are many kinds of excellence serviceable to education and many ways of achieving them. Only the rare person is exceptionally good in all things: teacher learn to do best what suits him most.

College Teachers' Preparation

A Professional Paradox. Considering their preparation, the professional performance of college teachers is unwarrantedly good—a circumstance which may have distracted from long needed improvement in pre-service training. A recent survey supports the empirical judgement that college teaching is not as good as it might be. The wonder is that it is good at all. The explanation must lie in the caliber of person attracted to the profession, the practical efficiency of current teacher-selection practices, imperfect though they seem, and the transfer values of scholarly training carrying over into development of new competencies. Otherwise it would be difficult to explain why a young specialist in mathematics, chemistry or Germanic literature can enter a profession whose speciality is educating youth, face responsibilities for which he is not well prepared, and acquit himself honorably and in time with distinction. Perhaps the discipline of winning a Ph.D. degree has greater selective properties than many of us suspect.

It is unnecessary to dwell in detail on shortcomings of present practice in preparation of college teachers. There is general agreement that the typical graduate program pursued by prospective teachers falls short of the mark: commendable as a means of training in specialized scholarship and contributing also toward broader discipline, it does not offer direct preparation for the fundamental professional responsibility—teaching. More serious than the omission of training in the technical aspects of instruction is a failure to impart broader concepts of education, human development, the learning process, and teacher's mission. These things the teacher must obtain for himself through experience. Yet while much can be learned on the job, college teaching is too advanced a profession to be mastered in route. In the first place, students learning from an apprentice teacher may not get the education to which they are entitled, though they respond to his eagerness and enthusiasm. Second, there is danger that the teacher will acquire more readily the technical skills of his craft than its basic understanding. Third, though no teacher can long maintain himself without an educational philosophy, it makes a great difference whether the philosophy is based on ascertained fact and tenable assumption or a mixture of empirical knowledge and doubtful opinion. What the self-prepared teacher may lack is not proficiency to maintain himself in the classroom but vision of the possibilities of education, a deeper sense of purpose, and realization of how it is attainable .

Despite weakness in preparation many teachers do a fine job. Alert and sensitive, they are able to capture the spirit of the profession and become accomplished craftsman. Teaching is not a standardized process conducted according to uniform "rules": there is freedom for individuality in approach and style , for personal discoveries and values . Existing gaps in the "science" of teaching can be filled only from personal experience. This affords added reason why many teachers succeed in training themselves. But self-training would progress further if it were based on more substantial and explicit earlier preparation, and many a teacher of moderate self-guided accomplishment would be enabled to reach a higher professional level.

An explanation of the gap between preparation and professional need is not hard to provide. The evolution of the college in educational function, organization, and practice has outdistanced developments in teacher-preparation. Scholarship is properly the principal ingredient in training college teachers; there was a time when, reinforced by capacity and willingness to learn by experience, it alone served the purpose. This is no longer true; the required preparation needs to be extended to include allied professional knowledge too important to be left to individual resources in informal learning. Even the expectation of continuing to enlist into professional service superior types of persons cannot compensate sufficiently for existing gaps in preparation.

Recruitment and Selection. Although practices in recruitment of college teachers are workable, they are not characterized by system, organization, or coordinated effort. With a membership now numbering some 200,000 and further increase in prospect, the time is approaching when the college teaching profession must consider a more deliberate and dependable long-range program of teacher supply along with clarified standards of selection. Assurance of continuity in staffing without sacrifice of quality cannot indefinitely be left to the conscience and enterprise of individual institutions, teaching departments, or administrators. Already in some fields, notably the sciences, it has become difficult to recruit first-rate persons against the competition of more remunerative opportunities in industry and government. A complicating factor is the decentralized and individualistic organization of higher education which, despite notable advantages, is a liability in recruitment. Regimentation in teacher-placement is undesirable: to legislate national or state certification requirements would certainly be unwise, and it is questionable whether even learned societies or regional accrediting agencies should undertake more than to *suggest* standards of teacher selection in any field. The answer may lie in voluntary working arrangements between undergraduate and graduate institutions.

If comprehensive provisions for teacher recruitment are still in the offing, an immediate need exists as Klapper has stated, for forthright assumption of responsibility by individual institutions. Centers of graduate study engaged in supplying teachers should, in addition to furnishing an appropriate type of preparation, make a vigorous effort to attract and identify students with interest and promise in teaching and accord them special attention. This is now being attempted by an increasing number of graduate institutions, but more rapid progress is contingent upon clearer understanding of the personal and professional qualities desirable in teachers, more explicit knowledge concerning what has been called the "sociology" of the college teaching profession, and agreement on the essentials of suitable training programs. Correspondingly, undergraduate colleges absorbing teachers need to cooperate more closely with graduate centers, advising the latter of their needs, assisting in recruitment efforts, and joining in formulation of training policies. A college should not look toward a single university or a small number for continuous replenishment of its staff; its working relations should be with a wide range of graduate centers possessing distinctive interests and strengths. Each college should try to maintain access to a corps of recruits whose interest and aptitude for teaching have been demonstrated and for whom an approved program of training has been provided.

Teacher-selection practices vary among institutions, and even criteria of selection differ in the emphasis and rigor with which they are applied. Apparently most institutions have well-defined standards of preparation at least in announced policy, and a generalized if broad description is possible. What is sought in a cadidate is evidence of quality as a person and fitness as a scholar demonstrated by some record of achievement and personal and professional recommendation; in only 21 per cent of over six hundred institutions was preparation in professional courses for collage teaching found to be considered "of great importance." Graduation from a "prestige" institution or high testimonial from a distinguished scholar is a telling factor, although a candidate may improve or impair his chances by the impression he creates in a personal interview. For appointment to senior academic positions scholarship requirements are correspondingly higher, over 95 percent of institutions insisting on the doctorate as prerequisite for a full professorship and possibly also further publication. Distinguished or "name" professors invited to join a faculty are not subjected to such close analytic scrutiny, their reputation and known achievement being surety for their worth. In general a teaching record is appraised whenever information concerning it is available, but, with beginners at least, a searching attempt to assess technical competence in instruction is not made.

Training and selection go together. More direct criteria of selection cannot be employed until the preparation of college teachers is itself more directly focused on fundamental professional needs. Until such time colleges must necessarily continue to choose the best educated, scholarly, and personable applicants, hoping that in time they will also come to be good teachers. When universities undertake more direct training programs for college teaching, colleges will be enabled to add to their criteria of selection a tested indication of instructional worth.

Essentials of Preparation. Universities have begun to experiment with programs of college teacher preparation. The programs vary in substance and form, and some time may elapse before any agreement is reached on essentials. Whether training takes the form of organized professional courses is at this stage less important than that there be direct, sustained preparation, including an attempt to screen candidates and to attract and encourage the more promising. In this spirit and without reference to formal organization, some elements likely to be considered essential in such preparation are here proposed in the hope of stimulating discussion of the subject.

One essential is knowledge of the function of the college. Without minimizing issues in theory or practice it is possible to convey an understanding of the educational role of the college and the manner of its fulfillment. This the prospective teacher needs, his own understanding being bounded by his experience as undergraduate and later as graduate specialist. The object of training should not be to indoctrinate with one set of principles but to expose prevailing views for examination. With this information and accumulating experience, the beginning teacher should gradually develop his own educational philosophy by discriminating selection of values and principles which he can approve. In the meantime he has some knowledge of the broader meaning of education, the relation of educational theory to social philosophy, the function of the college as a stage in the process of education, and his own expanded role as educator. These things do not come naturally to a graduate student engaged primarily in mastering and advancing a specialized field of scholarship.

A second requirement in preparation is introduction to study of the learning process and the nature and needs of college students as learners. Not much is known with certainty regarding the mechanics of learning on higher intellectual levels, and a good deal of accepted information is empirical or even speculative. But the increasingly assured facts, principles, and insights which the science of psychology has succeeded in gathering relative to the educational development of college students should be communicated to the teacher-in-training. Valid knowledge exists on the nature and growth of intelligence, personality development, dynamics and conditioning factors of human conduct, laws of learning, significance of individual differences, and nature and needs of adolescence. Even with existing gaps in knowledge there is more to be learned than the graduate student is usually asked to master within his period of preparation.

It should be possible to impart to the prospective teacher some basic understandings of human nature and the learning process. To learn, for example, to view the student in terms of his individual needs would be a great gain. To recognize human development as a continuous process would help the teacher start instruction from the point of actual student achievement, and avoid slippery footholds on assumed foundations. Awareness of problems in learning would foster more conscious selection and arrangement of teaching methods. Untenable notions regarding unlimited transfer of training, the inviolability of subjects of instruction, or the potency of sheer reason in dictating human conduct could be replaced with more reliable fact or theory. Once started on study of learning process, the new teacher could more easily carry forward on his own.

A third requirement in preparation is actual practice in teaching under the friendly supervision of an able teacher. The value of this in launching the beginner on a higher plane of professional effort is inestimable. Some things the new teacher needs to know can be learned only through personal experience, and it is better that unavoidable mistakes be made where they can be sympathetically noted, discussed, and corrected. Of even greater importance is the opportunity from the beginning to induct the prospective teacher in sound values of professional workmanship which he can later cultivate under his own direction. Emphasis in practice teaching should center on this rather than on correction of elementary mistakes. Many a self-trained teacher has learned the rudiments of instruction which acquiring any aspiration to higher levels of performance which could have increased his effectiveness immeasurably.

Jointly with practice teaching opportunity there should be some systematic study of instructional method. Technical knowledge is more easily acquired during experience than apart from it, and even in practice teaching stage only a beginning can be made. Emphsis at htis stage should be on fundamentals rather than technical niceties: how the teacher conducts himself in the classroom, objectives of teacher-student relations, main points in planning and organizing instruction, patterns of teaching and their uses, employment of teaching aids, and principal methods of evaluation. Whether such study is pursued informally or in organized courses, it should be related to each trainee's personal experience in teaching, and immediately applied. It follows that the practice teaching opportunity should be utilized for real teaching and not service as "helper" in clerical or routine chores; and that the experience should be graduated so as to enable the trainee to sample teaching problems step by step.

A fourth essential in preparation is information regarding the wider scope of the college teacher's responsibilities, their rationale, and the manner of their performance. This should afford a practical orientation to the tasks in which the new college teacher, almost from the beginning, may be called upon to share—in advising students, course planning, institutional research, and the like. The prospective teacher needs to know how to maintain proper balance among these matters: consideration of salient principles and, whenever feasible, opportunity to apply them in practice teaching experience should suffice. The fundamentals of educational counselling can be developed in a series of discussions, supplemented by observation of counselling procedure and personal contact with undergraduate students.

The art of curriculum making can only be learned through prolonged first-hand experience; what the trainee can acquire is some understanding of the curriculum as an instrument of educational policy, values in different fields of study, and ways in which subject matter can serve instruction. Other related functions of college teaching may be similarly approached, with greater emphasis on formation of attitudes sympathetic to their acceptance and later on-the-job mastery than on operational details.

Whether elements of training such as have been suggested are acceptable or others and better ones conceived, it is important that a more adequate program of preparing college teachers be instituted. The profession is already moving in this direction. The criticism made in 1947 in the Report of the President's

Commission on Higher Education is too vital to be ignored: "College teaching is the only major learned profession for which there does not exist a well-defined program of preparation directed toward developing the skills which it is essential for the practitioner to possess."

THE BEGINNING TEACHER

The Beginner vis-a-vis the Experienced Teacher. The beginner is under greater self-compulsion to develop than is his more experienced colleague. The advantages of youthful vigor and enthusiasm are heightened by an eagerness to succeed in the face of the challenge of probationary status. The fact that young teachers are sometimes found inadequate is less due to complacency than to fundamental shortcomings of capacity or training. The first years of teaching are often the best from the standpoint of growth.

If the "twenties" are the awkward age of college teaching, the "thirties" are the more dangerous: it is then that the leveling off process begins. Having gained a measure of stature and self-security from growing proficiency in his job, acceptance by colleagues and institution, and sense of ease with students, the teacher may be inclined to relax, trustful of future success without the necessity of constant exertion. Many a teacher has enjoyed a life-time of professional activity without rising above the level of journeyman in his craft. The danger is well-known and exploited in argument by opponents of the principle of academic tenure who, in obviating one problem, would create others. The answer is to induce continued self-growth by positive means, not by threat of economic insecurity.

While the danger of stagnation is real, its incidence need not be exaggerated. If one may judge by observation, the majority of teachers are not so affected: they remain alert to their duties, conscious of their need for growth, and anxious to improve. Seasoned teachers worry as much about an occasionally "flat" lesson as any conscientious novice. The beginner may work harder and "stimulate" his students more, but the experienced teacher has incomparably more to offer in instruction. It takes professional maturity to distil wisdom from knowledge, broaden perspective, and discriminate between greater and lesser ends. It takes art to conceal and the practiced teacher can actually influence students more by appearing to 'stimulate" them less. Yet the experienced teacher must continuously fight the temptation to slacken in growth.

Conditions Favorable to Growth. The beginners's objectives in growth differ from those of his colleagues with greater professional experience. Except in the small college the beginner is not at once plunged in *medias res* but allowed to confine his efforts to a few principal activities. It is expected that he acquit himself creditably in instruction, form good relations with students and colleagues, show sensitivity to the special character and purposes of the institution, and reveal in his own person promise of future development. If the beginner can satisfactorily demonstrate such capacities he will normally, unless institutional policy dictates otherwise, be retained. His subsequent objective should be not only to add to his institutional usefulness by increasing his range of responsibility but also to move gradually toward a higher plane of total accomplishment.

A factor conducive to growth is willingness to accept into one's professional province any responsibility pertinent to the education of students which one is qualified to perform, and to set out to learn it. It is important at the outset to establish a realistic priority of effort in terms of institutional needs and one's own capabilities. The most important thing is to become increasingly aware of opportunities, problems, and needed skills in teaching. Of next immediate importance is to accept normal auxiliary responsibilities in organized campus living, professional group activity, and administrative routine, and resolve to do them well. Following this in priority are the specialized institutional tasks to which the young teacher may be assigned by virtue of need or special qualification. The young teacher must not be impatient with these additional obligations nor underestimate their challenge.

A further requisite for growth is readiness to learn from others. The young teacher should be quick to avail himself of opportunities to learn, informally or otherwise, from teaching colleagues, administrative staff members, and students. It is a mistake to compare the scholarship of one's new associates with those on the front lines of university research: they are not competing with university scholars but using scholarship as a tool in educating students. Nor should the beginner indulge in comparison of his new academic surroundings with those previously experienced without reflecting on differences in institutional purpose, composition of students, and financial resources: teaching impecunious but able students in a struggling small college is often more professionally rewarding than working in a materially richer setting. A young teacher has something to give his new institution, more to get from it. He brings fresh knowledge and enthusiasm beneficial to students and colleagues, but can learn much from them about the use of knowledge in teaching. Helping to freshen their interest, he may in turn absorb their "know-how."

Means of Growth. Anticipating the beginner's needs, colleges have begun to make systematic provision for induction and early in-service training. At this stage the program is little more than rudimentary. A relatively ambitious effort may include, in addition to the amenities of social introduction, formal briefings by college officials on various aspects of institutional activity followed by opportunity for personal observation; specific colleges or large departments of instruction may hold instructional orientation conferences, or place the beginner for a time under the guidance of a more experienced colleague for informal consultation on such problems as may arise. In small institutions where new appointees are fewer and more widely spaced in time, it is easier for a department head or senior colleague to take a personal interest in a newcomer, supervising his immediate needs and fostering longer-range growth.

Whatever institutional provisions are formally made they can only be supplementary to the beginner's own efforts. The opportunities for learning are many, the place of learning is everywhere on the campus, and the agents of learning all those with whom he makes contact. Observing classes taught by colleagues and in turn inviting observation of his own, he can improve his teaching: talking with them and listening to discussion at conference and informal gatherings, he can acquire much of value in general teaching theory and practice and specific learning problems and needs of students. By studying the educational program of the institution and familiarizing himself with its aims, scope of instruction, and special features, he can become better informed concerning the requirements of his own job. Most of all he can learn from students by observing them in classes, talking to them informally, and dipping into record files;and by sinsitive assessment of their reactions to his teaching--not so much by direct expression of comment as by less direct means he can ascertain the direction of needed improvement.

These things may be done without neglect of principal pursuits or sacrifice of long-range interests to the expediency of immediate success in adjustment. An inordinate expenditure of time and energy in order to learn "much in a hurry" is not required; what is required is alertness to such opportunities as normally present themselves or may be created without strain, and resolution to apply what has been learned. In his eagerness to succeed, the beginner should be careful not to burden his colleagues with his presence: even the most sympathetic weary of engaging in "shop-talk," answering questions, or opening their classrooms to observers. One needs to develop professional patience. In many matters there is no substitute for experience, and some valuable accomplishments can be acquired only in the course of service. There is no quick way of becoming a seasoned teacher: one must work at his craft a long while and patiently absorb the lessons of his own and others' experience. Similarly, in order to become familiar with a complex institution one must live in it.

Except in limited ways the beginner cannot expect to share in the government of his institution—sit on its policy-making bodies, influence its actions, or administer its laws—until he has secured his position by earning the confidence of colleagues and responsible officials. Similarly he cannot exercise wider leadership among the profession and the public until he has come to be known. Opportunities will develop in time, and it is well not to hurry them too much. The young teacher can err in seeking to extend himself beyond the limits of his experience and accomplishment.

THE EXPERIENCED TEACHER

While no clear demarcation exists between the close of apprenticeship and the beginning of professional maturity, increasing experience gradually liberates the maturing teacher from problems which beset the beginner. As these problems diminish, the teacher is freer to concentrate on growth of a higher sort: knowing the institution, he can better help to improve it as a center of education; having learned the conventions of teaching, he is in better position to develop original techniques; feeling at home in a field of scholarship, he can with greater assurance move in less trodden paths.

The growth process does not proceed in mechanical fashion from the conventional to the original, from the imitative to the creative. The promising young teacher, regardless of his inexperience, is from the beginning an original and creative worker in many respects. But to establish one's mastery in a craft one must learn its rules, and this is the primary task for the beginner. The experienced teacher should not be content with applying the rules more expertly or reaching for "superior levels of the commonplace" but strive for qualitatively different and higher achievement. Education is improved both by doing familiar tasks better and by envisioning and attacking new tasks.

Improving Instruction. The better the teacher, the greater the challenge for improvement that he sees. Even the accomplished teacher will find worthy targets in the endeavor to effect better course organization, planning of instruction, conduct of lecture and discussion, guidance of study, and evaluation of achievement. However familiar the subject and fluent the instruction, teaching and study aids, practice exercises, and reading lists are never so good that they cannot be improved. Better ways of adapting teaching to the individual needs of student , engaging superior students in more exacting and enriching activity, and stimulating the slow or uninterested learner to better achievement can almost always be developed.

An equally important goal is learning to deepen and liberalize one's influence as educator. Extending the educational potential of one's courses and one's activities as instructor will lead students toward broader personal development. Success in such effort is proportional to the teacher's continuous self-enrichment as person and scholar, his broadening perspective in education, and participation in the cooperative life of his institution. He cannot afford to maintain an academically provincial outlook, nor isolate himself in the classroom or laboratory away from other academic responsibility. He needs to join with colleagues in discussions of problems of teaching, learning, and administration, become involved in educational issues, and keep informed of developments outside his own discipline. Academic isolationism has operated to prevent many a wellqualified teacher from attaining the stature of educator.

The profession of college teaching has so developed in general and specialized phases that, however much he is occupied in personal scholarly pursuits, the college teacher must regularly share in common discoveries, accomplishments, and problems. Issues such as those arising from increased enrollments are not the concern of one professional group but of all. No one can afford to ignore the contributions to general educational thought of John Dewey, Bertrand Russell, or Alfred N. Whitehead but even more specialized writings in educational psychology, curriculum, and evaluation must be sampled if the teacher is to remain abreast of his profession. The publication in 1945 of Harvard's General Education in a Free Society deservedly attracted attention, yet studies and reports of comparable significance by colleges, teachers' associations, and government agencies within the last twenty-five years have been all too neglected. The college teacher, for example, who has not discovered for himself the series of publications sponsored by the American Youth Commission misses an opportunity for an enlightening look into the minds of students. In recent years the profession has been active in promoting conferences such as those of the Association for Higher Education and the Survey of Medical Education. To the existing fund of periodical literature in higher education a journal of distinction has lately been added in Improving College Teaching and Learning. All of these, as well as publications by the Educational Policies Commission, the American Council on Education, and other agencies, deal with matters of urgent import to the college teacher. There are practical limits to opportunity to engage in active collaboration and even to gain information through reading, but the college teacher should eagerly divide his attention between activities in his own discipline and those in the wider field of education.

One gains in professional understanding through knowledge of students, and for this purpose the classroom setting alone is insufficient. The teacher needs to associate with students in out of-class activities. The need is admitted in principle, but as the teacher becomes more deeply involved in his primary and collateral responsibilities he finds it increasingly inconvenient to find time for "socializing" activity. The higher he advance in the profession, the farther removed from students he is apt to become. The result is that older faculty members who have more to contribute to students pass less time in such association than junior colleagues. A teacher's first business is with students, and whatever his eminence none can afford to be so busy as to be unavailable for informal association with them. Attending student' social events, participating in their activities, sharing their company at meals, inviting them to a weekly "coffee hour," accompanying them on excursions, or simply "visiting" with them during chance meetings are part of the normal routine of professional living. Students are pleased and benefited by these contacts, and teachers may learn much that is useful in teaching and conducive to mental vigor and alertness.

Productive Scholarship. Even the teacher who publishes little can by sustained pursuit of study, extracting knowledge and relating it to instruction, refresh himself and invigorate his teaching. The teacher who can periodically produce scholarly work of publishable quality—a report of a significant experiment or investigation, a monograph on a subject of importance, a learned paper—helps not only to advance knowledge but to infuse his instruction with a sense of excitement reserved for an originator or discoverer. Standing to profit most of all is the teacher who makes continuous productive scholarship an absorbing hobby while maintaining himself in other phases of his responsibility. The discipline of exploring a problem, determining a line of investigation, following through in research, organizing findings, and giving them clear and effective expression offers an unmatched opportunity for growth.

Those interested in dedicating themselves to productive scholarship should not make the commitment lightly. The exercise of productive scholarship is exacting, requiring an abundance of energy with which to satisfy also concurrent teaching obligations. A teacher should begin by realistically appraising himself and the circumstances under which he works. If by temperament he finds intensive application to a long-term task irksome, if he finds the company of people more congenial to his interest than solitary devotion to study, if writing comes hard and the discipline of learning to write is unappealing, or if the institution makes such professional demands as to leave little time and energy for systematic research and writing, perhaps he should explore other more promising avenues of service.

There is a great difference in personal investment between preparing an occasional piece for publication and producing a more extended work of scholarship: the latter is not often turned out by working weekends and during short vacation periods. One must be willing with real austerity to "strip down" to the essentials in living, foregoing many social and professional interests. Even the pressure of family responsibilities may have a bearing on the outcome. The implication is not that the productive scholar must prepare himself for a rigorous existence without the normal amenities but that, like the artist or creative writer, he must live under professional discipline, rationing himself so as to make productive work possible.

Growth through Civic Experience. Contact with the community offers an opportunity to be of service, a constructive outlet for the teacher's talent and energy, and a means of personal and professional enrichment. The community is a social workshop and laboratory in which products of instruction are used, raw materials for later instruction produced, new educational needs revealed, and provisions for meeting them tested. Many of the college disciplines, particularly the social studies, have their roots close to the surface of community living and are shaped in their growth by the immediate social climate. The teacher must derive nourishment from contact with the public environment outside the college. It is not enough to be a "student of society" in the abstract; the teacher needs to be close to people and to an understanding of them. From such proximity and understanding he will gain in knowledge of his students and the nature and possibilities of his subject. In the Middle Ages the "Seven Liberal Arts" were taught as dry encyclopedic knowledge divorced from events of contemporary life; only the unremitting efforts of dedicated scholars kept them from extinction. Today the liberal studies in the college program are richer from contact at all points with people and their ways. To an extent the work of the college teacher is by nature confining; all more reason why he—the physicist or the metaphysicist- should cultivate opportunity for community experience if he is to grow in capacity for liberal instruction.

Reciprocal Obligations of the College

Professional growth is not a one-sided undertaking. For its part the college has important obligations to fulfill if it would help the teacher realize his professional potentiality. Over and above its human complement of teachers and students the college has a corporate existence and character shaped, in some cases, over generations. It has influence and prestige carrying beyond the physical confines of the institution, and resources above those of material possession. The corporate life of the college should be so conducted as to encourage the development of students and teachers, and its strength brought to bear in their support. Of the many obligations which the college has to teachers, a few have been chosen for special mention.

1. *To employ wise policies of teacher selection, retention, and promotion.* Sound personnel policy is essential for the maintenance of a healthy institutional life. The best way for a college to achieve excellence is to find and appoint good teachers. Students would be better educated and teachers' professional development enhanced if the latter were selected on the basis of criteria more intrinsically related to their responsibilities. The right people in the right fobs do not need much external stimulation in order to fulfill their aspirations. In the absence of more reliable indices of potentiality it is the obligation of the college to recruit people with the highest qualifications of

intelligence, character, and training, trusting the probationary process to permit further evaluation of their fitness. The probationary period, usually of at least three years' duration, should be made a rigorous test of a young teacher's capability and longer range promise. Success should earn retention. Current practices tend to be inconsistent: on the one hand, some institutions release all but the most brilliant newcomers after a few years of service, while in many others, retention after a nominal probationary period is almost assured if the young teacher "seems all right."

Academic promotion policies are also in need of reassessment. The need for considering skill in teaching as a factor in promotion is self-evident, and in principle more and more colleges have come to accord it equal ranking with scholarly attainment. But good teaching is not as measurable an accomplishment as productive scholarship, and the practical result is to tip the scales in favor of the latter. This is professionally unfair and unrealistic. Without withdrawing recognition of acknowledged scholarship, promotion standards should in practice include good teaching and other professional attainments.

Although opportunities for promotion may necessarily be competitive, the principle of competition should not be carried too far. It is not a fruitful exercise to rank teachers of different accomplishment in different fields of instruction. A teacher should be appraised in terms of his professional contribution, and where a wider scale needs to be established, it should be weighted in terms of all of the teacher's functions and not a selected few.

2. *To afford adequate remuneration.* No person enters the teaching profession in order to become rich; but there is a functional relationship between adequate salary, job security and expectation of a sufficient retirement income, and maintenance of high standards of professional achievement. College teaching offers rewards sufficient to attract first-rate persons to the profession, but people cannot be expected to be single-minded in devotion to their job when its salary has to be supplemented by earnings from various part-time occupations College governing boards recognize the problem and do their best in the face of mounting odds, but its full resolution is beyond their

control. The matter calls for vision and statesmanship on high levels of public policy so that higher education may be granted the subsidy it needs without admission of outside interference.

Arguments for improving teachers' salaries are often presented as a plea for public generosity and civic idealism, as if proper compensation were a matter of upholding the prestige of a profession. Actually more fundamental laws of economics are operative. To get and to hold persons of high professional caliber it is necessary to take account of competing opportunities in the employment market. It would be catastrophic for American society if its colleges were staffed with teachers of mediocre quality satisfied with low-paying employment. The public would not long tolerate paying physicians reduced fees for inferior medical service nor low-cost housing that fails to stand up. The cost of maintaining education should be viewed in the same way; failure to do this presents even greater risks since a decline in the educational product is less perceptible immediately and more destructive in the long run.

3. *To foster a climate conducive to good teaching and learning.* On the whole American collages have done an exemplary job in supporting teachers in the exercise of their rights as scholars and citizens and in resisting intrusion of occasional repressive influences from outside. A comparable job needs to be done in making every campus a stimulating and productive place in which to live and to work. Absence of restraints is not enough' to be intellectually invigorating a college should be hospitable to new ideas, new projects and endeavors, and to change. It should not only use its people skillfully for its own ends, but encourage them to conceive and seek ends of their own, expressing their distinctive talents in professionally useful ways. It should promote sound orthodoxy and promising heterodoxy, and having tried some things and failed, try again. No institution can afford to rest on its past or present accomplishment. By continually reviewing its goals and the processes designed to serve them. Imaginatively assigning creative people to creative tasks, pursuing institutional research, sharing with other institutions the product of its experience

and learning, and being responsive to new developments in society, a college can retain its vitality and help its teachers to grow.

Much argument has centered on the extent to which faculty participation in institutional government is desirable. Faculty management has its limitations but also the incomparable advantage of broadening the scope of responsible college citizenship. It impels concern for educational tasks outside one's immediate sphere of instruction, and fosters civic pride and sense of professional belonging. Government by committees may be awkward, but the quality of ideas is improved through friction of minds, and in the long run coordinated group activity is more productive than streamlined individual effort. The atmosphere of democratically decentralized rule is wholesome for liberal education, and the freedom it offers for responsible dissent is an influence for growth. Not every college is in position to grant the organized faculty broad powers of educational authority, but so far as possible it should invest teachers (and students) with responsibility for the conduct of institutional affairs.

4. *To assign teachers to instruction and other service in ways that take account of their special capabilities, interests, and needs for growth.* Industry has learned the importance of placing the right worker in the right job; the college is perhaps more careful in initial selection of its people than in their subsequent specific utilization, even with regard to their primary responsibility in teaching. Assignment to courses often follows the path of least resistance, the basis of course allotment being continuity in status quo, teachers' indicated preference, and seniority, combined naturally with scholarly attainment. The result is to keep teachers in the same courses for a longer time than may be desirable, depriving them and others of an opportunity to extend their teaching competency. Young teachers are at a disadvantage in carrying a heavier burden of elementary or "leftover" courses and delayed from entering those for which they may be more suited.

Little within the supervisor's province of responsibility is more important than fostering the proper professional utilization of manpower. A teacher's satisfaction in his work and continued impulse for self-improvement depend upon the challenge and interest in his assigned duties. One needs to feel that the courses he offers are "right" for him and that, in general, his program of professional activity has been planned with care, looking toward his long-term good. Since institutional needs occasionally conflict with personal interests, it may be necessary at times to compromise to the extent of accepting a course lying outside one's sphere of preference. But a teacher needs to feel convinced that his long-term needs for growth are not being overlooked.

The paramount consideration in determining assignment to courses is that students shall have the best instruction available. Subject to this qualification, other considerations are admissible, chiefly the teacher's own preference, need for representativeness or balance in viewpoints, and training requirements of younger teachers. At this point the supervisor's insight into the potentialities of teachers and his leadership qualities come into evidence—in creating new and better growth opportunities and inducing colleagues to avail themselves of them. Some teachers are less venturesome than others in accepting new responsibilities, and may need to be convinced of their desirability. Particularly in the rapidly developing program of extra-instructional educational services it is possible for an alert supervisor to conceive new tasks promising to be useful to the institution and at the same time to engage special capacities of teachers.

From the teacher's viewpoint a good teaching schedule has—in addition to the intrinsic worth and challenge of its courses—variety, coherence, and balance. It is unwise to assign more than two "sections" of the same course lest instruction become routinized; it is equally undesirable to include completely disparate offerings so that the teacher has difficulty in finding a focus for scholarly interest and application. An ideal teaching schedule consists of perhaps three different courses, on different levels to enable the teacher to work with students over a range of educational maturity, yet involving a common area of scholarship or related divisions of that area.

5. *To maintain a reasonable work schedule and satisfactory conditions of work.* Within their financial capabilities colleges endeavor

to keep the individual service load down to workable size, and the vigilance of accrediting agencies and professional organizations has helped to enforce proper standards. College teaching should be distinguished by quality of production rather than volume of activity. A heavy teaching schedule, oversized classes, extra-instructional assignments, and burdensome "housekeeping" duties have an adverse effect on professional quality. Needing special protection are the ablest and most promising teachers and those whose distinctive interests require more painstaking application. Many an able young teacher has been checked in fulfilment of a promising career by being prematurely saddled with too many responsibilities. It is reassuring for an administrator to assign an important task to a person who invariably performs well, but it is more important that such work be apportioned fairly without excessive inconvenience to anyone. Exacting extra-instructing duties should be rotated among those able to manage them, and few should be exempt from the indispensable routine chores ever-present in an operation of institutional size.

Two common complaints of teachers concern the inadequacy of work space and secretarial assistance. Such things are hard to govern by educational principle, but in an institution's desire to expand its academic opportunities and services, space facilities for teachers are frequently overlooked. Spacious reception rooms and administrative quarters are much less important than assigned space in which a teacher can pursue work with a student, a colleague, or his own thoughts. Similarly it is false economy to use teachers in clerical tasks they are untrained to perform; it is cheaper to liberate them for professional responsibilities. The physical preparation of instructional materials—course outlines, bibliographies, study exercises, examinations—as well as necessary administrative reports should be the responsibility of a shared or centralized secretarial service.

6. *To orient the new teacher to his job.* A beginning has been made in this direction but the organized effort is far from adequate. Entering a new institution, even an experienced teacher requires systematic orientation to changed responsibilities and routines. A beginner needs more through in-service training not only in functions specific to his

job but also in broader professional practice. The college should provide a planned program of activities familiarizing the beginner with its educational aims, the nature and scope of its curriculum, essential information relating to students' background, current concerns and problems, and, in a more detailed way, with the teacher's individual responsibilities. This training should include planning and organizing instruction, preparing instructional materials and aids, proper use of various lesson patterns, guiding independent study, and evaluating learning. Training may be conducted in individual or group conference held in conjunction with actual supervision of the beginner in his job. If more general interest warrants the conferences may be organized on a large seminar basis with an invitation to participate extended to all faculty members.

7. *To give every teacher the benefit of constructive supervision.* Every professional person, regardless of maturity and attainment, needs at many points in his career the benefit of a colleague's advice help, or criticism. In the college such supervision has special character and requirements. It is exercised more by the teacher himself and a voluntary group of associates than by a the teacher himself and a voluntary group of associates than by a designated executive officer or senior colleague, its function is advisory rather than managerial, and it operates more indirectly, informally, and unobtrusively. In practice it must take account of the teacher's sometimes superior qualification in an academic field, of the rights of academic freedom and the dignity of the profession, and—not least—of the absence of standard criteria of merit. Nevertheless there is an indispensable place in college teaching for the "supervisor"— a dean, department head, or senior colleague—on whom rests special responsibility for promoting and aiding in individual and group efforts at self-improvement.

Observation of college teaching is better conducted under the auspices of teachers themselves, exchanging visits and discussing their own and one another's teaching problems. Instruction during such visits is less constrained and the subsequent conference between teachers more free of tension. Students becoming aware of the practice of faculty intervisiting will be less self-conscious. The supervisor's role is to stimulate interest in such a program, help organize and maintain it, and assist teachers in utilizing the results.

A Correlative means of supervision is systematic group discussion of teaching problems on a college-wide, department, and course committee basis, organized and led by teachers. Criticism of teaching practice and proposals for improvement, emanating from group deliberation and impersonally directed, have greater effect than those passing from supervisor to teacher—and hurt much less. The supervisor's role is to sponsor and support these conferences, promote participation, play an active though not dominant part in the proceedings, and assist in carrying out the proposals. The supervisor himself, meeting in informal sessions with individual teachers, can make direct contributions of inestimable value, whether in dealing with instructional problems of the moment or matters of longer range. On the college level such meetings should be free of official formality and didactic tone: they are explorations of ideas between equals.

Good supervision stimulates the initiative, imagination, and intelligent effort of others. College teachers need less to be corrected and guided than released for creative work. The college supervisor makes his best contribution not by trying to recast colleagues in his own image but by giving them leeway to develop in theirs. It does not much matter whether the supervisor is privately in agreement with what a teacher attempts: if the latter is convinced of the worth of an idea, provided no prohibitive consequences impend, the supervisor should accord assistance and support, although he is free to express his reservations. Some undertakings may not succeed, nut it is important that the teacher keep trying, and from the effort may come growth.

8. *To protect the teacher in the exercise of his professional duties.* This obligation may not need to be invoked of ten, but when a critical situation arises the institution should take an unequivocal stand. A college teacher is professionally dedicated to the task of stimulating thought and guiding it in the direction of truth, in pursuing scholarship and according it free expression. There are times when, in the practice of his calling, he may arouse opposition from public groups on grounds of offense to patriotism, religion, morality, race, or eco-

nomic belief. Insistent protest by even a small vocal group can make a large institution uncomfortable. It is easy then for the institution to make its public peace by assuring that the teacher will be restrained from further giving offense; but the proper course is for the institution to ascertain whether the teacher's action has been professionally correct and, in the event that it has been, to give him unqualified support whether or not it agrees substantively with what has been said or done. Only in this way can the teacher's (and the profession's) freedom to grow be assured. All too often a teacher's manner rather than substance of expression may be the cause of the difficulty; such offense in unnecessary, and steps should be taken to obviate its recurrence. Teachers are bound by the same obligations to good taste and civility as other persons and, when they become careless or insensitive it is the institution's supervisory responsibility to correct them and restore harmony.

An institution should be slow to intervene in matters of teacher student relations, yet avoid a policy of complete noncommitment. For a college to dignify every complaint against a teacher with a formal hearing would have the effect of fostering educationally undesirable habits: haggling about examination or course grades, for example, would be certain to increase. Solicitous parents may write to a college executive expressing grievance against this teacher or that; in trivial cases reply should be made without even notifying the teacher; in cases warranting more complete explanation the complaining letter should be forwarded to the teacher with a request for reply. Only when charges are unmistakably serious is thorough investigation justified. If a teacher is qualified to hold his teaching position, he is qualified to work his way out of the occasional difficulties that arise in teacher-student relations. The "official" judgment of the institution should not supplant the teacher's own judgment except for cause.

Teachers have been known at times to behave capriciously and to be guilty of unjustifiable actions in dealing with students. In such cases the institution has an obligation to rectify the mistake. Incidents in which students seem to have been treated unfairly should be investigated and, if the teacher proves to have been at fault, amends made to the student without degrading the teacher or compromising his future effectiveness. A good teacher grows from the mistakes he has made, provided they have been brought to his attention without incurring his lasting resentment.

SELECTED BIBLIOGRAPHY

Anderson, Paul R., " The Preparation of the Teacher in General Education," *Journal of General Education*, 3:98-106, January 1949.

Association for Higher Education, *Current Issues in Higher Education,* 1954, Proceedings of the Ninth Annual National Conference on Higher Education. Washington: National Education Association, 1954. 321 pp.

Blegen, Theodore C, and Cooper, Russell M., editors, The *Preparation of College Teachers,* Report of a Conference Geld in Chicago, Illinois, December 8-10, 1949, Sponsored by the American Council on Education and the U.S. Office of Education. Washington: American Council on Education, 1950. 186 pp.

Carman, Harry J., "Teachers of Tomorrow," *Association of American Colleges Bulletin,* 35: 306-16, May 1949.

Eckert, Ruth E., "Some Neglected Aspects in the Preparation of College Teachers," *Journal of General Education,* 3:137-44, January 1949.

Edmondson, James B., "Improving the Effectiveness of College Teaching," *School and Society,* 76:209-13, October 4, 1952.

Gilbert, Amy M., "In-Service Education of the College Faculty," *Journal of Higher Education,* 20:192-97, April 1949.

Gray, William S., ed., *The Preparation and In-Service Training of College Teachers,* Volume 10 of the Proceedings of the Institute for Administrative Officers of Higher Institutions. Chicago: University of Chicago Press, 1938. 230 pp.

Kelly, Fred J., ed., *Improving College Instruction,* Report of a conference Held at Chicago, Illinois, December 7-9, 1950, Sponsored by the American Council on Education and the U.S. Office of Education. Washington: American Council on

Education, 1951. 195 pp.

——, *Toward Better College Teaching,* Bulletin 1950, No. 13, Office of Education, Federal Security Agency. Washington: U.S. Government Printing Office, 1950. 71 pp

Klapper, Paul, "Problems in College Teaching," *American Association of University Professors Bulletin,* 36:53-63, March 1950.

——, "Professional Preparation of the College Teacher," *Journal of General Education,* 3:228-44, July 1949.

National Education Association, Research Division, "Instructional Staff Practices and Policies in Degree-Granting Institutions, 1953-54," *Research Bulletin,* 32:159-214, December 1954.

President's Report on Higher Education, *Higher Education for American Democracy,* Vol. IV, "Staffing Higher Education," 63 pp. New York: Harper & Brothers, 1947.

Reed, Anna Y. et al., *The Effective and the Ineffective College Teacher.* New York: American Book Company, 1935. 344 p.

Russell, John Dale, ed., *Problems of Faculty Personnel,* Volume 18 of the Proceedings of the Institute for Administrative Officers of Higher Institutions. Chicago: University of Chicago Press, 1946. 146 p.

Tead, Ordway, *College Teaching and College Learning: A Plea for Improvement,* frank Ellsworth Spaulding Lecture for 1947-1948. New Haven: Yale University Press, 1949. 56 pp.

Wilson, Logan, *The Academic Man: A Study in the Sociology Profession.* New York: Oxford University Press, 1942. 248 pp.

Woodburne, Lloyd S., *Faculty Personnel Policies in Gigher Education.* New: Harper & Brothers, 1950. 201 pp.

3
CURRICULUM OF THE COLLEGE

The curriculum is an instrument of education, the chief means available to the teacher for the accomplishment of his educational purpose. Over the years it has received much professional attention, yet not always with proper reference to the ends it is meant to serve. The subject matter of the curriculum tends to become absorbing in its own right and its essentially instrumental role to be forgotten. Disciplines of instruction appear to assume an independent purpose for existence, and the servant leads the master. Just as other instruments have at times outlived the needs which created them, so have portions of the curriculum sometimes remained after their usefulness diminished. Protected by tradition the curriculum has not always been subjected to the test of logic or practical sense.

It is difficult to determine when a curriculum is an efficient instrument of education and even harder to gauge its efficiency with precision: results in education are slow to become evident. They are not readily provable, and the final issue may remain in doubt. In recent years much effort has gone into redesigning the curriculum to adapt it to the needs of the times. The chances are that from this activity has resulted an instrument capable enough of serving its purpose; the probability is also that it can be further improved. Important for both current use and future improvement of the curriculum is an attitude receptive to recognition of shortcomings as well as merits, and not so restrained by tradition or by loyalty to a field of scholarship as to fail to perceive or take needed action.

To laymen a profession is supposed to hold no secrets for it practitioners; those in the profession know better. It should be admitted that there is much relating to curriculum concerning which knowledge is lacking, in which professional procedure is based on trial and error, hypothesis, or simply faith. We behave sometimes as if there were no curriculum problems that greater resources of money or manpower could not solve. Such self-assurance is not justified; it would be healthier to acknowledge that in many respects our approach toward assembling, organizing, and conducting a program of study is experimental and tentative.

The Teacher's Concern with the Entire Curriculum. The college teacher is often so engrossed in immediate tasks that he is unable, except in an incidental way, to spare the time for cultivating familiarity with the college program as a whole. Except where problems impinge upon his own or his department's courses of instruction, he is unlikely to be concerned with what are sometimes called "curriculum matters." Beyond the scope of his courses his knowledge of the organized course of study may be limited. First his professional training was not planned to focus attention on problems in curriculum; then, following his entry into teaching, his chief preoccupation was naturally with immediate preparation for instructional and other responsibilities. Thus the pattern was set. It is not unusual to find teachers of several years' service with an institution who have only casual acquaintance with its patterns of offerings, and, summoned to college-wide curriculum service, even experienced teachers are astonished to discover how much hard work as well as disputation can take place behind the closed door of a conference room.

Yet, next to teaching, there are not many matters more deserving of the teacher's attention and concern. In order that he may teach his students properly, he needs to be aware of the larger educational experience in which they are involved, of the relations among its component parts, of its values and shortcomings.

Furthermore, acquaintance with the curriculum in general terms is in itself insufficient. One should know the curriculum intimately enough to understand its shared use as an instrument of education: its rationale, the principles underlying its operation, its purported goals, major component elements, manner of operation, and determinable achievements. The teacher should, moreover, be interested in learning how the program came to be, recent developments or changes, and curriculum undertakings under way. Whether or not directly engaged in curriculum activity, he is not without influence in formulating policy and determining its future success. Often it is the collective judgment of the faculty which decides whether a curriculum proposal is acceptable, and the support furnished by the faculty which makes the difference between the success or failure of an innovation. The teacher has an obligation to use his influence responsibly to good effect.

Some Attributes of the Prevailing Curriculum. While there is no "typical" college program, it is possible to describe attributes common to programs in most institutions. In important respects the contemporary American college is distinguishable from the institution of several generations ago or even from comparable European institutions today. To check the pertinence of these attributes one has only to relate them to the institution he serves or to others with which he may be familiar. In recognizing the existence of common characteristics, prevailing differences in curriculum features of institutions need not be minimized. So much has been written on the subject that listing and brief explanation may suffice.

1. *Comprehensiveness.* The range and variety of knowledge encompassed within the college curriculum is "encyclopedic." Practically every major field of learning is represented by a course or courses, in some instances at several levels of study. The compact body of liberal disciplines which almost to the time of the Civil War "consisted chiefly of studies in Latin, Greek, mathematics, logic, and moral philosophy, with occasional smattering of Hebrew and elementary physics and astronomy," has given way to a program of extended dimensions. To the traditional subjects—classical languages and literatures, mathematics, philosophy, and physical science—modern languages and literatures, the biological sciences, the social sciences, the fine arts, music health, and physical education have been added, and the increase of knowledge within each subject has led to multiplication of courses of instruction. Most recently even liberal institutions have been introducing studies in such occupational fields as business, home economics, journalism, social work, and teaching. So extensive is the college curriculum that a student can hope to master only a fraction of it.

The vast expansion in the scope of knowledge that has taken place in modern times is not the only reason for the comprehensiveness of the curriculum. In every age the sum of organized learning has been much larger than that which the college could or cared to include in its program. Much of the time, however, the theory under which higher education operated placed a premium not on inclusiveness but on selectivity of learning; under formal discipline, for example, a few well-chosen formative subjects could accomplish the purposes of college education. When this theory lost ground, a formidable barrier against less discriminating admission of studies was removed. Under the advancing pressure of science, social science, and new professions, and with the mounting enrollment of students with differentiated interests, the gates were further opened and in a short time the college curriculum became virtually a panoramic representation of man's knowledge.

2. *Number of separate offerings.* The amount of knowledge enclosed by the curriculum inevitably presents problems in organizing instruction. Paralleling scholarly and research practice in the different fields of learning, curriculum disciplines have tended to be organized and conducted in limited allotments, within the larger boundaries of departments, divisions, and "schools" of instruction. The number of separate course offerings in liberal colleges alone, if a cumulative nonduplicating list could be assembled, would run well into the thousands. A single large college may have twenty-five or more departments of instruction and may list upward of five hundred or six hundred courses; a large one with several branches may have twice the number. In one semester a student may pursue six or seven courses, and in four years of study "complete" between fifty and fifty-five. A mathematical credit system keeps track of the student's progress through the forest of studies and indicates when he has accomplished enough to merit graduation.

College teachers are aware of the difficulties inherent in this proliferation of studies. The condition is not an outcome of design but of evolutionary development to which a number of influences contributed: the increasingly specialized nature of scholarship, pressure for admission of new fields of learning, desire to satisfy the differing interests of students, introduction of the elective principle, and others.

Teachers themselves are not without responsibility, as all should admit who have at various times pressed for inclusion of a particular course representative of their specialized interest.

3. *Disparity among courses.* Equally evident is the discrepancy among courses in range and depth of subject matter and in structure. In effect there is no common yardstick by which a course is definable. In the same semester and for an equal number of credits a student may be enrolled in a "general" course of broad content, a specialized course of delimited area but considerable depth, and a "tool" course in speech, writing, foreign language, or mathematics. In his junior year he may take courses less rigorous than those pursued as a freshman. Some courses are logically self-contained units, others a framework of convenience enclosing selected beginning and terminal points for instruction, as, for example, "History of Europe from 1815 to 1865." Most courses are specifically within one field of learning or department of instruction, others are interdisciplinary. The duration of courses varies among and within institutions, and may range from a "quarter" of six or eight weeks to a period of a year or two.

There is no virtue in uniformity as such, and some disparity among courses is necessary and desirable. Differences in levels of study, conduct of instruction, and outcomes of learning should be cultivated if we are to provide students with variety of learning experience. Weakness occurs when diversity is fortuitous rather than planned, when no definite standards obtain as to what constitutes good course of study.

4. *The elective principle.* Most liberal colleges adhere to the elective principle. They differ in the degree of elective freedom granted, the nature of elective offerings, and the manner in which student selection of courses is regulated. Elective study is commonly associated with "concentration" in a major field of study, and represents a recognition of the worth of different varieties of learning experience as well as a practical concession to the divergent interests of the students. The realistic alternative to limited election is not a uniform course of study for all students but either multiplication of specialized colleges or greatly curtailed enrollment in higher education. It

is no coincidence that pressure for elective study developed when the colleges began to attract more students and that the recent growth in enrollment has been accompanied by an expansion of elective opportunity.

Further justifying the elective principle is the theory that higher education must fulfill also an exploratory function, that is, enable the student to explore himself in relation to various fields of learning. Elective opportunities are not limited to the field of the student's "major" concentration but are present to some extent in other phases of the program of study. No single feature is more characteristic of the contemporary American college and its concept of higher education than the elective system.

5. *The prescribed core.* Paired with the elective principle is the complementary practice of designating a portion of the curriculum as "prescribed." Prescriptive offerings vary widely among institutions in substance, form, and extent. In some cases prescribed courses may be few, consisting of several "tool" subjects and content courses such as "History of Western Culture" which are judged indispensable. More often the prescribed program is of greater extent, containing representative courses from major divisions of study embracing the humanities, science, and social science without a definite organic interconnection. The prescription may be stated in terms of listed courses or as a required "distribution" of credits among given course groupings or "areas" of study. The sum of prescribed course credits may range from a small fraction of the total needed for graduation to more than half.

The prescriptive principle is founded in the belief that a common body of educational experience is basic to the development of all students regardless of individual differences, and that the best interest of each requires that a balance be maintained between common and differentiated study. The prescriptive principle as such has not incurred as much criticism as its elective complement. The problem is to determine what constitutes proper balance and, even more serious, to identify and assemble the elements of a good prescribed core.

6. *Internal regulation.* The multiform nature of the curriculum im-

poses a need for greater institutional regulation of study than may in principle be desirable. American institutions of higher education have been criticized as being over-regulated: there are rules governing admission to courses, attendance, fulfillment of prescriptions, choice of electives, preparation of programs of study, retention or dismissal, and eligibility for graduation. To institutional regulations departments of instruction may add requirements for their own "majors." Having satisfied the college foreign-language prescription a student may be faced with an additional language requirement set by his elective department; or, having selected a field of concentration, he may find himself pursuing patterns of elective courses not primarily of his own design. Extensive use is made of the device of labeling courses prerequisite to others, though the strict necessity of such linkage may not always be apparent.

Some regulation is necessary to safeguard coherence and continuous progression in study and balanced education. Amid the variety of curricular offerings it would be unsafe simply to turn the student loose to shift for himself. Unrestricted election of studies could readily degenerate into the practice of sampling courses at random or, contrarily, into overspecialization. But the prevailing abundance of regulation does lend a "lock-step" quality to college education. In an attempt to break the lock-step some colleges have taken measures to insure greater individual freedom in programming and progression in study, using for this purpose placement and exemption examinations, comprehensive tests of achievement, and independent reading courses.

Curriculum Strengths and Weaknesses

The foregoing discussion of general curriculum attributes suggests both strengths and weaknesses. It is well to make an explicit distinction between the two, since current proposals for reform threaten at times to sweep away much that is good along with the elements that should be eliminated.

Strengths. 1. *Adaptability to individual needs.* The college curriculum has evolved in a manner responsive to the needs of a mixed student population. Its value lies not only the richness of its offerings but also in their adaptability to students. Though the reality falls short of the ideal there is inherent an effort to make available to each person an appropriate education. A science-minded student can, with adequate guidance, develop his potentiality in science and at the same time secure a broad training in the humanities and social sciences. The musically gifted student, the artist, future mathematician, psychologist, or teacher can similarly select studies consistent with his special aptitudes while pursuing others addressed to the demands of more general education. The student without pronounced aptitude or interest has a chance to explore his capacities in several fields of study. No single common course of study could serve all these students, even were it possible to prescribe one which would meet with general approval. In the absence of indisputable authority indicating otherwise, a diversified, multipurpose curriculum seems best.

2. *Dynamic quality of the program.* Whatever its failings the curriculum of the American college is alive, responsive to change in society and to the growth and development of knowledge. Advances in scholarship and its application to the service of mankind are reflected in adaptations of the course of study. It is not true now, as it may have been in past periods, that institutions of higher education are out of touch with intellectual and creative progress in the world outside. Without surrendering its function of conserving the best in tradition, the college is involved in the discovery and acquisition of new subject matter. To be sure, not everything admitted into the curriculum has proved worthy of retention. But the prevailing experimental approach to curriculum making is wholesome, and the willingness to change, appraise, and change again is evidence of professional alertness and determination to improve.

3. *Intellectual freedom.* The elective principle has introduced a radical change in the concept of curriculum and in basic educational philosophy. Liberal education can hardly stress freedom as an objective without admitting freedom into the learning process, and without opening up a wider intellectual universe for investigation and study. A closed system of thought, whether it relates to science, political philosophy, or educational theory, is intellectually confining; minds do not operate at their best within strictly delimited boundaries. What-

ever advantages the older fixed curriculum may have had in greater order clarity, it also approximated a closed system of thought which in time became involuted, narrow, and illiberalizing. For long periods the liberal college curriculum was liberal mostly in name; the most creative intellectual work in the eighteenth century was done by individuals who broke away from the barren fields of institutional learning. The current curriculum is open-ended, fostering a variety of approaches to education and encouraging experimentation. The goal is education for every student, but associated with it is a healthy assumption that what is good education for one may not be good for another, and that our chances of determining a *uniform* good education for all are negligible. A philosophy of education which is realistically cognizant of the limitations of its own claims to truth and which is willing to try to educate different individuals in different ways is compatible with the goals and interests of democracy.

4. *Elective influence on instruction.* Where the student has a measure of freedom in choice of studies, the effect upon instruction is bound to be good. This does not mean that teachers consciously engage in competition for trade or need a competitive incentive in order to teach their courses well. A degree of competition for the interest of students is healthy. Choosing teachers and courses was an ancient prerogative of university students and, although historical records attest to abuses, it is regrettable that at least in American colleges this privilege was for a long time withdrawn. Both teachers and students acknowledge that a different spirit exists in elective as against prescribed courses, the difference being not wholly attributable to the greater selectivity and maturity of classes, or the teachers' fondness for their courses. Voluntary student enrollment and participation in course activity is itself a factor for good morale which facilitate the teacher's task and improves its effectiveness. Too many prescribed courses have the unpleasant habit of "going dead." The small element of competition introduced by the elective system, while insufficient to threaten teachers, serves to put them on their mettle We take pride in keeping up the level of enrollment in our elective courses, and perhaps subconsciously work harder to make the experience rewarding to students.

Weaknesses. Some weaknesses in the educational program result from the functions it seeks to fulfill, and are an extension of properties which have been identified as "strengths." The difference between "strength" and "weakness" may be only a matter of the degree to which a condition exists; carried to extremes, a commendable practice may engender its own problems. Thus, a profusion of curricular offerings allowing an opportunity for enriched educational experience may also be confusing to students; a pluralistic approach to education may be necessary and justified but may foster undesirable conflicts in aims and purposes. Good educational principles do not in themselves insure against difficulties and abuses in practice.

1. *Difficulty in organizing for the student a balanced, unified, and coherent program of study.* The wealth of course offerings is in a sense embarrassing. From this diversified domain it is not easy to carve out individual programs of study which meet the specifications for good education. A program of study is not merely a succession of courses; it implies relevance to purpose, internal coherence, balance, and continuous progression of educational experience. While curriculum regulations may be helpful in insuring at least minimal adherence to principles of program organization consistent with individual variations, the problem of planning and shaping a pattern of study for each student remains. The student may be unable to plan such a program for himself, or may be influenced by preformed interests to concentrate on some fields of learning to the neglect of others. For the lazy or indifferent student there may be too much opportunity to "shop" for easy courses, and to assemble a program of study that is hardly true education. A mediocre student can find courses suited to his mediocre abilities, and be graduated without ever having been challenged to rise above mediocrity. These are not hypothetical limitations; they are apparent in the records of many students.

2. *Lack of clarity in aims of studies.* The curriculum may at times resemble a patchwork of courses unrelated by any unity of purpose or common sense of mission. Instruction in different courses may be guided by mutually irreconcilable aims or, in some cases, by no clearly definable aim at all. In the final analysis the choice of instructional aim

is made by each teacher. One teacher of literature may guide his instruction so as to center on developing appreciation and independent reading interests; another may concentrate on literary and biographical facts of authorship, content, and style. A science teacher may conduct his course with a view toward acquainting nonspecialists with some fundamental discoveries and concepts of science and methods of scientific procedure; another may labor to produce prospective scientists, and a third may not go beyond stressing memorization of the contents of the textbook and laboratory manual. Furthermore it is not exceptional to find teachers indulging in classroom criticism of studies whose purposes do not suit them: the historian may express dissatisfaction with a less "disciplined" social science, and the teacher of philosophy find fault with "bread-and-butter" subjects which have invaded the academic field. To the student on the receiving end of these doctrines, the aims of college study just seem confusing, if and when he stops to think.

Though return to a monolithic curriculum structure is hardly desirable, some clearer definition and greater consistency of educational purpose in specific course offerings would be helpful. A diversified curriculum need not be a disorganized one. Different approaches to instruction can be maintained provided they are known, identified, and coordinated as far as possible toward common ends. However much we differ in educational philosophy, our professional goals are not situated in diametrically opposite directions and we more often agree than disagree on desired final outcomes.

3. *Too much "splintering."* The tendency has been to divide and subdivide areas of instruction, creating narrower, more intensive, and more specialized units. Pressure from professional schools and a desire for academic prestige have operated in the colleges to promote the admission of technical and advanced courses more appropriate to graduate levels of study. The weakness is evident in purely humanistic as well as quasi-professional offerings. Some of the "splinter" courses are of questionable value as instruments of general or liberal education. Even the teacher who pursues broader objectives of instruction than those directly implicit in a course title is handicapped

by having to work within the confines of overspecialized subject matter or technique.

It is true that the world's knowledge has come to be embodied within specialized fields of learning, but the curriculum need not faithfully mirror this design. The shape of the curriculum should be influenced by its function, which is primarily to utilize disciplines in educating people. To a certain extent the curriculum must conform to the existing organization of learning, but it is free also to create new syntheses more suitable as educational tools. Colleges have begun to combine and reorganize their offerings so as to present fewer course units, of greater scope and substance. The effort thus far has centered more on basic or "general education" courses than on elective studies. A cursory review of electives in some large college will disclose many which are still narrow and overspecialized in content.

4. *Dissatisfaction with prescribed studies.* For reasons which have been noted and for others, the conventionally prescribed courses have not provided a satisfactory core of general education. Growing by accumulation rather than design, they have increasingly encroached upon the total college program; as new fields of study developed, departments of instruction tended to strengthen their position in the curriculum through the medium of a required course or two. Unrelated to each other, prescribed courses reflected some of the common weaknesses in college studies and displayed further shortcomings of their own. Often organized as an "introduction" to a field of study or as a "general" offering upon which later specialization could be based, they were apt to be pursued without much interest and taught without much interest and taught without enthusiasm. Perhaps with this in mind, some colleges deliberately cut back their prescribed studies to a minimum composed chiefly of essential tool subjects.

Yet a substantial element of common education is necessary, along with the complementary need for some differentiated training. General education does not necessarily postulate that courses must be commonly prescribed, but since advanced studies tend to be so divergent, a foundation of common learning offers greater assurance of a balanced liberal education. Acting on this belief, colleges have been experimenting with new "programs of general education."

The precise meaning of "general education" is difficult to determine since the term has been used in various ways. Essentially the "general education" movement represents a renewed effort to design a core of studies which would meet the common requirements for educating people and at the same time provide each student with an effective foundation for further differentiated training. Departing from the conventional subject-bounded course organization, the programs seek to arrange new syntheses of learning in fewer and larger blocks of study. Instead of offering limited samplings of knowledge from many different subjects, an attempt is made to bring the student into contact with representative problems in a few major fields. The interrelationship of disciplines is recognized and brought into the content of courses, and greater care is used in maintaining lateral coherence among studies. The task of formulating such programs, involving as it does a break from tradition, has not been easy; hardly any are without defects discernible to those responsible for their operation. But the experimental effort is promising, and the motives for it sound.

5. *The credit system.* The danger in attempting to record educational progress through a quantitative system of credits is patent: it lies perhaps not so much in the device itself as in the inferences it may foster. As a method of assessing the orderly progress of large numbers of students through courses of study essentially dissimilar and incomparable, the credit arrangement is feasible enough; but as a way of gauging the actual accomplishment of a specific student it is without much value. The number of course credits a student has earned reveals little concerning the extent and quality of his educational development. Learned and Wood's study indicated that assumptions regarding students' real knowledge made on the basis of their credit standing are hazardous. Yet the student's progress through the course of study must be charted, and no better alternative to the credit system has yet presented itself.

The weakness of the credit system may be offset in a variety of ways. One is simply by flexible organization of study schedules and close guidance of students, enabling the college to know and evaluate students as individuals. Another is by computing for each student a special credit rating indicative of his qualitative worth along with the usual numerical total of credits completed. A third is by use of comprehensive achievement examinations as measures of progression; a number of institutions are currently utilizing such examinations with reference to prescribed studies. Elective field of concentration, or the total college program. Prepared with skill and care as valid instruments for determining educational growth, comprehensive examinations are an effective offset to the limitations of the credit system. The practical deterrent to their habitual use is that such instruments are hard to devise, and their preparation is laborious and costly.

A Balanced View. In the face of interlocking strength and weakness it is difficult to maintain a balanced view of the curriculum. Some educators, unfavourably impressed by its shortcomings, have advocated complete revamping, looking toward a simplified, more logical and coherent sequence of studies, one which would minimize specialization, and exclude offerings not in the liberal tradition. Before supporting such proposals it would be well to consider the difficulty of finding an alternative serviceable to as many students in as many ways. For all its shortcomings the present curriculum does a remarkable job; and though imperfect in practice, its underlying principles are more in harmony with the needs of the student population than an attractively simplified, uniform course of study conceivably could be. (The reference is to the comprehensive liberal college serving a heterogeneous group of students; existing specialized colleges are not faced with the same problem and do not show these shortcomings in the same degree.)

Much can be done to improve the college curriculum. As one reviews the immediate past it is heartening to note how much has already been done to revise it and strengthen its effectiveness. Despite its size and awkwardness the curriculum has proved adaptive to change. If progress is slow at times, the slowness is more attributable to opposition by vested interests than to scarcity of promising ideas and proposals. Curriculum improvement will come only as it is actively fostered by teachers careful to distinguish the good from the bad and willing to venture experimentally into untried ways. There is no certain remedy by which to secure a good curriculum; easy formulas are apt to conceal deep pitfalls. Only in patient, continuous. Cooperative trial is there assured hope of success.

How the Curriculum Came to Be

Even a brief account of the development of the American college curriculum shows the interplay of modernism and tradition, resistance and gradual accommodation, controversy and compromise. The early American college was in most instances church-related and guided by religious purpose, though not exclusively a school for the ministry. In addition to training an educated clergy, its avowed aim was to perpetuate the higher learning in the persons of an educated class of English gentlemen. The curriculum emphasized religion, the languages of religious learning, logic, natural philosophy, and elements of mathematics. Necessarily the program of study was prescribed. By the end of the Colonial Period a trend toward greater secular interest made itself noticeable, reflected by the establishment of nondemominational colleges and the reorganization of studies in older institutions. In 1779, under urging by Thomas Jefferson, the College of William and Mary revised its program, substituting new professorships in political science, medicine, and modern languages for professorships in Divinity and Oriental languages, and adding new studies in law, fine arts, and natural history. With the development of state universities in the early nineteenth century the secular influence became dominant, expressing itself, among other ways, in greater willingness to open the curriculum to admission of new studies.

A hundred years ago the college curriculum was a simple affair with a clearly organized structure of studies. Though earlier the University of Virginis and a number of other institutions had experimented for a time with the principle of limited election, by the middle of the nineteenth century a single fixed pattern of study, distributed over a four-year period, prevailed almost everywhere. Several institutional—notably Harvard, Yale, Dartmouth, Rochester, and Michigan—had crganized separate schools or sequences of study leading to the B.S. degree. The Bachelor of Arts course, however, was the recognized liberal program, consisting in the main of Greek and Latin, mathematics, philosophy, religion, physical science, and history. A number of professorships in modern language and literature had been established but these subjects were still on the fringe of the curriculum. Biology, social science, music, and fine arts had not yet been introduced. Disciplines were not organized and conducted in course units but offered as broad fields of learning in graded sequence. The heart of the curriculum was the classical subjects studied for the full four-year period; subjects of secondary importance such as physical science and history were fitted into the program whenever convenient, sometimes with intervals between periods of study.

As indicated earlier, the limited range of studies was not a reflection to the paucity of knowledge in the world outside; it was the effect of deliberate principle consistent with what had evolved as the prime objective of the college—training through mental discipline. As mental discipline was then understood, it was not necessary to have many subjects as instruments of education: a few "formative" studies could serve the purpose. Those with the strongest claim to disciplinary values were the classical languages and mathematics, regarded as ideally complementary in the kinds of training they afforded the mental faculties. Scientific studies were judged respectable and practical useful, but not of sufficiently high disciplinary quality to warrant the award of the A.B. degree to students pursuing a science-centered program.

As the nineteenth century proceeded it became more difficult to resist the pressure of new studies, chiefly in the expanding fields of science; and once the barrier of the traditional curriculum had been breached, new subjects entered one by one. Gradually and of necessity the elective principle entered one by one. Gradually and of necessity the elective principle was developed. In the years between 1870 and 1910, under the leadership of Eliot of Harvard, Barnard of Columbia, Andrew White of Cornell, Jordan of Stanford, Harper of Chicago, and others, the issue was fought out and a decision finally reached. By 1910 the elective system in one form or another had become accepted by the great majority of American colleges.

The principal argument used by proponents of the elective system was that an enlarged curriculum, more nearly representative of the many fields of learning, would better serve the educational interests of students; the elective system itself was the device for holding students' programs of study to manageable size. Support of the elective principle was offered even on disciplinary grounds: it was argued, for example, that by limiting the range of studies for each students, more thorough scholarship and better mental discipline could be secured. The new studies were themselves affirmed to have disciplinary value.

The victory of the elective principle was ultimately assured by the evident social and cultural importance of the new studies, the changing educational needs in a democratic society under rapid industrialization, and the upward pressure upon the college of a large new high-school population for many of whom the traditional studies held no special interest. In the twentieth century it became difficult to defend a limited and exclusive curriculum on any grounds. Thus were admitted many of the "newer" subjects now in the college program. After 1890 organization by departments was effected in order to facilitate course instruction by competent specialists. Colleges developed different arrangements for combining prescribed and elective studies, but in one manner or another their curricula assumed some of the general characteristics previously discussed.

Recent Practices in Curriculum Reconstruction

In comparison with its predecessor the modern college curriculum has enjoyed little stability. In a sense its evolution has never ceased: under constant scrutiny by college authorities it has changed almost from year to year through the addition, withdrawal, substitution, and reorganization of courses. Aware of inherent difficulties and problems almost from the time of the inception of the elective system, colleges have been experimenting with ways and means of strengthening the curriculum. In recent years the effort has been intensified and its reach extended. No longer content with piecemeal change, institutions have undertaken basic alteration in curriculum design. Indicative of this effort is the general-education "movement" aiming at an organic reconstruction of the basis of liberal education. Although current curriculum revision is not limited to general education, the latter is representative of the spirit and principles guiding the effort.

The general-education movement is widespread; in 1939, a yearbook of the National Society for the Study of Education spoke of it as "the current ground-swell in American colleges and universities." Certainly numerous colleges have been experimenting with the general-education programs and several such programs will be summarized in the pages immediately following. These are not represented as typical or necessarily superior, but as indicative of the kind of curriculum thinking and practice taking place.

Relative to these accounts some general observations suggest themselves. No two programs are identical in content or organizational pattern. But in various way all center attention on the study of contemporary society and its major institutions, and on the responsibilities and problems of intelligent social living. Paralleling this emphasis on social understanding is almost equal stress on science in the modern world and on self-cultivation in the humane and esthetic arts. The subject matter is selected and taught in such a way as to enhance its liberalizing values vis-a-vis its specialized training potentialities. No effort is made to "cover" all disciplines either through multiple samplings or comprehensive survey courses. Prescribed introductory departmental offerings have given way to three or four large courses each identified with a major division of learning. An attempt is made to find new syntheses of subject matter and elements of integration within studies among them. As a might be expected, different methods of fostering integration are being tried, some(e.g., at Boston University) more pronounced than others. The tendency is to keep the programs under almost constant surveillance, resulting in steady modification of course contents. Omitting much relevent information pertaining to honors work, comprehensive examinations, remedial instruction, and the like, the following synopses will dwell principally on component courses.

COLUMBIA COLLEGE

The Columbia college curriculum as now constituted did not originate as a unit but developed gradually the period from 1919 to the present; a large portion of the course of the study in the first two years is devoted to orientation courses in the three areas of the humanities, the sciences, and the social sciences. There are requirements also in the field of English composition, foreign languages, physical education, and hygiene. The description which follows is restricted to the three orientation courses.

Contemporary Civilization A and B, a two-year sequence in the social sciences, represents a pooling of effort in subject matter and instruction by the Departments of Economics, Government, History, and Philosophy. The objective of the course is to reveal the nature of the past and to expose the insistent contemporary problems of the present which our tradition—the living past—can help us understand. In the freshman year the course starts with the breakup of the Middle Ages and undertakes an analysis along three lines of inquiry. How have people made a living? How have they lived together? How have they understood the world and their relation to it? In the second year some insistent problems of the present are raised for consideration. It is evident from the nature of the problems studied that none of them can be fully understood and solved in isolation from the others or if only one aspect is singled out for special investigation.

Humanities A and B is a two year sequence in literature, music, and fine arts taught by the Departments of English, Philosophy, History, Classics and the Modern Languages. The object of this course is to introduce the students to the several "languages" of the arts, in the belief that those arts are effective in increasing the range and power of the mind. In the freshman year the students pursue a prescribed course featuring reading and discussion of portions of more than forty selected "great book"; in the sophomore year they have the option of continuing the sequence course or taking in its place other courses in more specific subject fields.

Science A and B was originally organized around the concepts of matter, energy, and radiation; the study of the earth as a part of the universe; and the development of the plant and animal life. This course was offered as an alternative to specific courses in particular sciences. Laboratory work was an integral part of the course and was designed to permit the students to acquire a body of facts by direct observation. In 1946 it was recommended that an integrated two-year course in the natural sciences be required of *all* students, that the teachers be prepared to conduct instruction throughout the entire course, and that the subject matter of the course should range from the principles underlying the behavior of gross and microscopic bodies to the nature and activities of living organisms.

The requirement in effect at the present time may be summarized as follow:

One two-term course from each of any two of the following groups: (a) mathematics; (b) astronomy, chemistry, physics; (c) botany, geology, psychology, zoology.

COLLEGE OF THE UNIVERSITY CHICAGO

The college of the University of Chicago has been engaged in constructing an effective curriculum in general education for about twenty-five years. The curriculum is still undergoing revision, but the general aspects differing most markedly from the traditional liberal college programs may be described.

Students are normally admitted to the College upon completing two years of high-school study; following a four-year course of study in general education they qualify for a bachelor's degree. Achievement is not measured in terms of courses completed or credits earned but by passing comprehensive examinations in a number of subject fields. Attendance in these courses is optional and students may take the comprehensive examinations whenever they feel themselves sufficiently prepared. The core of the program is a group of three courses, each of which is prescribed for three years: Humanities, Social Science, and Natural science. There is no requirement of advanced or specialized work in a given field. A schematic summary of the course of study follows:

First Year	Second Year
Social Science 1	Social Science 2
Humanities 1	Humanities 2
Natural Science 1	Natural Science 2
English	Mathematics

Third Year	Fourth Year
Social Science 3	History
Humanities 3	Observation, Interpretation, and Integration
Natural Sciences 3	
Foreign Language	

The Humanities sequence is organized with a view to training students in the exercise of the disciplines which contribute to an intelligent appreciation of the arts. While maintaining distinctions between the proper role of the humanities and that of other areas of knowledge, instruction seeks to avoid too narrow a conception of humanistic subject matter and method. The sequence of three courses is aimed at the following objectives:

1. Increasing the experience of students with the great products of the arts by the examination of a considerable body of the best works in the fields of literature, the visual arts, and music.
2. Training student is the exercise of analytical methods appropriate to humanistic ends.
3. Training students in the use of the arts of criticism which will enable them to recognize some of the differences in values ascribed to works ... and, in the light of this recognition, to make responsible and sensitive criticisms.

The three-year Social Science sequence includes study of American political institutions, personality and culture, and freedom and order. *Social sciences 1* selects for study a number of situations in which the American people have had to face critical problems of government. Students are expected to develop skill in reading and interpreting original documents and some historical sense of the American democratic tradition. *Social Science 2* explores the possibilities and limitations of studying human nature and society in a scientific way. Study is centered upon the relation of an individual's personalty to his culture though its concern is not alone with the students' society and culture but with societies in general and with widely contrasting types of the culture. *Social Science 3* attempts to foster the habit of deliberating rationally on problems of public policy with the help of the analytical disciplines of political science, political economy, political sociology, ethics and social philosophy. With respect to each major problem the students are encouraged to assemble what they know of the historical background, the philosophic arguments concerning the ultimate values, and the scientific theory and facts for the purpose of drawing or appraising conclusions on practical policy.

The three years of the Science sequence are divided about equally between the physical and the biological sciences. The topics chosen for treatment are representative of these two major fields but not exhaustive. An attempt is made to relate the work of the science course to problems and matters which are the main responsibilities of the other courses in the program. The unit elements of the course are not, strictly speaking, topics but problems, and are treated with considerable emphasis on detail and questions of evidence and interpretation. The laboratory work is distinguished by a paucity of written instructions. Student teams are expected to formulate the problem to be solved, develop the details of experimentation, and proceed, on the basis of their own plans, to obtain and interpret data.

All students are required to take a course in the *History of Western Civilization* and one in *Observation, Interpretation, and Integration,* both of which are offered in the fourth year. These two courses strive to effect integration of the curriculum: the one historically by focusing attention on genesis and development, the other philosophically by concentrating attention on intellectual analysis and methodology.

There are also prescribed courses in mathematics, English composition, and foreign languages but they are more limited in scope than the three principle sequences.

HARVARD COLLEGE

There was widespread feeling in the faculty at Harvard that although the curriculum made adequate provision for the "concentration" in a given field, it did not assure adequate distribution of the students' educational experience over all the major fields. The Harvard Report discusses in detail theory of general education and the desired outcomes of education, and recommends methods of achieving these aims.

It is assumed that general education is distinguished from specialized education not so much in the subject matter as in method and outlook. The curriculum is viewed not as a collection of courses but as an organic whole whose parts join in expounding a ruling idea and in serving a common aims. It was felt necessary first to decided what traits of mind and character contribute to responsible social living; and then to choose the elements of knowledge which may be expected to nourish them. The traits singled out for emphasis were: to think effectively, to communicate thought, to make relevant judgments, and to discriminte among values.

The Report of the Harvard Committee recommended the introduction of a substantial intellectual experience common to all students and also that the principle of specialization be retained so that students might be enable to gain a more thorough mastery of a segment of learning. The curriculum as finally adopted prescribes during the first two years of study:

1. Three elementary courses in general education, one from each of the areas of Humanities, Social Sciences, and Natural Science.

2. Additional courses outside the field of concentration to achieve a total of six. The courses satisfying this requirement may be selected from the group of elementary courses in general education from the second-level general education courses offered by the committee on General Education, or from department course offerings judged suitable for general education. The students are given considerable latitude in selecting courses in each area from a list of equivalent alternatives.

The outline of the elementary courses in general education is as follows:

THE HUMANITIES

1. Humanism in the West
2. Epic and Novel
3. Individual and Social Values
   I. In History and Drama
   II. In Fiction and Philosophy
4. Ideas of Good and Evil in Western Literature

THE SOCIAL SCIENCES

1. Introduction to the Development of Western Civilization
2. Western Thought and Institutions
3. The Growth of Modern Western Society
4. Institutions and Culture in the West

THE NATURAL SCIENCES

1. The Physical Science in a Technical Civilization
2. Principle of Physical Science
3. The Nature and Growth of the Physical Sciences
4. Research Patterns in Physical Science
5. Principles of Biological Science

None of these courses is of "survey" nature and no attempt is made to treat exhaustively the subjects under discussion. The humanities courses are organized around problems revealed in ancient and modern literature. The science courses center on different portions of the fields of science. The social science courses range from a straight course in the *History of Western Civilization* (*Social Science 1*) to one of sociological content and organization (*Social Science 4*). There is no formal attempt to intergrate the subject matter of the various courses. It is felt that the nature of the three fields themselves provides a measure of integration which will be reinforced whenever two courses make contact with the same subject matter.

The second-level general education offerings are designed to fill in some of the gaps in elementary courses and also to provide course which do not readily fit into an established department. The second level offerings are as follow:

THE HUMANITIES

111. Classics of the Christian Tradition
113. Type of Art: The Representation of Nature in European and Asiatic Art
114. Art in Man's Environment
116. The Spirit of the Renaissance

THE SOCIAL SCIENCES

111. History of Far Eastern Civilization
112. Human Relations
113. The Impact of Science on Modern life
114. Interpretations of American Institutions.
115. Economics for the Citizen
116. Introduction to the Civilization of India
118. Democratic Theory and its Critics
119. The Structure and the Growth of Law
120. Fundamental Human Rights
127. Introduction to the Civilization of the Middle East

THE NATURAL SCIENCES

111. Organic Evolution
112. Introduction to the Philosophy of Science
114. Human Behaviour

In addition to the prescription in general education, the students must complete a year's work in English composition, engage in supervised physical training in the freshman year, demonstrate a reading knowledge of a foreign language, and satisfy an elective concerntration requirement.

COLGATE

The Colgate curriculum contains a core of courses devoted to problems drawn from the following fields: natural sciences, public affairs, philosophy and religion, area studies, music and the visual arts, literature, English communication, and the American Idea in the Modern World. Students are also required to demonstrate competence in a foreign language and satisfy a concentration requirement. In the "core" courses instruction is based so far as possible on actual "cases" or concrete problems. In seeking the solutions to these problems it is intended that the students exercise their powers of initiative in exploration and analysis, as well as their capacity to teach and to learn from others. The following are brief descriptions of some the core courses.

Problems in Natural Science investigates problems significant in the development of the physical and biological sciences the ways in which the problems have been attacked, the development of scientific theories, and the verification or rejection of such theories.

Problems in Public Affairs treats some important problems in the area of social organization and discusses concrete cases in industry, labour and economics, and social, governmental and international relations.

Problems in Philosophy and Religion defines problems of meaning and value and explores possible answers by examining the chief ideologies, philosophies, and faiths that lay claim to the belief and loyalty of Western man.

Area Studies. The objective of this course is to help the students to understand and appreciate problems which lead to conflict in the modern world, and to relate these problems to the position to the United States in the world.

The American Idea in the Modern World offers an analysis of contemporary American aims and values through an examination of our fundamental cultural documents and practices to determine the validity and effectiveness of the "American Way" in the current conflict of ideologies at home and abroad.

BOSTON UNIVERSITY

The college of General Education of Boston University has developed a two-year course of integrated general education, the purposes of which are summarized thus:

1. To attain through a study of our cultural heritage and that of other cultures a frame of reference which will enable the students to apply a broarder perspective when they meet contemporary social problems.
2. To develop the habit of reaching decisions on social problems through the give and take of the democratic discussion method.
3. To give the students experience, not only in the habits of "scientific thinking" but training in evaluating the social implications and the consequences of rival theories.

The special distinction of the program is in its attempt to develop a comprehensive integration of subject matter in contrast to the more common tendency towards limited integration. The aim is to unify the courses of instruction so that material drawn from all fields is synchronized and correlated at every possible point. An effort is made to bring before the students actual cases and problems and to discuss them in all their relevant aspects. The major elements of the program are as follows:

Human Relations. This course seeks to give the students knowledge of themselves and the society in which they live. Beginning with a study of the nature of man, the course proceeds to analyze some factors which have been involved in the evolution and institutional development of contemporary Western civilization.

Political Economy. Political and economic phenomena are treated as they are found in society, together. The principles of economics and politics are applied in both historical and contemporary situations.

English and Humanities stresses straight thinking, clear writing, and effective speaking. It aims to help the students arrive at an understanding of the worth and dignity of man as revealed in literature and the humanities.

Science. The purpose of the course is to give a clear understanding of the achievements of the principle sciences, to demonstrate the relationship between the laws of science and the world of nature, and to promote understanding of the scientific methods in order to show how scientific development has made for cultural progress and growth.

Guidance is a required course with three major objectives. It aims to help the students: (1) meet various problem of a personal, social, vocational, and educational nature; (2) determine, analyze, and understand their interests, aptitudes, abilities, limitations, oppotunities, and needs; and (3) acquire sound occupational information in order that they may make wise vocational choices and decisions.

TECHNIQUES OF CURRICULUM REVISION

Curriculum revision is not an exact science or fine art; there are no strict rules of producedure to be followed. Rather, it is a careful process of applying balanced judgement supported by educational principles and looking squarely at the results. There are so many variables in education that its courses cannot be predicated with certainty; result become evident in experience only after experience has been made possible. An important function of the curriculum planner is "to make educational experience possible" and to do what he can to assure a reasonable degree of success; that is, to invite and accept ideas whatever their origin, develop and improve them, and put them to work in the Curriculum. It helps if the Curriculum planner is hospitable to proposals for change, is venturesome rather than overcautious, recognizes the merits of a proposal as well as its defects, and uses his professional talents to minimize foreseeable difficulties. Most of us have strong convictions about the value of some college disciplines as compared with others; in working on curriculum matters it behooves us to keep our prejudices under control and prevent them as far as possible from colouring our judgment.

There are positive principles of operating procedure which are important, though the manner of their application must be influenced by the particular curriculum problem at hand. If the problem, for example, is to reassess an institution's prescriptive offerings and recognize them "from the ground up" practically every known principle of curriculum-making will be brought into use, and even new principles may have to be devised. If the problem is limited to deciding whether a single course offering has merit, fewer considerations will be operative. Each curriculum task presents a fresh challenge to creative endeavor. It is not possible to list a routine "series of steps" by which curriculum revision can be accomplished, but attention can be directed to a few considerations which are practically necessary. In listing these considerations in the following discussion, the numerical order has no significance.

1. *Relevance to educational aims.* Neither the whole nor any portion of the curriculum can be appraised without reference to the educational purposes it is meant to serve. Though educational aims can be evaluated without reference to a stated body of subject matter, the latter cannot be weighed independently. It is not enough to say, "Here is a

proposed course in Political Theory; it traces the development of concepts of the state and the relation of the individual to the state held by representative philosophers and political thinkers from Plato to John Stuart Mill; the subject matter seems attractive and there is no other course offering like it; let us, therefore, adopt it. " Explicitly or otherwise, the question should be raised, "How does the proposed offering relate to the aims of our college as we understand them?"

Investigation of this question may reveal that the proposed course serve well the college's purposes and might be satisfactory if effective instruction were assured. On the other hand, study of a proposal for a course in "Field experience in psychiatric social case work" may produces a less favorable finding although the substance of the proposed course is substantial enough and its appeal to some students strong. Courses with sectarian leaning, excessively professionalized or specialized offerings, and those too advanced for undergraduate study can be spotted quickly by checking their relevance to the aims of the college. This is not the only criterion by which the validity of an offering can be established, but some of the disorder in the current curriculum might have been avoided through stricter adherence to this principle.

Institutional aims are themselves subject to examination. If the aims are stated so generally that they cannot serve as an effective criterion of relevence, it may be persumed that the curriculum and instruction also suffer because of this vagueness. Such a statement of aims needs to be reformulated in more explicit terms if it is to serve as other than academic window-dressing. It is disheartening to be confronted with a set of aims stated grandly but unrealistically in view of the actual needs and realizable possibilities of the institution's student population, or lordly references to "higher spiritual value" affording little direction to educational process. Where clearly-defined purposes prove chronically inhospitable to new learning, they should also be opened up for examination by the faculty, since a static curriculum is almost certain to depreciate in vitality.

The curriculum maker deals as much with educational aims as with program content and organization. Often he must concern himself with principles and issues of educational philosophy for which no assured basis of judgment exists. In these circumstances he does the best he can, relying upon his own convictions and beliefs and such evidence as he can secure; admitting into consideration also the points of view of others. But he cannot proceed to the practical details of curriculum development without facing the question, "what educational purpose is this meant to serve?"

2. *Ascertaining or verifying the need for change.* Curriculum revision is regarded with annoyance by some college teachers as symbolizing incesscent tinkering and love of change for its own sake. Not until the teacher is himself invested with responsibility for curriculum study does he come to appreciate its importance and to develop zeal; in its pursuit. Yet to the extent that curriculum makers fail to establish the need for change and to convince their colleagues of this need, they overlook an essential aspect of their obiligation.

Curriculum revision should not be undertaken until convincing evidence points to the need for change. Frequently the first awareness of need is not by the constituted curriculum-making "authority" —a teachers' committee in a department or college or a specialist curriculum director—but by those involved directly in teaching and learning. Pressure for change from teachers or students may take the form of criticism of the existing offerings or constructive formulation of alternatives; in either case it is up to the responsible curriculum personnel to verify the need for change before taking further action.

The most fundamental kind of curriculum change does not, however, usually originate in this way. Concerned with immediate teaching and learning problems in their courses, teachers and students seldom have the broadest view of curriculum objectives and attainments. For this the curriculum maker is in better position: maintaining contact with proceedings in specific courses, he can also see the curriculum as a whole, from different angles and without the proximity which sometimes distorts prospective. Curriculum shortcomings and possible methods of improvement may be more apparent to him than to colleagues on the scene of action. Some of the most promising ventures in general education have grown out of recommendation by small, centrally-selected faculty committees which utilized the advantage of a "standoff" view. The most creative contribution the curriculum maker can make is to take the intiative in fostering curriculum improvement, explain and justify his proposal to his colleagues, and convert an indifferent faculty to open-minded cooperation. This is even more important than sitting in judgment on proposal submitted by others and perhaps supposing their development.

One method of detecting shortcomings and determining need for change lies in study of the related ends and means in education. Not all of the college's offerings were specifically designed to suit the purposes they now serve: traditional disciplines have been readpted, studies originally patterned by specialists for specialized ends have been refitted, and others have for a long time been substantially unaltered. There are bound to be defects of omission and commission. By relating the accomplishment to the goals it should be possible to discover where some of the defects lie. The reasonableness of this procedure must be admitted unless one chooses to argue that education is a mystical experience with no visible connection between activity and outcome. At the risk of incurring hostility by being too specific, it might be mentioned that the conventional freshman composition course with its theme writing and handy manual in language mechanics is less than an ideal way of developing the art of written expression. Perhaps also other typical offerings in introductory science, mathematics, and foreign language, in content or course organization, fall short of their purported objectives. One way to tell is to look them over.

In this sensitive job it is better for the curriculum planner to forego a priori judgment in favor of a more scientific approach. There are signs by which curriculum weakness may be spotted: poor morale of students or teachers with reference to certain course, repeated expression of dissatisfaction, persistent decline in enrollment, irregular attendance or excessive drop-outs, high incidence of failure or of easy success, failure to continue elective study in the same field, or evidence of background deficiency in later studies. Weakness may reside in instruction rather than curriculum, and it is necessary to distinguish between the two.

Once a trouble spot is located, the portion of the curriculum affected should be scrutinized and an attempt made to assemble all pertinent information. Talks with students, teachers, and counselors, analysis of students' programs and academic records, review of course syllabi, outlines, and study materials, and reliable standardized tests may serve to establish more precisely the nature of the difficulty and sometimes suggest the needed remedy. If curriculum change is contemplated, the evidence of weakness should be publicized to the extent that the faculty is convinced that a problem exists, but *not* in such a way as to place any particular teacher or group of teachers in a defensive position.

Verification of assumed need for change is no less essential when the curriculum maker deals with fully formulated proposals previously sent up "through channels." The fact that proposals may originate in faculty departments and carry departmental endorsement is not a certain indication of their necessity. Some departments are more eager for change than others, and without curbing the constructive efforts of their teachers it is nevertheless important to keep department offerings within workable bounds and assure reasonable stability. It is unwise to add, exchange, or withdraw courses except for good reason, and in advancing a proposal for change the reason should be indicated. If evidence cannot be furnished by those originating the proposal it should be sought by those responsible for promulgating further action. Indication of needed change is not always based on a weakness calling for correction; it may represent an extension or reinforcement of existing strength.

3. *Preparing or developing a curriculum proposal.* Curriculum change is not only method of improving a college program. More can sometimes be accomplished by redirecting the aims and methods of instruction, improving guidance services, enriching extracurricular activities, extending opportunities for individual study, or strengthening evaluation procedures. The various contingencies should be explored for their possible contribution to the solution of a problem. For this

reason it is well for a "Curriculum committee" to work in concert with other college agencies performing representative institutional function. Frequently curriculum change is and should be correlated with changes in other phases of the educational process.

Assuming that curriculum change is necessary, how does the curriculum planner proceed to formulate and develop his ideas? Analyzing the process is somewhat like analyzing thought itself, and the result is apt to be equally indefinite. Good curriculum planning is the product creative use of intelligence, utilizing such informational resources as may be available, moderating itself by careful judgment, but necessitating eventually a "leap into the unknown." Effective curriculum change seldom consist in reproducing courses offered elsewhere, and where little precedent exists, not even imitation is easy. It is no accident that current experimental programs of general education, while resembling each other in underlying ideas and some general features, differ in detail of content structure, and emphasis. Each reflects the separate creative efforts of its authors—their ideas, hypotheses, and tentative solutions. There are and will continue to be "standard" offerings, but recent curriculum revision has sought in the main to get away from standardization.

The curriculum maker does not approach the constructive phase of his task in an attitude of naivete. His knowledge of the underlying factors creating an unsatisfactory curriculum situation may suggest alternative courses of action and point the way to a corrective plan. Beyond this is the "beacon light" of educational purpose which helps in determining a sense of direction, and general principles of teaching and learning which help to maintain even experimental effort on a safer course. The known needs and capabilities of students also guide the curriculum maker in the exercise of initiative and original thought.

While the curriculum planner is not absolved of final responsibility to think for himself, he can to some extent be guided by pertinent information. It is useful to know how other institutions are dealing with comparable problems in oder to check or verify certain assumptions, gain insight into possible procedures, or discover and avoid unanticipated difficulties. A canvass of research studies will disclose findings on disputed matters such as the efficacy of large versus small group instruction, the merits of laboratory versus nonlaboratory science training, or the values of integration. Standardized tests in fundamental subjects may reveal deficiencies in students' learning which must be considered in any eventual curriculum proposal. Talks with students and teachers or systematic canvassing of their ideas may produce good suggestions. By gattering and analyzing such information, reflecting upon it, and "living with it," the curriculum maker will be aided in crystallizing his own ideas and strengthening his convictions.

Consideration of proposals espoused by a department and submitted for higher approval to the college-wide curriculum agency presents fewer difficulties. Such proposals should not be merely "rubber stamped." Even after the desirability of curriculum change has been estabilised, the proposals should be analyzed, studied, and improved in every way possible. Proposed course offerings should be scrutinized for suitability of content, range of learning covered, coherence and clarity of organization, appropriateness to instructional level, and articulation with other offerings—down to such relatively minor technical matters as course title, catalogue description, allotment of credits, and qualification for admission. Further revision, however, should not be attempted except in consultation with the colleagues originating the proposal, and with their concurrence; where objections to revision are offered, they should be carefully weighed, and if necessary a compromise effected that is agreeable to all concerned. Nothing is so annoying to teachers engaged in curriculum planning as to have a central curriculum committee highhandedly reject or alter their proposals. Yet the function of this committee is too important to permit the passive endorsement of all proposal received.

4. *Design and Structure of courses.* Inevitably the curriculum maker is faced with the problem of determining what constitutes the essential attributes of a course. Course offerings in the various discipline may differ widely in form as well as substance. To the teacher of mathematics accustomed to teaching a closely-knit body of subject matter, an art, music, or home economics workshop, a physically education course, or even one in social science may seem a loose array of

planned activity without internal system and logic. No teacher can afford to think in this way, least for all one who is involved in curriculum activity. Merit in the design of a course cannot be judged by the measure of its conformity to a standard pattern.

What, in essence, is a course? It is a body of learning experience for students, selected from established fields of scholarship (and other forms of endeavor), organized and presented in such a way as to serve the maximum educational needs and interests of the students. Each course is in effect a synthetic creation, an artifact conceived and executed by teachers. No course is any less artificial than any other, although some have become "naturalized" by usage. Many teachers, at one time or another, have been given the opportunity to develop a course out of the raw materials of scholarship and professional experience; such a course can be as respectable as another long sanctified by tradition.

Viewed in this light a course assumes certain obligations of functional rather than formal propriety. In the first place, the design of a course should be suited to its avowed purpose. Lecture, discussion, reading laboratory, or practicum courses are not interchangeable at the curriculum maker's will; nor can the optimum range or depth of a course be determined to serve as a standard for others. A course which aims to provide an overview of a field of learning, let us say An Introduction to Anthropology, is necessarily of broader framework and looser internal construction than an intensified specialized offering in the same field. A course which seeks to develop proficiency in an art, the use of an intellectual method, or a group of skills must emphasize opportunity for individual student performance, perhaps at the expense of subject-matter coverage. Performance courses and those more purely conceptual have different criteria of organization, and in as much as difference between such courses are often a matter of degree an almost endless variety in course design is possible.

Secondly, whatever its external form the course should meet the specifications of a good "learning experience for students." The subject matter must not only conform to the requisites of scholarship and be relevant to the purposes of instruction, but should also challenge the students' interest and be suited to their level of competence. The course should be "full" but not so overloaded in content that the task completing it in the specified time of study is hopeless. Topics of study should be related to each other and arranged in an oderly progression learning, from the easier to the more difficult, the simpler to the more complex, or from less to greater student self-dependence. The adaptability of the course to newer and more promising teaching methods should be surveyed, since much can be done suggest effective method of instruction while the proposal is under consideration. Without changing its substance or emphasis, provision can be made for greater reliance on laboratory or field work, audio-visual instruction, case study, individual student research, or other types of suitable procedure, thus facilitating if not ensuring better instruction. Finally, the course should be adaptable to the use of reliable method of evuluating students' learing.

5. *Evaluating curriculum innovation.* The subject of evaluation in its general application to the educative process will be discussed in a subsequent chapter; at this point the reference is specifically to evaluating the results of curriculum change. No curriculum project can be so carefully prepared and instituted that its success is assured in advance. There is an element of risk in every curriculum undertaking, and the bolder its reach the greater is the risk involved.

A curriculum planner's task is not done until he has arranged for suitable evaluation of the projected program or offering. In fact, it would be well for him not to consider a plan as ever "completed" or "finished," but to accept continuing responsibility for assessment of its effectiveness. Every curriculum innovation should be viewed as experimental, not only in the sense of its being subjected to the test of performance but also in its susceptibility to continued adaptation or change.

The manner of evaluation depends upon the nature and scope of the curriculum activity. A single new course offering can be evaluated fairly simply. An instructional "log" recording the teacher's day-to-day impressions of the course—accomplishments, problem encountered, difficulties unresolved—can form the basis of conferences with curriculum planners out of which will develop suggestions for further improvement. A survey of students' reactions, preferably conducted and reported by the teacher, can furnish important supplementary information. A formal inventory of student achievement through examinations, problems, and work exercises can at least partially reveal the extent to which the avowed objectives are being met. The students' performance in related or advanced courses contributes further evidence.

Evaluation of a comprehensive curriculum undertaking is more complicated. It may be necessary to prepare a formal plan of evaluation as saying approaches from different directions. A new program of general education, for example, may in part be evaluated experimentally by comparing the performance of matched groups of students in "new" and " old" offerings: this is a laborious procedure which is, however, useful in furnishing objective evidence. Along with this, comprehensive examinations may be administered measuring proficiency in subject matter and growth in power. Questionnaires, survey inventories, or check lists may be employed to take soundings of students' attitudes toward the new courses, the nature and extent of their participation in assigned study, their interest in independent activity, and the carry-over into other kinds of learning. Analysis of students' programs of study and transcripts of their academic records may show whether satisfactory articulation, orderly progression, and creditable accomplishment are being maintained. An important index of evaluation is, of course, the continuous estimate by teachers participating in the program, their evident interest and enthusiasm. A pratical plan of evaluation containing several of these feature may be fashioned according to the available time and resources of the institution concerned.

SELECTED BIBLIOGRAPHY

A College Program in Action, A Review of the Working Principles at Columbia College, by the Committee on Plans. New York: Columbia University Press, 1946. 175pp.

Association for Higher Education, *Current Issues in Higher Education,* 1953, Proceeding of the Eighth Annual National

Conference on Higher Education. Washington: National Education Association, 1953. 292 pp.

Butts, R. Freeman, *The college Charts Its Course.* NewYork: McGraw-Hill Book Company, 1939. 464 pp.

Carmichael, Oliver C., "Contemporary Trends in the American Colleges," *Association of American Colleges Bulletin,* 36:488-93, December 1950.

Cohen, I. B., and Waston, F. G., *General Education in Science.* Cambrige: Harvard university Press, 1952. 217 pp.

Eisenhart, Luther P., *The Educational Process,* Chapter II "The Curriculum" and Chapter III, "Programs of Concentration." Princeton: Princeton University Press, 1945.87 pp.

French, Sidney J., ed., *Accent on Teaching.* New York: Harper & Brothers, 1954. 334 pp.

General Education in a Free Society, Report of the Harvard Committee. Cambrigde: Harvard University Press, 1945. 267 pp.

General Education in School and College, A Committee Report by Members of Faculties of Andover, Exeter, Lawrenceville, Harvard, Princeton, and Yale. Cambridge: Harvard University Press, 1952.142pp.

Graeffe, Arnold D., *Creative Educatrion in the Humanaties.* New York: Harper & Brothers, 1951.199 pp.

Hofstadter, Richard and Hardy, C. Dewitt, *The Develpoment and Scope of Higher Education in the U. S.* New York: Columbia University Press, 1952. 254pp.

Jordan, Dravid Starr, *The Trend of the American University,* ChapterI, "The Evoluation of the College Curriculum." Stanford University, Calif.: Standford University Press, 1929.126pp.

McGrath, Earl J., *The Humanities is General Education.* Dubuque, Iowa: Wm C. Brown Co., 1949. 308pp.

Millett, Fred B., *The Rebirth of Liberal Education,* Chaspter II, "Experimental Programs and Courses." New York: Harcourt, Brace and Company, 1945. 179 pp.

Morse, H. T., ed., *General Education in Transition.* Minneapolis:

University of. Minnesota Press, 1951. 310 pp.

National Society for the Study of Education, *General Education,* Fifty-First Yearbook of the Society, Part I. Chicago: University of Chicago Press, 1952. 377 pp.

Severighaus, A. E., Carman, H. J., and Cadbury, W. E., Jr., eds. *Preparation for Medical Education in the Liberal arts College,* Chapter 8, "Some Ventures in College Education." New York: McGraw-Hill Book Company, 1953. 400 pp.

Stevens, David H., *The Changing Humanities.* New York: Harper & Brothers, 1953. 272 pp.

Stickler, W. Hugh, ed., *Organization and Administration of General Education*: Dubuque, Iowa: Wm C. Brown Co., 1951. 431 pp.

Stickler, W. Hugh, Stokes, J. P., and Shores, L., eds., *General Education: A University Program in Action.* Dubuque, Iowa: Wm C. brown Co., 1950. 280 pp.

The Idea and Practice of General Education, An Account of the College of the University of Chicago, by Present and Former Members of the Faculty (F.C. Ward et al.). Chicago: The University of Chicago Press, 1950. 333 pp.

Valentine, P. F., ed., *The American College,* Chapter 6, "General Education Programs." New York: Philosophical Library, 1949. 575 pp.

4

PRINCIPLES OF METHODS OF TEACHING

Teaching as Craftsmanship. There are few teachers who do not take pride in a well-taught lesson, a skilfully-developed lecture, or a course which is challenging to students. Colleges rate "exceptional skill in teaching" high among the criteria determining faculty promotion. Students prefer a well-taught course to an easy one. Craftsmanship in teaching is highly valued by all concerned in education. There is no scarcity of good teaching in the colleges, although from the nature of the commodity supply can never equal demand. Yet college teachers are strangely reluctant to submit their instruction to critical examination; indeed, they tend to be suspicious, if not disdainful, of all talk of teaching "methods".

To an extent this attitude is understandable. By frequently overstating their case, proponents of instructional method in and out of schools of education have not endeared themselves to their academic colleagues. In the preparation of the teachers for the lower schools, emphasis on pedagogical technique has tended to detract from mastery of sturdier subject-matter disciplines. Furthermore, methodology does not occupy the same position of importance in higher education as on lower levels: college student are more mature, and more independently competent in learning. It would be a mistake for college teachers to expend their energies more on procedure than on substance of instruction, yet the two are so closely allied that to neglect the former is to hurt the latter.

The college teacher will admit that technical skill in teaching makes a difference in student's learning, and that in actuality wide variations exist in quality of teaching performance. He will also admit that his own teaching has improved with experience, in part "naturally " but more largely as a result of deliberate painstaking effort. This is tantamount to admitting that craftsmanship in teaching is necessary and can be developed. All that systematic attention to method can hope to accomplish is to expedite and reinforce the process of self-improvement.

There is more concerning method of college teaching than the profession has thus far been able to determine. Of the many good college teachers, few have reached the limit of their potential skill; the lack is not in motivation but in definite knowledge of what constitutes instructional excellence and how to achieve it. Successful teaching is too often a fortuitous occurrence; why a class period or an entire course turn out exceptionally good we may not always know. Not until an art or science can be reduced to some basic components separable for investigation and controlled use will its mastery be pursued with assured hope of success. In the case of college teaching this is easier said than done.

At this stage of development in the art of science of college teaching, a formal course in "method" can serve no more than a rudimentary purpose- to acquaint beginners with a few of the essentials. Much beyond this we cannot go. Even gifted teachers have found difficulty in disclosing the secret of their accomplishment; translated into words, the magic of their performance disappears. This much we can say: craftsmanship in teaching is a difficult and elusive art, compounded of moral, intellectual, and esthetic ingredients, and of many technical skills involving operation with ideas and with people. The difference between a novice and an expert teacher is similar to that between an unskilled and a master workman. The sooner a teacher sets out to master the challenges of his craft, the more valuable will be his service to his profession.

What Is Teaching? In essence teaching is stimulating and directing learning by students. Contingent upon the subject of instruction, learning may be stimulated and guided in different ways toward different ends; but whether the subject is comparative anatomy, Latin philology, or music, teaching is no more than helping the student to acquire knowledge, skills, ideals, attitudes, and appreciations leading to his changed behaviour and growth as a person. Giving a lecture, leading a discussion, demonstrating an experiment, preparing a good examination, and other procedures in teaching are instrumental to this principal function. In the main good teaching takes its cue from the requirements for good learning.

It is impossible to encompass within one definition the meaning of good teaching. Certainly one criterion relates to ascertainable achievement in learning, that is, to the extent to which students learn what they are supposed to learn. Many of the desired outcomes of instruction can be formulated in advance; a teacher of organic chemistry may want his students to learn the structure, properties, and uses of certain organic compounds and, in the process of learning them, to acquire scientific interest and understanding. The greater the student's success in attaining these outcomes, the better has been the teaching. Not all the outcomes of instruction, however, can be proconstituted; in every case there are collateral products deriving more from the human contact than from the nature of the subject. Two teachers offering the same course may achieve different results in the ideals, attitudes, habits, and human values they help to foster. To the extend that they contribute to the educational development of students, these incidental learnings must also be considered in estimating instructional effectiveness.

Student are not taught separately but in classes containing from ten or fifteen to as many as several hundred. Although instruction is imparted to a group it must necessarily aim at individuals. The end result of learning is individual: from the same instruction students will learn different things and progress in different directions. A further measure of teaching effectiveness, therefore, is in the ability to strike the right chord of common learning need in a group of students, yet remain sensitive to the many deviations from the common need and provide for them in instruction. What is realistically possible depends of course upon the size of the group, but the need for attending to the individual is never absent. Even in a large lecture class the skilful teacher can make student feel that he is speaking to each of them personally, both by the substance of his message and the manner of its communication. In smaller recitation, discussion, or laboratory sections a requisite of good teaching is to complement common group learning with the development of each student's special aims, capabilities, and interests.

By definition a teacher is a specialist in working with people; the speciality becomes an art as the teacher becomes more skilful in helping people to educate themselves and each other. This holds true for individual students as well as for groups. It is the mark of the beginner in teaching that he tells the student what the latter wants or need to know; the more experienced teacher will help the student to learn for himself; the accomplished teacher will design his instruction from the outset with the aim of developing the student's resources and motivation for intellectual self-dependence.

The advantages of group instruction do not lie only in making possible a more economical management of the school or the college. Although in some respects group instruction may restrict maximum individual accomplishment, it has compensations in learning. Some things students can learn better than from each other than from the teacher, and others they can gain *only* through group participation. Ideals, attitudes, and modes of desirable social behavior can be learned more effectively through such activity than in individual sessions with a teacher. In many courses—particularly in the humanities and social sciences—even the substantive content of learning may be deepened and enriched by sharing ideas in group discussion.

Skill in teaching is reflected in the ability to utilized the resources of a group to promote the greatest possible interchange of learning. The good teacher works through the medium of the group, liberating and directing its energies; he plays upon the capacities of students to stimulate each other, to set examples in the exercise of initiative and provocative thought, and to add to the substance of instruction. Often he encourages the students to take a leading role, being himself content provide support and guidance. There are instances in almost every course when students' contributions excel anything the teacher himself could have initiated, and as a teacher gains in skill he learn to formulate his teaching plans so as to avail himself of such occurrences.

There is a quality of good teaching which may be termed aesthetic. In every field of work the artist is distinguished by his quest for perfection and his pride in quality of production; he may not always succeed in his purpose but his performance is rarely ordinary. Whatever his objective he does not neglect the rules of good workmanship or fail to invest his work with distinction. Artistry in teaching adds another dimension of value to its other contributions toward students' accomplishment in learning: long after the subject matter of a course is forgotten, the teacher as a craftman may be remembered. As for the teacher himself, no small portion of his professional reward is the satisfaction derived from the sense of a job tastefully done.

There are many styles of teaching, and each teacher's should be suited to his own person and circumstances. Possibilities of distinction are inherent in whatever accomplishments the teacher possesses in marked degree—broad erudition, specialized mastery of his field, competence in research, ability to organize information, skill in exposition, effective individual approach to students, talented group leadership, and even personal qualities of poise and affability. Around one or more of these a characteristic style of teaching may be built; but good style cannot be maintained without attention to fundamental conventions. Regardless of how superior a teacher's scholarship, he still requires almost daily preparation of instruction; no matter how friendly a teacher's relation with students, he cannot surrender his objectivity of professional judgement.

Certain "ground rules" of teaching need in particular to be respected. Of small nature, they are occasionally disparaged as symptomatic of the "pedagogical mind," but actually are a token of more solid virtue and distinction. The teacher, for example, has an obligation to observe the same properties of conduct that he expects of student. Punctuality in reporting to class, in keeping appointments with students, in reading and returning written assignments, in grading examination papers, and any other commitments the teacher makes to students may not be cheaply regarded. The student likes to know his standing in a course, as does the teacher in his own professional affairs: after the student has had a chance to demonstrate performance he should be apprised of its worth. Students like, teachers, may carry too heavy a work-load: without compromising his standards, a teacher can be considerate in estimating and timing his assignments. Ordinary academic housekeeping chores—maintenance of attendance records, preparation of grade reports, requisition of materials and equipment—relished by none, should nevertheless be accomplished with promptness and orderly economy. It is unseemly for a teacher to spend ten minutes of a class period at midterm in taking attendance—as if he was meeting the students for the first time. Teachers are deceived if they regard such minor considerations beneath their concern. Though not the basic measure of good teaching, they cannot be neglected with impunity.

Creative Use of Teaching method. Essentially every teacher creates his own teaching method. In terms of his personality and experience, the purposes and subject matter of instruction, and the students he teaches, each follows the procedures he judges suitable, choosing and adapting available techniques or devising, when necessary, new ones. One cannot teach well by copying a method which proved effective for someone else. The distaste with which reference to "method" is commonly received would be lessened were this recognized.

The distinction between method and technique is worth emphasizing. A technique is the procedure or device through which a teacher seeks to accomplish wholly or in a part a specific instructional purpose. There are many techniques—in lecture, discussion, questioning, experimental demonstration, laboratory work, audio-visual presentation, independent study and research, testing, and others—each subject to flexible rules of operation. The number of possible techniques is not unlimited, although new ones are constantly being developed and familiar techniques modified. Every teacher necessarily employs a number of techniques, serially or in combination, their choice and manner of use depending upon his general method of instruction. The latter is a composite style or quality of teaching, a characteristic mode of instructional behavior reflecting one's own values and educational philosophy. One's teaching method influence not only the choice of techniques and the manner of their use but also goals of instruction, selection and emphasis of subject matter, and relationship with students. The variety of possible teaching methods is unlimited, there being as many variations as there are the teachers.

The choice of techniques is influenced by the method which the teacher elects or is impelled to follow. There are those, for example, who lecture as little as possible, preferring less formal processes of group learning. Others rely upon the Socratic manner of questioning because they feel it suits their intellectual temperament. A devotee of audio-visual aids will find occasion present instructional films, filmstrips, and recordings, whereas a colleague in the same course will manage well without them. Mimicry and dramatic representations are sometimes effective devices, but not for the teacher with limited acting talents. One teacher will conduct a course in Shakespearean drama mainly through interpretative reading, another will prefer group discussion of character, plot, philosophical sense, and literary style. The scholar will create opportunities to direct his students toward individual research, the bibliophile to books, and the scientist to the laboratory.

We tend to adopt a method of instruction consistent with our capabilities and the subject of instruction, but usually do not go far enough in systematic self-analysis to enable us to develop a mode of instruction indicative of our best efforts. The choice of method is apt to be too casual, and we are often content to use the approach and techniques which most readily suggest themselves. As a rule we do not expend on method a sizable fraction of the intellectual energy we devote to scholarship. The creative use of method does not presume preoccupation with process to the neglect of substance. But it does presume a conscious attempt to develop a style and manner of instruction well-fitted to the personal and professional resources of the teacher and the possibilities and requirements of the teaching situation. It implies a willingness to experiment with new forms of teaching in an effort to find those which serve best a given purpose.

Factors Influencing Method. Some of these factors have been mentioned in the foregoing discussion. Without attempting a detailed exposition it may be useful to summarize the most important of them.

1. *Method should conform to the objectives of liberal study.* In almost every field of learning there is a difference between teaching the dedicated specialist and the interested generalist. The difference is especially apparent in music and the fine arts where specialization presumes not only a compatible interest but also a degree of aptitude granted to a comparative few. The number of people with a lay man's interest in music or arts is legion. Teachers in these fields have adjusted successfully to their separate constituencies of learners; it would not occur to a teacher, for example, to treat in the same way students in a course in music appreciation and those in an elective in Advanced Harmony. Emphasis in instructional method would be, on producing on the one hand an informed and critical music loving audience, and on the other skilled and sensitive musical specialists.

A similar distinction should exist in teaching history, mathematics, science, and other college disciplines. Most students in these fields do not seek to become specialists but to gain values useful in personal development. It is wrong to assume that this purpose can be served by the same methods of instruction employed with specialists: the same method *may* be appropriate or they may be inappropriate altogether. A safer course of action is to start by keeping in mind the goals of liberal learning, then to select or design methods which promise to be suitable. We have mistakenly tended to assume that imparting the liberal values inherent in the disciplines of science or history is same as training for a career as scientist or historian. Excellent training in historical method and independent historical research may be quite unrewarding to the students interested in enlarging his knowledge of past events in order to gain in understanding of the present.

Progress has been made in accommodating teaching method to the needs of liberal learning. Coincident with changes in the content of general education have been changes in instructional approach, emphasis, and technique. In many places science instruction for the general learner has come to rely more on the lecture-demonstration and less on individual laboratory work; the use of mathematics to explain principles and scientific relationships are kept to a minimum; exercises in problem solving are subordinated to an understanding of the problem and the factors entering into its solution; the applications of science are directed towards illuminating the larger world of experience rather than the inner recesses of science itself; there is a more conscious effort to relate the subject matter of science to other fields of learning. Much as the specialized scientist may deplore some of these developments, they are necessary for the education of many students. Rigorous, intensive training in science is better reserved for science "majors".

In its own way mathematics instruction has attempted a comparable modification of some of its general offerings.

There is little use in grumbling about the average student's lack of skill in mechanical routines or in rushing him into further ill-understood techniques. Instead, we accept the student and his preparation as incontrovertible data and begin by discussing the reasonable character of the elementary mathematics which he formerly knew largely by rote. After a brief introduction to the essential logical ideas which are fundamental to any appreciation of mathematics, the evolution of the number system and the essentials of elementary algebra are discussed from a mature and reasonable point of view. After this foundation is laid, the book provides an elementary but critical introduction to several of the most important branches of modern mathematics, without, however pushing any chapter so far as to strain the student's technical equipment. Applications are discussed throughout, but the discussion is restricted to applications which are within the student's grasp rather than to allow it to degenerates into a Sunday Supplement article on the Wonders of Science.

For sometime modern language instruction for the nonspecialist has sought to subordinate mastery of grammar and linguistic structure to fluency in conversation, ease of reading, and appreciation of literature and culture. Indeed in most subjects instruction has been adapted to the purposes of the general learner as distinct from the incipient specialists. But much remains to be done.

2. *Method should be adapted to the capacity of the learner.* No honest teacher is willing to give his subject less than its due in instruction: no teacher wants to cheapen his subject by offering it at low cost in

output of study or by simplifying teaching in a manner unbecoming its dignity. We tend to believed that a student who undertakes to learn mathematic or philosophy should learn it in the way it is presented by the mathematician or philosopher. We dislike to compromise our ideals by accommodating instruction to the inadequacies of some students.

Yet common sense suggests that there is no point in teaching a subject unless the student is prepared to learn it. It does little good to give the most beautifully organized lecture if the students are unable to follow intelligently and take notes discriminatingly. At the expense of some disfigurement of his lecture an experienced teacher will take steps to insure that students comprehend its substance. Techniques of instruction can be changed more readily than the student's capacity to learn, and the teacher who would teach must take realistic cognizance of this fact.

Adapting instructional method to the capacity of the learner involve first of all determining the right the level of instruction. A discipline can be taught on several levels depending upon the intellectual maturity and receptiveness of the students. Elementary Greek will be taught differently to students with previous training in Latin and to a class of foreign-language beginners. General physics can be offered on a higher level to learners with a background of college science, mathematics. Second, it involves formulating or choosing proper instructional media. In teaching freshman, for example, it is necessary to realize that they may be insufficiently trained in listening prolonged discourse, in extended writing, in the use of library resources, reading list, or even a textbook. These considerations should not deter the teacher from attempting to use more advanced media of instruction than those to which the student has become accustomed, but they should alert him to the necessity of concomitantly preparing and training the student for their use. Third, adaptive instruction involves continuous flexibility in the planning and conduct of teaching. A course outline judged suitable in the planning stage may in practice prove too inclusive; it is more advisable to adjust the outline than to insist on "covering" the planned subject matter at the expense of sound learning. An exercise assigned for study may contain difficulties or hazards in learning unanticipated but the teacher; it is better to alter the assignment *in cursu* than to invite a confused or slovenly performance.

Shaping instructions to the capacity of the learner involves the teacher in the problem of individual differences. Whatever the nature of the course and the size of the class a few basic principles of method cannot be neglected. One is to attempt to know the students as far as possible as individuals. Even in a large lecture group the teacher may obtain pertinent information regarding the composition of the class by a survey of college records and a preinstruction inventory of the students' background of achievement and readiness for learning. In a smaller recitation section, a little time devoted to identifying students as individuals will facilitate adaptation of instruction. Devices such as self-introduction by students, brief individual interviews with the teacher, preparation of class "registers" listing a few pertinent facts about each person, and short, frequent work assignments and test exercise in the early weeks of instruction will help the teacher to learn Who's Who academically. The effort to know the students should persist throughout instruction, with the object of distinguishing abler students who can profit from enriched study, poorer students who require special assistance, and those with special goals and interests in study.

A second principle relates to the desirability of long term planning of instruction. Even when a comprehensive course syllabus is available, instruction formulated on a day-to-day basis is not readily adaptable to individual needs. The teacher requires the advantage of longer perspective and greater time for preparation to avail himself of possible opportunities for adjustment of subject matter, methods, and materials of study. When instruction is viewed at longer range, it is also easier to detect and minimize difficulties awaiting learners, and to effect by preventive measures what might otherwise require correction and reteaching. A related third principle concerns the superiority of large topical arrangement of study over small-unit organization. The former facilitates advanced planning, make possible greater variety and flexibility in method, and affords more room for differentiation.

A fourth principle of teaching pertains to the advisability of experimenting with procedure in teaching individual students and small group. The tendency is too often to fall into the pattern of the lecture, lecture-discussion, or common assignment of study when more individualized instructions is feasible. Although the lecture and discussion, form the backbone of instruction, their use can often be supplemented by individual and small-group conferences, and differentiated reading, study, research, and laboratory assignments. Some courses are more successful if conducted *principally* on this basis. The values are not only in the greater adaptability of instruction but also in added student interest and the probability of more through learning. The development special "honors" work with abler students has been in this direction, and the same principle should be extended as far as possible to all students.

3. *Method should be in accord with sound psychology of learning.* Even on the college-level the significance of motivation as a factor in learning may not be ignored. Intuitively many teachers have sought to make instruction interesting, to foster in students a pleasurable feeling towards the study in which they are engaged. But the importance of motivation transcends the elements of immediate interest and satisfaction: self-identification with an activity is a necessary condition for learning. Some talented writers admit that they find writing would be arduous, but so thoroughly identified are they with a self-imposed mission that to discontinue writing would be unthinkable.

To help students identify themselves with the subject of study is inherent the task of instruction. Conscious striving to make a course interesting is only a small portion of this task. Looming larger is the obligation to convey a sense of purpose and personal meaning: "What is this course to me? Why am I studying it?" A student can plunge into the study of a science, become involved in factual memorization laboratory work, the solution of numerous problems, and even complete the course with a satisfactory grade without ever discovering what he was supposed to obtain from the course. This is not learning, and directing such experience is not teaching.

There are various ways of motivating instruction, and the most effective are those which succeed in developing a lasting sense of purpose. To motivate teaching is not to cheapen or popularize it. The precise, even-toned scholar who can relate his discipline to the meaningful experience of students does more to motivate instruction than the exhibitionist who indulges in theatrics. Growth in teaching skill involves among other things, progression from extrinsic modes of fostering interest to deeper, more genuine, and intrinsic ways of bringing the student into intellectual communication with a subject. At its best motivation is gradual, unobtrusive, continuous, and cumulative in its effect.

The foregoing is illustrative of one principle of sound psychological doctrine. There are many others, and while the teacher cannot be expected to deal with all psychological *minutiae,* he should be guided in instruction by an awareness of some of the paramount facts and principles of learning. The importance of proper emotional conditioning, the law readliness, configurational or "whole" (as against piecemeal) learning, appeal to understanding rather than rote memory, multisensory impression, spaced repetition or practice, and the need for expression of what has been learned bear particular examination. There is no reason to fear that adherence to these principles will cramp the teacher's personal style in teaching or conflict with any beliefs and convictions he may have concerning the goals of instruction.

College teaching is apt to be negligent in two respect: in its use of spaced repetition and of direct experience. In some subjects of instruction—for example, mathematics and foreign language—learning is cumulative and repetition inherent in the organization of the subject matter; in such cases, the "law of exercise" tends to take care of itself. In other subjects, such as the social sciences, repetition must be more deliberately provided if retentive learning is to be as assured. The tendency in college teachings is to assume that, once understood, a fact or idea will be "learned" or retained. This assumption is not tenable even with able students, and partly accounts for the fact that college seniors may know less of the salient content of a subject than they did as freshmen. Opportunity for repetition at spaced intervals should be forthcoming, not only by straight forward recitation but also through interesting study exercise and problems.

Much of instruction is verbal and conceptual where it could be more concretely based in reality. There is nothing wrong with concepts except the danger of their being misunderstood. Words are often imperfect carriers of meaning, and the teacher who stakes his entire outcome in teaching on the efficacy of language communication takes an excessive risk. Experimental learning is not possible in all course of instruction, nor is it desirable in any course to keep instruction too long on a perceptual, personal-experience level. But in many subject opportunities exist to strengthen instruction by grounding it in real experience, and to elevate and refine concepts by relating them to the world of sensory fact. Demonstration and laboratory exercise in science are an effort to do essentially this. Field and workshop activity can be utilized more extensively in foreign language study, the fine arts, psychology, practically all the social science with the partial exception of history, philosophy, and most of the professionally oriented disciplines.

4. *Method should be suited to subject matter.* The subject-matter factor in method helps to explain why teaching procedures cannot be pitted against one another, nor evaluated without reference to their instructional setting. It helps also to explain why teaching techniques cannot be prescribed in a general way: what is valid in one case may be invalid in another. It is impossible to decide, for example whether lecture instruction is in itself good or bad: in the "right" subject a gifted teacher can, with appropriate technical aids and some marginal differentiation in study, accomplish much by lecturing to a large class.

What constitutes appropriate teaching technique will vary from course to course and among elements of study within a course. Administratively a course may be labelled lecture or laboratory or recitation or workshop: this tends to identify the principle manner of instruction and perhaps determine the size of the class. But within each course different types of teaching procedure will inventiably be employed.

However individualized a course of instruction, it may be desirable occasionally to recall students from their separate tasks in order to clarify a common problem by a brief lecture. In a lecture course it is frequently useful to interject short question-and-answer and discussion periods. In so-called recitation or discussion courses teaching techniques need particularly to be varied so as to conform to the requirements of different elements of study. The criterion in shaping method of subject matter is not so much general category of the course as the precise type of learning inherent in a particular situation. For purpose of method it is superficial merely to identify a course as one of the humanities, fine arts, or physical science. A single course in any field may involve visualization of simple and complicated objects of sensory experience, concept formation and relationships, acquisition of skills, development of attitudes and appreciation, problem solving, changes in personal behavior, and the like. Each type of constituent learning may make its own demands in suitable teaching procedure.

5. *A teacher's method should suit him personally and capitalize on his special assets.* It would be most unfortunate if all teachers tried to be equally witty or solemn, outspoken or reserved, pliant or uncompromising, or followed standard teaching practices. It is a good thing for student that teachers differ in personality and temperament, in conception of their instructional obligation and in their method of fulfilling it; it is good also for teachers. Common values and ideals such as integrity, kindliness, love for learning, and respect for students may be variously expressed, and for every teacher that form of expression is best which is most consistent with his nature.

Studied unorthodoxy can be as bad undeviating conformity. Excessive individualism among teachers in distracting and confusing to students, and inimical to the fundamental purposes of education. For a students, to work with one or a few teachers markedly unorthodox in their professional ways is probably a salutary experience; to deal with none but professional eccentrics may be good clinical training but is not education. A teacher should not strain to be different: healthy individuality develops naturally from self-awareness and a conscious endeavor to use one's potentialities to advantage without violating the canons of good teaching and sound learning.

Whichever method a teacher uses should show that teacher at his best. We are not all the same stripe, nor equally gifted in all the capacities useful in instruction. Some of us are humorous, others merely tell jokes; some lecture effectively, others talk at great length. Fortunately teaching is broad enough to accommodate many aptitudes and to afford expression for different talents. It involves upon us to discover in what ways we can be most useful, to perfect ourselves in these respects, and to make them the personal hallmark of our teaching.

Usually the teacher has latitude in the choice of his instructional procedures. The quick-witted person with self-assured mastery of his subject may elect to engage in a running "give-and-take" discussion with students, developing the course structure as he proceeds; another with less poise or experience or who on principle rejects this procedure may choose a more orderly presentation and sequence of instruction. There is room for the "permissive" teacher and one who prefers stricter class regulation, for the "artist" and the "scientist," for the practical man and the theorist. Students appreciate a teacher not for everything he does but for the things he does well: and in fact this is where his greatest professional contribution lies.

Levels of Teaching

Mention has been made of a "college level" of teaching; actually there exists not a level, but levels. Levels of instruction differ with courses, classes of students, and individual learners. Even the term "levels" is inaccurate, suggesting a succession of plateaus rather than a continuous progression. Students' growth in learning power is steady, gradual, at a given time perhaps imperceptible. To parallel such growth, instruction must also be elevated continuously.

A distinguishing factor among levels of teaching is in the degree of responsibility for learning assumed by students; or, stated differently, in the measure of self-dependence which students exercise. Growth in intellectual self dependence is manifested by increasing mastery of the tools and resources of learning, ability to acquire, relate, and organize information, reliance upon one's own judgment as against that expressed by others, and ability to formulate means to make use of these developing powers of the students in progressively greater measure.

Growth in intellectual independence, though to some extent a function of maturation, may be greatly aided by instruction. Contrarily, using infantile teaching methods may serve to keep students longer on infantile levels of learning. A good teacher is not content merely to keep pace with the students' natural development, accommodating his instruction to what they can comfortably do. Students respond to teaching which aims at higher levels of performance than they can reach unaided. There is pedagogical wisdom in the remark attributed to the late Professor Morris R.Cohen, "I am not at their heads but where their heads should be."

Determining Levels of Instruction. To determine the extent of students' reach, one must know where it begins. Unless the teacher can estimate their competence in learning he will be working in the dark. Students' academic status as freshmen or juniors offers a clue toward developing an appropriate mode of instruction but is in itself not a sufficiently definite and reliable indication. Before an appropriate course of instruction can be charted a more precise estimate of students' abilities as learners needs to be obtained.

In trying to take the intellectual measure of a class the teacher may have to be content with something short of perfection: particularly in basic or general courses students are apt to be distributed over a wide range of competence. It helps if, at the outset of instruction, the teacher undertakes to learn what he can of the students' previous preparation and present readiness, and if, in the early weeks of a course, he continues to temper his teaching to their revealed capabilities and needs. A teacher can sensitize himself so that he realizes almost instantly whether he is operating above or below the students' reach, and can then raise or "tone down" his instruction accordingly.

To plunge immediately into the new subject matter of a course is neither wise nor economical teaching practice. It is better first to "get the feel" of a class—become acquainted with students, ascertain what they bring to the course, how well they are qualified to proceed, and in what manner they operate. This may be done in part by informal discussion, and when feasible by more formal "pretests" of learning. In the first weeks of the term it is helpful to make frequent short assignments of study tasks, grade them promptly, and be guided by the results. Successive weekly quizzes near the beginning of a course may be more informative in this respect than those given later. Effort to gauge the appropriate level of instruction should be continues, and instruction continuously adjusted as students develop in intellectual power. To discover that students are below normal academic expectation is not to abandon hope of teaching a course as it should be taught; it is a greater challenge to find suitable means of bringing the students up to a desired a desired standard of performance and to help them improve further.

Finding a common level of instruction for a class of students is at best a compromise, a matter of striking a common mean which may fit no one precisely. As instruction proceeds, however, it should be possible to determine individual deviations and introduce appropriate variations in instruction as circumstances permit. A common level instruction should not be geared to the brightest nor to the dullest but seek to maintain proper balance among all students. The difficulty of doing this with a lecture class of a hundred or more students has been acknowledged: it is the principal drawback of the lecture method. Yet teaching wholly by lecture is not typical of American colleges, and more usual-sized class sections permit greater deviation from the common mode.

Appropriateness of Teaching Procedures. Some teachers do exceptionally well with advanced students in specialized study but have no comparable success with beginning students in general course; others show the reverse capacity. The explanation is not in any inherent peculiarity of the teacher or in the caliber of the students; the reason is often in the instructional method the teacher is impelled to follow whether by intuitive preference or deliberate choice. More skillful selection from a wider range of teaching procedures, and more flexible use of them can promote better results on any teaching level. The validity of a teaching procedure is a function of the instructional level for which it is intended.

A discussional type of procedure for example may be appropriate for students in introductory social science, but uneconomical and even tiresome in an advanced course with students capable of self-directed learning. A lecture course, often used to introduce students to a field of study, is better adapted to students with greater demonstrated interest, scholarship, and capacity for independent work. Intensive laboratory training is needed in preparing science specialists, but may be less fitting for students interested in acquiring a layman's view of science. A common textbook may help to fix the structure and substance of a course, or it may hobble learning. A routine of frequent quizzes may be serviceable on one teaching level, puerile and unbecoming on another.

Progression in teaching can be gauged by yardsticks conforming to students' growth toward independence. One is the role of the teacher himself: as instruction advances the teacher becomes less of an expositor, discussion leader, lesson "hearer," and prime mover of learning and more of an adviser, guide, critic, and study supervisor. Except in lecture courses and in some subjects where teacher dominance may be unavoidable, instruction should become progressively less teacher-controlled and more student-centred.

A second yardstick is the relative emphasis on common and differentiated tasks of learning. Advanced instruction should provide a greater opportunity for students to conceive, plan, and execute differentiated tasks according to their individual purpose, interests and aptitudes. A third criterion is the quality of students' learning that is, whether learning is primarily assimilative and reproductive or original and creative. Good teaching on any level affords students some opportunity for an original contribution, but advanced instruction should extend this opportunity. Learning should proceed less by recitation and more by preparation of research papers, original experimentation, literary or artistic production, problem solving, or the application of knowledge to the conduct of real experience.

Progression Within a Course. Whatever the starting level of instruction the teacher should attempt to raise it during the course. Such advance becomes more likely when it is translated into conscious purpose. Thus at the beginning of a course in political science students may be unable to write a satisfactory paper of reasonable length; instead of circumventing this weakness the teacher can set out systematically to improve the students' writing performance. Following a half-dozen carefully prepared, short papers students may be able to show substantial improvement. Those who at the beginning do not know "how to read a book" (meaning the textbook) can be taught to do so before the course is completed. To commence on a simplified level does not imply that it is necessary to continue and terminate instruction on the same level. Correspondingly, if a teacher can begin instruction at an advanced stage it should be his satisfying obligation to carry it even higher.

At times one must exercise great forbearance with students who *should* be ready for advanced instruction but patently are not. At such times it is necessary to reflect that the blame may not rest entirely with the students, that teachers in schools and colleges are not always mindful of the importance of graduating instruction, and that somewhere along the line the students' training has been neglected. The teacher may recall his own experience as a beginner in independent scholarship or teaching when he became aware of limitations not previously recognized which he later successfully overcame.

Large and Small-Group Instruction

A point frequently at issue is the extent to which teaching efficiency is influenced by class size. Earlier experimental studies concluded that under typical instruction measurable achievement of subject matter is not adversely affected by large classes, certainly not to the extent commonly assumed. What these studies could not show is the effect of failing to meet individual needs and foster specialized aptitudes and interests. A teacher cannot get to know each student as well in a class of forty as in a class of fifteen, although he may present his subject as effectively and the resulting average achievement in subject matter may be as high. If to educate is to help each student learn not only common subject matter but also subject matter to some extent differentiated by his interests, then teaching a large group imposes a handicap on teacher and students.

To a degree the argument as between large and small-group instruction is theoretical. The typical college is apt to have both, not from professional choice but from financial and administrative necessity. The best that can be said for having some oversized classes is that within budgetary limitations the resulting economy makes possible the staffing of important courses with inherently limited enrollment, and the allocation of manpower to essential educational services. It would not be sensible to insist on a maximum class size, let us say, of twenty-five students if in doing so we were prevented by insufficiency of manpower from offering seminars in Greek literature or philosophy to five or six students. Under prevailing circumstances a teacher should be prepared to teach large as well as small sections, adapting his teaching method to the opportunities and limitations of class size.

Fitting Group Size to Subject Matter. A prior obligation, however, is to fit the size of the group to the nature and demands of the subject. Granting the pressure of budgetary necessity, all courses do not lend themselves to large-group instruction. The more personal a subject, the more it affects the student's individual purposes and interests, the greater the need for small-group instruction. The problem may be stated in this way: "In which subjects of study will small-group organization offer the greatest benefit to instruction and in which others can large classes be formed with the least possible loss in instructional effectiveness?"

A course in art history can be taught by a competent art historian making effective use of visual resources to a class of a hundred or more students, particularly if common lecture instruction is supplemented by small-group discussion; a studio or workshop course in art cannot effectively be taught except to a small class. General psychology on a descriptive level, combining lecture, demonstration, and some discussion can be offered in large-group instruction, but an advanced experimental course for psychology majors may require a small study group. In all fields of study some courses are less suitable than others for large-group teaching, the measure of their unfitness being in the degree to which instruction involves attention to individual needs, adaptation to differences, and mastery of complex skills or techniques.

Adapting Instruction to Class Size. Once a class has been formed its instruction is the teacher's province. Unfortunately at times class size has made little difference either in method or quality of instruction: some teachers do not get to know students in a class of fifteen much better than in a class of fifty. Yet more than any other consideration the desirability of knowing the individual student justifies small-group instruction.

In a small group students can learn more from the teacher, from each other, and by themselves, and to a greater extent fulfil their needs. It falls to the teacher to take advantage of these possibilities in his choice and use of teaching method. Lecturing from a platform to a class of six students would not appear in most instances a sensible procedure, yet unvarying daily discussion does not seem imaginative either. The teacher has many techniques to choose from: he can combine occasional brief lecture with more frequent discussion and, where possible, learning by firsthand experience; partition the group into smaller teams for purposes of research, experimentation, and reporting; individualize instruction by separate assignment of each student to projects, problems, and creative tasks. He is, in short, free to depart completely from the usual routines of instruction. Though normal complaint concerns the work "load" imposed by large classes, the small class with its vast possibilities of instructional accomplishment imposes the greater burden.

Large classes, on the other hand, considerably restrict the teacher's freedom in use of method. Unless he has assistants to guide and supervise individual student activity, he must rely mostly upon his skill in presenting subject matter, devising suitable study exercises which can be checked and graded, and preparing good examinations. He is more or less committed to the lecture as the principal technique of instruction, punctuated by such intervals of discussion as he can manage. The practice of dividing a large lecture class into smaller discussion and study groups, each with its own student chairman, has been employed in some instances with notable success but its general feasibility may be questioned. Nevertheless it is helpful to approach large-group instruction with awareness of how its more limited opportunities can be exploited. If the lecture method is used it ought to be as skillfully as possible, with safeguards for securing and holding attention, satisfying a range of interests, and anticipating difficulties in comprehension. Audio-visual teaching resources should be canvassed, and reading lists, study references, and exercises prepared for those who need reinforcement in learning. Appraisal of student achievement should be frequent and the results anaylzed for elements which may require reteaching. Even with a large class the lecture need not be the sole technique of instruction. Every lesson may point up activities that students can pursue leading off into special side roads of interest. It is surprising how well one can keep track of individual students in even large class when he put his mind to it.

PLANNING INSTRUCTION

The need for preparing for instruction is too evident to warrant justification. The self-respecting teacher will not meet a class without having reflected in advance on the substance of the lesson, checked on elusive details of fact, and assembled accessory materials. Most likely he will have proceeded further, shaping in his mind specific procedure, salient points of discussion, and supplemental student activity. All this is performed as a matter of professional routine. In some cases preparation is necessarily more thorough: a lecture in Constitutional Law may require extended research and precise documentation; an experimental demonstration may involve setting up complicated apparatus and a preliminary trial-run; the simplest field trip usually demands detailed preparatory arrangements.

Were the teacher the only factor in the situation, preparation for teaching could be essentially a matter of refreshing one's scholarship with only casual reference to the mode of instruction. But there are students to be considered, and they complicate the picture. Each situation involving learner is different from every other, and the fact that a course has been taught successfully in the past does not assure that it is being taught successfully in the past does not assure that it is being taught successfully now. The experience a teacher has gained improves his prospects for success in future instruction. But like the experienced general who must plan each campaign differently, the teacher needs to approach each new term as a separate challenge. The values of experience are dissipated if the teacher merely stirs up memories of past performance, resuscitates old notes, and relies on further improvisation to see him through. Planning instructional method is no more fundamental than preparation in scholarship, but it is a second requisite for effective teaching.

Planning of instructional method involves deliberate selection among the possible techniques of teaching. Laxity in this respect helps to explain why teaching so often falls into conventional molds of the lecture, discussion, or recitation: these are most "natural" and easiest. Referring to the lecture as "the characteristic method of higher education" Schueler thus explains its frequency of use.

It is easier to lecture, not to lecture well but just to lecture, than to engage in almost any other kinds of teaching activity. The professor faced with the necessity of teaching the effect on world trade of currency devaluation, or the influence of Freud on the novel of the twentieth century, finds it simplest to prepare a lecture which, once delivered, can be assumed to have 'covered' the subject. The problem of considering the relationship of his students, as individuals and as a group, to the subject, the ways in which they may react to it, and the ways which may be used by the teacher to bring them closer to it and to stimulate and guide the working of their minds, introduces into professor's preparation and into his classroom procedure that most complex of all variables, a consideration of the student and how he can best learn.

It is precisely this variable which creates the necessity for systematic planning of teaching procedure.

To plan methodically is not to plot in detail every aspect of instruction but to concentrate on a few basic questions. Which of the possible ways of teaching these topics are most promising and feasible? What kinds of teaching aids would be helpful and are attainable? What sorts of study or learning experience would be beneficial to students? What special assistance are students apt to need and how can it be provided? In what ways can instructional outcomes be evaluated? Involvement in such planning impose no commitment to inflexible procedure but makes possible a more conscious design for instruction. It does not inhibit desirable spontaneity, since the latter is sparked more by self-assurance than by temporizing uncertainty.

To an extent instructional planning has to be conducted at long range. Few teachers would commence instruction without envisioning the course in its entirety, outlining a tentative course of study, assembling a bibliography, selecting subjects for special investigation, determining a general mode of procedure, and programing course highiights. As an overview of instruction this is sufficient, but as each major topic of study is approached more detailed planning—at closer range—is necessary. If a course in Economics includes a unit on the "rise and development of corporations" encompassing several weeks of study, the teacher will find it advantageous to have the unit planned as a whole, centering on such questions as previously suggested. This will not only afford him sufficient time to formulate desired techniques and secure such teaching aids as may not be close at hand but also enable him to determine more specifically the learning potentialities of the entire unit, the progression from lesson to lesson, and the opportunities for individualizing instruction.

Long-range planning helps the teacher to organize instruction on the basis of large units of subject matter. A single class period is seldom in itself a complete instructional unit: more often it is part of a larger whole, the composition of which is more apparent to the teacher than to the students. Conducting instruction in terms of large subdivisions of subject matter enables the student to operate more intelligently through awareness of the interrelationships of constituent parts, and greatly facilitates diversification of instructional procedure. The teacher can better determine when to use lecture, discussion, formal recitation, small-group study, individual library or laboratory work, field trips, and at which points to pause for testing achievement and possible remedial teaching.

Some planning on a day-to-day basis is desirable. Plans do not develop exactly as conceived, and modifications may be necessary. It is well, therefore, to review the plan of the next day's work—how the juncture with the preceding lesson is to be made, the extent of the new lesson, and some of the details of content and technique. Few things are as exasperating to students as unneeded repetition of earlier instruction of unexplainable gaps in subject matter resulting from hazy recollection of what was previously treated. It is especially advantageous to make a last minu te check of factual details, reference materials, technical aids or equipment, and instructional notes. Fifteen minutes devoted to such preparation may make the difference between impressive, workmanlike teaching and fumbling, apparently extemporaneous performance.

Instructional planning takes place in advance of, immediately prior to, and during instruction. Plans should not be so fixed that they cannot be modified or even altered in the course of teaching. An unexpected occurrence—a significant event, an emergent problem in learning, a change in students' attitudes or interests—may affect the value of a prepared plan, making it less promising than a revised mode of operation which suggests itself on the spot. A teacher should take advantage of "targets of opportunity" as they arise, and not feel bound to the restrictions of the original plan. The purpose of planning is to promote the best use of the teacher's resources in instruction, not to hinder or confine him.

5
INSTRUCTIONAL TECHNIQUES

It is proposed to review in greater detail some techniques of instruction mentioned in the preceding chapter. The goal is as before: not to reduce fine teaching to a technical operation but to feature technical workmanship as one of the qualities of superior instruction. If attention to technique has any value in college teaching it lies in the varied and imaginative uses which may result, not in the pursuit of any prescribed routine. Every teacher has the right to do things differently.

The subject of teaching technique has lately been receiving attention in college circles and in the last few years a considerable literature has accumulated. The signs point to an intensification of interest. Systematic information on college teaching practices is more available than formerly, but is not yet adequate. The ensuing discussion is bound to reflect limitations, other than those attributable to confinement of space, which the authors are frank to acknowledge.

There are those who belittle technique, insisting that apart from the requisites of scholarship good teaching is largely a matter of following common sense. The position has some merit. Not all teaching problems derive from shortcomings of technique or require technical expertness for their resolution. Personal failings may create difficulties in teaching: remove the cause and you eliminate the difficulty. The lazy teacher who "ad libs" his way through a course needs conscience more than pedagogy. A teacher's voice can intimidate students, make them nervous or fidgety, or put them to sleep. Distemper or arrogance will breed hostility in return, and excessive joviality may produce disrespect. These are not aspects of technique but qualities of behaviour governable by common sense. They influence instruction, as—conversely—engaging personal qualities may go a long way toward compensating for technical shortcomings.

On the other hand, technical considerations contribute much to quality of teaching, sometimes accounting for the difference between success and near-failure. Most difficulties in college instruction arise not from personal failings of teachers but from the peculiar demands of teaching and learning on college levels. Such problems cannot ordinarily be resolved by attention to duty and the precepts of common sense: they require specialized knowledge and technical skill. To help the teacher impart his instruction with better, effect is all that technique aspires to do.

The number of available techniques in teaching precludes any attempt at comprehensiveness in review. We propose to deal with relatively few—those which are common and by this token important: lecture, discussion, laboratory or workshop procedure, smallgroup and individual instruction, remedial teaching, and some specific devices associated with their use.

Lecture

The lecture is so common in college teaching that we forget it is a procedure uncharacteristic of pre-college instruction. Modern secondary education avoids the pure lecture form, preferring techniques which involve students more actively in the learning process. On college and adult levels of learning the lecture is appropriate, particularly after students have been trained in its use. Despite distinctive limitations it is economical of time at a stage in learning when time is of the essence. Its advantages in making accessible to large groups of students the instructional services of an incomparable scholar or teacher and in the economical deployment of manpower have been mentioned earlier. Despite some question as to its popularity the lecture system is securely established, and sooner or later most teachers become initiated into its use. For that matter every teacher at times employs the lecture in some form, whatever the structure of his course.

The use of the lecture does not require apology. In many circumstances it is the most appropriate form of instruction, and occasionally the *only* appropriate form. It is not feasible to compare the lecture with another mode of instruction as if the two were interchangeable: in the right course and with the right person a single semester of lectures can be more instructive than several years of independent reading and unlimited group discussion. To open up a field of study, draw attention to its vital elements, distil the essence of many years of productive scholarship, bring students abreast of developments in the forefront of research—for these purposes the lecture is invaluable. To listen to a lecture can be a thrilling experience from which the student may gain ideas obtainable in no other way. But, possibly to a greater degree than other forms of instruction, lecturing presumes a high order of intellectual competence on the part of learners.

Conduct of the Lecture. Lecturing to a group of several hundred students in a large hall with the aid of a public address system involves a considerable feat of teaching, if the lecture is viewed not only as a means of presenting information but also of effecting learning. A course of instruction may be defined as "students and teacher working *together* in a sustained way in a common field of study." It is with respect to the italicized word in this definition that difficulty with the lecture technique usually occurs. For a poised, articulate, well-prepared person to "deliver" a lecture, once he has become accustomed to the presence of a "mike," is not hard; what is more difficult is to keep working with the students—to establish contact quickly, pace one's delivery to their capacity to follow, make proper allowance for note-taking, anticipate difficulty or slowness in comprehension, round up mental stragglers, clinch an important point before advancing to the next, relieve fatigue, boredom, or the strain of listening, and at intervals provide opportunity for audience participation.

To achieve a good lecture one must be sure to remain in continuous contact with the audience or learning group. Some audience participation is indispensable, the difference between this and other forms of instruction being in this respect more in degree than in kind. In a lecture, opportunity for student participation is not as frequent, prolonged, or widely distributed, but there must be regard for the principle that learning through listening needs reinforcement in self-activity. To compensate for the restriction of students' verbal expression, the lecturer must learn to *sense* how students are responding in thought to what is said. Like other modes of instruction, the lecture should provide intervals for clarification of thought, assimilation of ideas, and respite from close concentration.

Naturally and informally a mood may be created at the outset which is favourable to the establishment of rapport with students. One device is, before beginning the lecture, to exchange a few words with students within conversational reach on almost any subject that comes to mind—a topic of world news, an item of college interest, an afterthought on the last lecture, or how they fare in the course. Engaging in this friendly gossip will help foster a sense of ease and remind students that the person before them is *their* teacher, and not a stranger addressing them from a platform. Instruction may begin with a few questions providing a brief flashback to the preceding lecture or relating to the day's work; directed to students in various quarters of the room and enlisting the attention of all, the questions will help the audience to merge as a learning group. After a few minutes of such discussion the lecture itself may get under way, starting slowly and gaining in tempo as students become absorbed in listening, but not exceeding the rate at which they can reasonably follow.

A lecture should seldom be presented in one unbroken discourse. Unless exceptionally interesting, a long lecture strains the capacity for concentrated listening, causing intermittent wandering of attention and loss of continuity in thought. In preparing the lecture it may be well to organize it in several blocks or units, each presentable in not more than fifteen minutes of continuous exposition; as each unit is completed, it may be punctuated by a questioning or discussion period of two or three minutes. This should suffice not only to close ranks among the listeners but also to reveal points of difficulty in comprehension which merit further explanation or reteaching. Little is gained by advancing when a breach in understanding has developed. The lecturer should school himself to stay in front of his audience but not to run away from it. By being sensitive to symptoms of audience reaction, even those represented by listening posture, he can estimate how his instruction is registering.

As a rule the exposition should be concluded before end of the class period so as to allow some time for general discussion. This is the time to gauge audience response, tie up loose threads of thought, and review a salient points. Students should be trained to recognize the importance of this interval for summing-up so that there will be no gathering of books and coats and scraping of furniture to distract attention. It is worth explaining at the beginning of the course, the proposed organization of the lecture period and emphasizing the function of the summary discussion. Students need training in the technique of large-group setting are diffident about asking a question or offering an answer before a large audience; they should be encouraged and helped to do so. Where the lecture-hall is so large as to make it difficult for the student to be heard, the lecturer may have to assist by restating the question or answer.

In holding audience attention throughout the lecture pace of delivery is important. There are times when the atmosphere of a lecture, particularly one dealing with an abstruse or technical subject, may become uncomfortably close. It is then that a sudden change of pace is helpful in reviving the listeners' attention: a brief interruption, a glance around the room, and an interpolated remark by the lecturer may have the effect of breaking audience tension. Observing his audience as he speaks, the lecturer notices that students are becoming listless, that there is shifting in the seats and some inattentiveness; instead of digging harder into the subject, the lecturer would do better to pause, smile, and suggest that this may be a good time to take a "breather," answer questions, or clear up any matter of difficulty. Or the lecturer may say nothing, merely halting momentarily to let the audience settle down and resuming when attention has been restored.

In sum, what are some of the mechanics of good lecture performance? Assuming that the lecture has been well prepared in substance —first, making contact with the audience at the outset and fusing it into a learning group; second, maintaining this contact throughout the lecture through quality of substance, manner of presentation, and intermittent involvement of the group in active participation; third, providing a discussion period at the conclusion of the lecture to elicit audience response and for summary purposes; fourth adjusting the tempo of the lecture so as to gain and hold maximum attention.

Lecture Outline. A useful guide to instruction and serviceable also in directing study is the course outline arranged topically in an order conforming to the lecture sequence and including lists of readings and recommended study activities. Such an outline facilitates good lecture organization, saves time in daily preparation, and provides advance notice to the student of whatever is forthcoming. Last minute determination of lecture content—of items to be emphasized and others to be touched in passing—can be troublesome. Some teachers solve the problem of coverage by endeavouring to include within the allotted time everything of possible value, drowning the subject in a flood of detail; others ramble as the spirit moves them. The outline embodies a systematic effort to define the scope of instruction with regard to order and emphasis. It serves as a standard of relevance binding the lecturer to the subject, but not so tightly that he is prevented from making necessary adjustments.

An outline presented on the blackboard immediately before the start of each lecture is not a substitute for a course syllabus issued earlier to students, since it fails to provide a needed overview of the course and an opportunity for specific pre-lecture preparation. Although a course outline is necessarily less comprehensive in detail than one prepared for each lecture it has greater instructional value, especially if it can be supplemented by a brief blackboard synopsis developed during the lecture.

Lecture Assignment. For students to obtain maximum benefit from a lecture, individual participation in study should both precede and follow it. On their own initiative most students would not engage in preparatory study, hence formal assignments may be necessary. The lecture should be conducted on the assumption that the assignment has been fulfilled (even if an occasional quiz is required to enforce compliance), and that students are prepared to receive a higher order of instruction than would be possible without such preparation. Unless the lecturer proceeds on this basis, students will not pay much heed to the assignment and lecture time will be expended injudiciously in attempted "full" coverage, or the lecture will be in part repetitious of what students have already acquired. The lecturer has enough to do in dealing with essentials, supplementing common information sources, clarifying meanings and relationships, and investing the subject with added educational dimension without traversing ground which students are competent to explore for themselves.

The post-lecture assignment of study furnishes needed opportunity to differentiate instruction. This is something for which the lecture proper is not well adapted: occasionally the lecturer may relate a comment or question to particular students with special interests, but for the most part he cannot deviate from a common direction. The study assignment can be organized so as to afford latitude for special capabilities and interests. Readings and learning exercises can be differentiated in quality and extent. Beyond a common minimal level compatible with respectable achievement each student is free to proceed as far as his educational resources permit. The extent to which the lecturer is able to pursue differentiated instruction depends upon the size of the class, the availability of professional assistance, and his own resourcefulness in assigning and evaluating learning. Where the lecture is coupled with smaller-group conference or recitation, more can be accomplished in this respect.

The post-lecture assignment should not recapitulate knowledge already canvassed by the lecture. Repeating the same information without lapse of time detracts from interest and attention; rather, the study assignment should seek to extend and enrich the substance of learning. A lecture dealing substantially with an explanation of principles may be followed by study problems involving applications; one opening up a subject to general view may be followed by an assignment leading more intensively into special aspects. Assigned study can fortify instruction more effectively through enrichment than repetition.

Audio-Visual Aids. The effectiveness of a lecture, as of other modes of instruction, may be enhanced through the use of audio-visual devices. Not all teachers respond to such devices with equal enthusiasm: the addicts "overdo it," whereas others forego opportunities for their profitable use because of lack of familiarity, or timely preparation, or indifference. It pays to explore the aids available for teaching a course particularly through lectures, since verbal exposition alone, however lucid, has its shortcomings. Long ago science teachers discovered the value of demonstrational aids and some have since raised skill in demonstration to a high art. Aural representation has become common in music, as has visual representation in the fine arts; courses in appreciation could hardly be conducted without recordings, slides, or films. Similar accessories are widely used in the social sciences, and lately the value of recordings has become apparent to teachers of language and literature. The use of audio-visual aids in instruction is increasing, although inconvenience in securing them has been a limiting factor. Colleges have begun to develop film and record libraries as adjuncts to their extensive book collections, and teachers have become more systematic in tracking down available materials

The justification for their use is their anticipated contribution to instructional effectiveness. Unless the teacher is persuaded that such contribution may be forthcoming, there is no point in resorting to them; the elements of novelty and extrinsic interest which they add to a course are not in themselves sufficiently important. Granting their potential worth, the question is "How are they to be used?" As a rule it is better that they be introduced within the instructional context than detached from it. The demonstration of an experiment should be made at the point where it is needed to clarify or establish a scientific principle rather than reserved for the end of the lecture; a film should be presented when it is timely to the subject under discussion. Film showings occupying a full class period should be bracketed by discussion in adjoining class periods in order to tie them closely to instruction. It goes without saying that audio-visual aids should not be so spectacular as to focus attention upon themselves and detract from the substance of learning.

A teacher should be familiar with the aids he plans to use. Many a science teacher has come a cropper through failure to rehearse an experiment or check apparatus in advance. Films should be previewed, and recordings pre-played. Where "live" radio and television programs are to be related to instruction, it is well to learn as much as possible concerning their substance, technique of presentation, and points of relevancy to the course, so as to guide students' listening or viewing. Technical equipment should be checked by the teacher or a qualified operator: it is discomfiting to have a defective projector break down in the middle of a film showing, leaving the students bemused and the teacher to extemporize as best he can. Such minor mishaps have a way of inhibiting further reliance on technical aids, with possible disadvantage to instruction.

Appraising the Lecture. Evaluating one's own lecture performance is not easy, yet an occasional systematic effort may be rewarding. No one technique is sufficient, but several techniques used conjointly can reveal to the teacher a clearer picture of himself. A direct method is to reproduce the lecture on a recorder and listen to it afterward. Recovering from the first mild shock of hearing what sounds like an unfamiliar voice, the teacher can proceed to analyze his performance, noting diction, style of delivery, mannerisms of voice and speech, lucidity of thought and expression, and quality of organization. It pays to be more critical than tolerant, cataloguing faults for future correction. The obvious limitation of this technique is that the teacher may not always be able to recognize his merits and shortcomings.

Students' reactions, direct or indirect, may be of assistance in self-appraisal. It is a wholesome and sometimes chastening experience to gather a sampling of students' lecture notes and look them over; although ordinarily more indicative of the students' than of the teacher's failings, they can furnish leads for the improvement of instruction. A student questionnaire is a tricky device, but prepared strictly as a diagnostic instrument and not as a popularity poll, it may be helpful in pinpointing unsuspected strength or weakness. Experienced teachers are more apt to resort to indirect estimates of student reaction than to solicit direct comment: while justified in principle, this practice is less likely to furnish the specific diagnostic clues a teacher requires in order to perfect his performance.

An exchange of visits with a colleague, if possible one lecturing in the same course, is always helpful. Participating at the audience level, the visitor is better able to analyze students' reactions and judge instruction objectively, noting similarities and differences with respect to his own and gaining ideas for his own as well as his colleague's improvement. Allowance should be made for individual in teaching, and no attempt should be made to promote imitation or large-scale borrowing. An informal conference following the exchange of visits will be beneficial to both teachers.

Related Conference or Recitation. Customarily the large-group lecture is paired with the smaller-group conference or recitation. Theoretically the two techniques complement each other, combining to form a balanced learning experience. A weakness in the arrangement grows out of the need for assigning different teachers to the several conference groups, with the result that coordination between lecture and conference becomes difficult to maintain. Conference teachers have been known to run ahead of the lecture, to lag behind and in some cases to plot an independent course. These instances may be a typical, but they dramatize the difficulty and also suggest how it may be obviated.

The lecturer and the conference teachers constitute a team, performing their separate roles in relation to a common task. It is desirable, first, that they plan the course together: a teacher cannot teach effectively unless he is in accord with the way a course has been designed; each colleague's ideas should be weighed, and a consensus reached which is reasonably acceptable to all. Second, it is necessary that conference teachers maintain contact with the lectures, if possible through personal attendance, otherwise by frequent joint meetings of teachers. Liaison through a common course outline is effective only when the outline is sufficiently detailed and the lecturer is careful to follow it or consult with his colleagues on any major deviation. Third, lecturer and conference teachers should remain in instructional harness, treating not the same specific items but the same general topics. The proceedings of the conference need not invariably follow the lecture: on occasions, by agreement, the conference may be used to introduce a subject rather than develop it. But, whatever the plan, instructional activities should always be correlated.

The purpose of the conference is to offer types of instruction which the lecture itself is not able to effect. In part it supplements the lecture by elaborating content, digging into details, clarifying explanations, and providing exercises in application; but mostly it is follow-up of individual learning. This is the time to direct individual study, measure progress, assist the slow or temporarily disabled, and work with the superior or those with specialized interests. The conference also gives students a chance to respond to learning to a much greater degree than is possible at a lecture.

For the conference teacher to employ the lecture technique is as inadvisable as repeating the lecture content. His instruction should be more informal and intimate, following the student's leads in questioning and discussion and being responsive to his needs. Discussion should not be aimless, yet move freely within the limits of the subject and occasionally beyond them. Contrasted with the necessarily controlled conduct of the lecture, "permissive" instruction is all the more welcome. Though group discussion may predominate, a definite portion of time should be allotted to meeting with students individually for consultation on their problems.

Some teachers utilize the conference hour primarily for recitation that is, for hearing lessons and ration student performance. As an evaluation procedure this is costly in time: there are more economical ways of assessing achievement, some by the lecturer himself. As a method of teaching it is uninspired. Some questioning by the teacher is profitable as a means of fixing essential information or dispelling common misunderstanding. But an entire session devoted to quizzing students becomes either a tense ordeal or a boring routine. The first few minutes of the hour may be devoted to an oral or written quiz, after which instruction should become more nourishing. Once or twice in the course the full period may be used for an extended evaluation exercise.

Discussion

The teaching procedure most frequently employed is the discussion. It blends with other modes of instruction such as the lecture, recitation, or student report into various patterns the common feature of which is shared colloquy. Essentially it may be defined as an effort to have students learn by thinking and talking together as a group, and developing through the group process a shared appreciation of subject-matter. This mode of instruction suggests itself whenever the important outcomes of a course are derivable from common deliberation and exchange of thought following from and leading to individual reading and study. It is the method likely to appeal to the teacher who subscribes to "no method." It holds its popularity deservedly, but is by no means as casual and artless a technique as its practice sometimes implies.

Like the lecture, the discussion offers special learning opportunities not equally realizable through alternative techniques. It enables students to advance in creative thought by their own efforts, to make progress as a result of their own and others' response to the stimulus of questioning and volunteered expression. It enables students to enrich their own conceptions by reacting to those of others. If the level of discussion is high enough, even the teacher learns by being involved in such a process. A second great benefit is found in the opportunity it provides for training in collaborative effort. Discussion is not the only form of group learning, but like others it makes possible the development of attitudes and skills which contribute to collective accomplishment without which academic training, however intensive, is one-sided. Not alone in exchange of thought but in solving problems and carrying out missions or assignments in study, members of a discussion group can be taught to work together in small or large combinations.

A good talk is not necessarily good teaching. Some fine discussions take place in anterooms, cocktail lounges, and midnight soirees in girls' dormitories, but their educative quality is not always assured. The animated tone of a discussion, the extent to which it elicits participation, and even the worthiness of the subject are not alone the test of good instruction. At times we all find ourselves entering a classroom not as well prepared as we should like" yet we can meet the class, engage in a "stimulating" discussion, and terminate the session with most of our self-respect intact. There in lies the danger in teaching by discussion: in the comforting delusion that if a teacher is sufficiently master of his subject, the need for careful preparation is not so compelling. "I do not find in my teaching any correlation between the way I prepare and the success of the success of the subsequent discussion," a young instructor stated recently. By a superficial criterion of "success" the statement may be judged true: as an exercise in teaching, an unprepared discussion which turns out effective is an accident. The sin is not in the occasional unavoidable failure to prepare; it is in the specious generalization that lively conversation is good teaching.

The test of instructive discussion lies in a few commonplace questions. "Through this discussion what have students learned that they could not otherwise have known?" "How far has this learning advanced them toward mastery of the subject?" "In the time spent in discussion, was maximum use made of opportunities to learn?" "Could learning have been better effected through different instructional means?" Focusing attention on considerations of learning effectiveness as distinct from external stimulation reveals some of the greater challenges facing the teacher.

Teacher's Role in Discussion. This must vary with the teacher's personality and the philosophy of teaching to which he subscribes. A forceful person becomes a strong discussion leader unless he is careful to exercise restraint. The proponent of the "nondirective" methods necessarily subordinates himself to the group, using his authority as teacher sparingly. The Socratic teacher remains in the center of discussion, directing thought through his line of questioning. It is difficult to define the teacher's role other than by suggesting that, insofar as he may lean toward one extreme or the other, he runs the risk of either suppressing group thinking or dissipating its values through aimless drifting.

From the standpoint of learning, a satisfactory role is that which fosters the students' initiative and gives free rein to their ideas without surrendering the teacher's responsibility for keeping the discussion within the bounds of relevance, impelling deeper and more incisive thought, and at critical points contributing information which the group itself cannot produce. Speaking to their fellows and not to the teacher alone, students should carry the burden of discussion, their remarks reflecting responsible and cohesive thought. An idea once given currency should be pursued until its inherent contribution has been realized. Students should feel free to differ with one another and with the teacher, provided they speak responsibly. The teacher may participate on an equal; basis but is further obligated to help students perceive deeper meanings and relationships, to insist on probing ideas fully, to evaluate, criticize, and even on occasion to take up the reins of a discussion and alter its course.

Make an effort to study your own role the next time you lead a discussion. Do you literally or figuratively confront the student when he speaks so that he feels bound to address himself to you, or by your attitude do you encourage him to share his ideas with the class? Do you remain in the background of a discussion permitting students to assume control, or do you unobtrusively exert your influence to raise the quality and level of group discussion and incline it toward more productive effort? In short, what is the substance of your contribution? Whatever your chosen role, improvement in its performance presumes awareness and disciplined control of what you are doing.

Planning the Discussion. As in other forms of instruction, planning a discussion involves attention to technique as well as subject matter: how to select and arrange subject matter for clear and orderly development, how to begin the discussion, what sort of questions to ask, what instructional aids to prepare, what supplemental learning activities to introduce, and how to terminate the lesson this last being based on the proposition that a good discussion should be effectively concluded and not simply allowed to expire.

Preparing the lesson need not be expensive in time if the daily plan is part of a longer-term arrangement: for certain of the activities the stage will have been set in advance; others will require last-minute attention. The practiced teacher knows how to telescope his planning procedure, designing the main outlines of the lesson in a few strokes. Reviewing the subject matter, he can simultaneously cast it in a form suitable for presentation; from the many questions which suggest themselves, he will select the few most interesting, thought-provoking, and pivotal; supplemental learning exercises—study assignments, student reports, panel discussion, demonstration, a film showing— will most likely have been arranged in advance and can now be worked into the plan; for an appropriate lesson ending he may propose a problem, exercise in application, creative project, summary or critical evaluation. Over a period of years a teacher will accumulate a store of teaching materials, illustrative aids, and study activities from which he can quickly select those suitable for the immediate purpose. The daily plan need not be written out, although it is helpful to append notes to such subject-matter, as one may require a memorandum of procedural items which may otherwise escape the memory.

Common Teaching Aids. Like the actor in the theatre, the teacher is provided with props designed to assist him toward more telling performance. The most commonplace are black board and chalk. Judged by the use to which these accessories are sometimes put, one of their common functions seems to be to let the teacher work off accumulated nervous energy. The stick of chalk is mistreated— now broken in two, juggled, dropped, picked up, juggled again—to the evident amusement of the class. The blackboard is also misused— to pound home a point (literally), scribble and quickly erase a word, or draw a cabalistic design; without pause in speech a teacher will whirl to the blackboard, write and noisily dot a word, and whirl back to face the class, seemingly pleased by this gymnastic performance.

The blackboard is made to be used in less dramatic and more controlled fashion. Except when blackboard exercises are customarily part of instruction (as in some mathematics courses), it should not be utilized for extended writing; a lengthy lesson outline, assignment, or series of examination questions are better presented through the medium of the individual copy. When representation to scale or precision in diagramming is desired, free-hand blackboard drawing should not be attempted; carefully prepared charts, large enough to be viewed by the class, can do the job better. The blackboard may be used for a brief lesson outline to guide instruction; for a terminal summary outline of discussion; to develop a problem or exercise illustrative of a principle or point of instruction; for rapid free-hand drawing of sketches or diagrams not requiring precision; and for deliberate accentuation of key items in instruction.

The mimeograph or duplicating machine is another serviceable instrument, utilized by some teachers to excess, by others hardly at all. It is well to remember that prior issuance of instructional materials to students is conducive to a more intelligent approach to learning and independent study. On the other hand, materials should not be issued unless they are germane to instruction, and never so freely that they cannot be assimilated; students learn to discount quantities of mimeographed materials to which little reference is made later. A practical suggestion relative to the physical preparation of mimeographed materials may not be out of place: such preparation should be handled by a skilled professional typist. Some "home-made" productions we have seen belie the worth of their content and offer a poor example of workmanship for students to emulate.

Questioning. Much of the real success of teaching by discussion hinges on the quality of the questioning, that is, the intellectual substance of the questions and the manner in which they are presented. Unless the discussion is completely spontaneous and "nondirected," its path will be controlled by the kinds of questions propounded; even a student-centered discussion presumes a line of inquiry initiated by someone. Class sessions that should have been taut with interest have been known to languish for lack of skilled exercise of the questioning technique.

Not all important questions projected during a discussion can or should be prepared in advance: such a practice might result in holding the group too rigidly to a fixed path of learning and inhibiting spontaneity of expression. The wiser course is to formulate key questions, insert them at appropriate points in the discussion, and have others in readiness to submit as necessary. A discussion which "takes hold" generates its own questions, emanating more often from students than from the teacher. The greater the teacher's mastery of the subject, the more significant his questions; the more accomplished the group, the more challenging the questions it will set for itself. The substantive quality of questioning is a function of thinking, and as such is impossible to achieve by prescription.

Questions vary according to the function they serve. There are teaching questions which elicit from students information tributary to learning; thought-provoking questions which generate ideas radiating in many directions; drill questions which prompt repetition of learning for the sake of better retention; test questions which seek to assess the amount and quality of learning; problem questions which challenge power in application and use of knowledge; attention-getting questions aimed at reviving the drowsy or recalling the inattentive; and rhetorical questions which the teacher asks without expectation of an answer, as a way of varying his form of utterance by breaking the monotony of the declarative sentence. The various types are generally not interchangeable, although a question may serve more than one purpose.

Within limits the form of a question follows its function. A thought question may be short or long, but as a rule will not be in " Yes-No" form, call for a cryptic reply, or by its working suggest the answer. On the other hand, drill questions may be of a brief, rapidfire order, evoking responses correspondingly short; the premium is not so much on determining the correct response as on issuing it promptly. A "why" question presumes more considered reflection in responding than does the usual "when" or "what" question. There is an element of skill in fashioning the form of a question to the nature of the response sought; a disappointing answer is often traceable to an ill-adapted form of question.

Variety in function and form of questioning lends interest to instruction and increases its effectiveness. No discipline consists wholly of facts to be assimilated, or ideas to be reflected upon, or problems to be solved; each is a synthesis of mental operations requiring for their sustenance different kinds of stimuli and instructive aids. We fall too readily into a characteristic pattern of questioning which may not do justice to the variety possible or necessary. A lesson pivoting on a few general thought questions may be slow-footed and somnolent unless the subject itself is exceptionally evocative; it can be enlivened by introducing a change in the character and pace of questioning. A recitation progressing by a succession of brief, pointed questions may become disjointed and tiresome for lack of a substantial theme; it can be improved by pursuit of more thoughtful inquiry.

The manner of stating the question influences the quality of response. A question is a directive to thought: it should be clear in intent and precise in expression. Whatever difficulty it possesses should be inherent in its thought, not in its wording: many questions one hears in a college classroom are not intrinsically challenging once their language has been decoded. Directive terms such as "discuss," "indicate," "describe," "explain" lack sufficient definiteness to be of good service. A question should be a single, compelling invitation to response, not a cumulative spray or shower of invitations. Center your attention on questioning technique the next time you observe a colleague in action. Does he state the question, stop, and await the answer, or does he follow it in quick succession with another, and another—each succeeding question designed to clarify the original but serving only to blur its memory? A sensible question, clearly worded, does not need to be paraphrased or embroidered. And how often do you encounter the teacher who does not wait for the student to answer but supplies the answer himself? Conversation is disconcerting when the questioner insists on answering his own questions, and gradually the other participant subsides into the role of listener. Students may not be quick to answer a question but they should have the opportunity of coming to grips with it. Be patient in hearing out a student.

Questions should be adapted to the level of instruction; as a course progresses the character of the questioning should be elevated. It is by asking himself questions that a student learns to master a subject. The questions addressed to him in instruction should increasingly challenge his understanding, insight, grasp of relationships, appreciation, and critical evaluation of the content of study. It is evidence of growth when at the end of a term of instruction a group can engage in spirited deliberation of questions of much higher content value than those characteristically introduced at the beginning.

Some Specialized Techniques

Laboratories and Workshop. Laboratory work has long been a feature of instruction in the natural sciences, and under one or another designation the workshop principle has similarly been applied in teaching the fine arts and music, creative writing and dramatics, and numerous technical and applied studies. Recently the terms "laboratory" and "workshop" have been generalized and expanded in use, and in various form are associated with courses in psychology, the social sciences, foreign language, home economics, health education, and preparation for teaching. The essential principle involved is learning by doing, with the burden of course activity placed upon the student working under the teacher's direction. Although not identical, the two techniques have features in common, and for the sake of brevity in this discussion will be treated together as "laboratory instruction."

The values of laboratory instruction for the student lie in the opportunity to experience a learning situation at first hand, to translate theory into practice, to develop, test and apply principles, and to learn methods of procedure—with greater reliance on his own power and with greater freedom from the restrictions which group work often imposes on the individual. For the teacher it is a chance to observe the student in action, assess his worth, correct his mistakes, and guide him in a promising direction. An incisive question or two may reveal whether the student appreciates what he is doing or is trying to follow instructions without comprehending them; a little encouragement or special help may kindle or intensify interest in learning and provide the basis for independent accomplishment in the future. In some subjects laboratory instruction is a necessary complement to lecture, discussion, and other verbal media of teaching; in special experimental or technical courses it may serve as the basic procedure. Although laboratory work does not preclude organized large-group effort, it is more often conducted as individualized or small-team activity.

A danger in laboratory instruction stems form the normal temptation to which a busy or preoccupied teacher is subject, namely to conduct his own work while leaving students to do theirs. Teachers have been known to absent themselves for portions of a laboratory period in order to carry on other pressing work or to remain seated at their desks, accepting interruptions from such students as apply for help. Even good students need supervision, and poor students may fail to recognize their mistakes or be unwilling to admit them. Unsupervised activity may nullify the benefits which the laboratory is supposed to afford and instead promote poor work habits. A mediocre student is more likely to solicit help from another student than from the teacher, and come away with faulty or incomplete information or with correct "answers" which are not fundamentally understood.

Laboratory instruction presumes skill in teaching different from that involved in the conduct of lecture or discussion. The premium is not on a careful exposition or development of course content but on the ability to guide the student in the creative accomplishment of tasks without depriving him of the chance to do his own work and, at the same time, without allowing him to commit serious mistakes. Just the right proportion of reserve and readiness in advancing suggestions is necessary; the teacher must "size up" the student to know at which point to offer help, when to withhold it. Preparation for laboratory instruction is essential, but the preparation consists in thinking over what the students will be doing, the preliminary verbal instruction they will require, the difficulties they are likely to encounter, and some of the questions by which the quality of their performance can be appraised and their learning experience improved. Preparation should also concern itself with ensuring accessibility to needed equipment and materials and arrangement of proper conditions for work.

A science student, for example, pursuing a laboratory investigation has an opportunity to relive the experience of the pioneer research worker who originated the hypothesis, developed the experiment, and confirmed his discovery. A laboratory manual which outlines in detail the experimental procedure to be followed and requires the student merely to furnish answers deprives him of intellectual challenge and potential profit; the teacher who stands at the student's elbow and prompts him at every step achieves the same effect. To be instructive, the laboratory manual should be so prepared as to state the problem to be investigated, fill in the necessary background, suggest a general mode of procedure, and leave to the student the task of formulating a precise plan of investigation, setting up the experiment, and reaching significant conclusions. The teacher can make a personal contribution by observing the student at work, occasionally helping him over a hurdle, and leading him by question or quiet suggestion to realize greater learning possibilities in what he is doing.

Speaking generally, sufficient use is not being made of the opportunity to train students in the technique of team and paired investigation. Much of the current research in science is conducted on an organized team basis, and while each member of the team needs to be a skilled research man, he must also know how to work in concert with others. Students need practice in the joint planning of an investigation, in fairly apportioning the work, in coordinating experimentation, in checking one another's results. Particularly is this true in workshop activities where the pooling of effort by several students makes possible an attack on problems of greater magnitude or significance than could be entrusted to a single person. The recent development of the workshop as a technique of in-service training in several professions has underlined the value of such collective effort. It is surprising how unprepared students are to engage in shared undertaking at the beginning, and how rewarding can be the results in learning once they have been trained to overcome this handicap.

Small-Group and Individual Instruction. To teach a seminar or direct a small number of gifted students in advanced study is for many teachers a prized objective—a respite from the struggle with oversized classes and their component of indifferent students, and a chance to apply their scholarship in the interests of those who can and will learn. Even apart form higher-level work with "honor" students, tutorial or small-group instruction is often preferred to the more conventional class arrangement. Yet teachers engaged in such instruction will testify that few tasks can be more exacting of energy and skill, though the experience itself is stimulating.

Some individual or small-group work is indispensable in a college program. However attentive to individual needs a teacher may be in ordinary class instruction, there are practical limits: somewhere and at some time— particularly in pursuit of his chosen field of concentration—a student deserves to have the teacher's attention focused solely on himself. Second, in order to make the most of their talents, superior students need at times to be liberated from working in group harness. Third, some of the most valuable courses attract few students, and if they are to be offered at all, must be conducted for a small constituency. Finally, many teachers are of the opinion that tutorial instruction is an invaluable aspect of formal educational experience or at least that, without the values gained from persistent individual contact with a teacher, a student's education is impoverished.

Teaching a few students could be a lazy man's pastime. What makes such teaching arduous is trying to use it as an opportunity for a new and different kind of instruction. To conduct a lecture or discussion with a small group of students is simple, but what a wasteful method of teaching them! On the other hand, if the teacher resolves to help the students make the most of their capabilities, there follows an almost endless process of getting to know them, encouraging and guiding their special endeavours, thinking with them, patiently correcting their faults, and seeing them through the accomplishment of their purposes. Every thesis adviser knows the extent of the discipline involved in supervising a student's research project while trying to understand and strengthen it in terms of the student's own ideas. It is easier for the teacher to try to fashion the student in his own intellectual image than to penetrate the student's mind and work with what is there. Yet the latter is more in the nature of what is required if the student's potential is to be fulfilled.

With respect to technique of small-group instruction an almost endless variety presents itself. The teacher ,may use to advantage every common technique and add others of his own invention. The group may work as a unit, as individuals, or in combination. A brief assignment directing students to authenticate an historical date or event can lead to fascinating investigation, discussion, individual reports, analysis of documents, and side-trips in research. The class can meet in the library and conduct an intensive examination of source materials. Microfilmed documents can be brought into the classroom and viewed there. Other classes may be visited, teachers invited in for consultation, or a correspondence initiated with scholars outside the college looking toward an exchange of information. More work can probably be done outside the classroom than within it, and the teacher must be thoroughly prepared to use to maximum advantage discussion and conference time.

In tutorial or individual instruction emphasis is on the special purposes and needs of the student in relation to the realizable opportunities of the course. It is unseemly to proceed as if the student were an audience to be addressed; or to map out the course as for a large group whose individual capabilities and goals are not readily ascertainable. The individual student is not there primarily as a listener, and his needs in instruction can be identified. Planning should be cooperative with respect to content and method of learning. The student should be invited to formulate his purposes in study, develop a method of attack, and outline a suitable program; the teacher should consider these proposals and improve them through ideas drawn from his greater knowledge and experience. The contract made, the burden of activity should then be on the student, with the teacher assessing and guiding progress, opening up new avenues of exploration, refuelling the student's interest and ambition. Individual instruction can be an exciting interplay of minds or a deadly sequence of stilted recitation, depending upon how the teacher interprets the two roles in the partnership.

Remedial Teaching. However skilled the instruction and diligent the student, there will be occasions when remedial teaching is necessary. No matter how carefully students are selected for admission to college, there will be some with special disabilities in learning which require correction through clinical methods. There are able students who for some reason have not learned to spell correctly, punctuate a sentence, or perform basic arithmetical operation; intelligent young people who have never learned how to study; otherwise fair students with pronounced difficulty in mastering a foreign language, mathematics, or science. Though it may be intermittent remedial teaching is an inherent feature of classroom instruction. On an institutional basis most colleges find it desirable to operate with organized facilities for systematic correction of special disabilities, such as speech, reading, and study "clinics" and remedial workshops.

Whether remedial teaching is conducted by the teacher in the ordinary course of instruction or by a specialist working from a central college facility, the underlying principles of successful remedial treatment are the same: to identify the disability, ascertain—if possible—its cause, and develop suitable corrective measures. Remedial instruction is essentially individual: occasionally it may be possible to group students with common disabilities, but even in such cases, though the symptoms are similar, the causes and needed remedies may be different. A student's failure which on the surface seems attributable to laziness, indifference, or neglect of study may turn out to be rooted in psychological factors, or traceable to some serious fault in earlier training. The causes of persistent disabilities are not easily identifiable; and though the teacher should not be quick to speculate on possible hidden origins, it would be a mistake to accept the obvious surface explain that the student has failed to apply himself industriously, and that a compensatory period of study will correct the condition. Where long-standing disability exists, it is untenable to assume that reteaching alone will supply the corrective.

The teacher is not omniscient concerning the students he teaches. The best he can do is to try to determine from available evidence the possible cause of a student's difficulty, and devise an appropriate way of dealing with it. If the evidence points to a physical or psychological cause the problem should be referred to physician or psychologist; the teacher should not attempt to fulfill the role of psychologist any more than he would that of medical practitioner. In most cases the causes will be less complicated and mare amenable to instructional treatment; in such instances it should be possible to plan with the student a program of remedial teaching designed for his special needs. A student may be deficient in compositional skill simply because he has never mastered the mechanics of sentence structure. In a college student such ignorance may be deplorable, but good sense suggests that it is better to spend less time in shedding tears and more in developing with the student a graded sequence of writing exercises aimed at helping him unravel the mystery of the sentence. So also in the treatment of difficulties in foreign language, mathematics, science, music, or anything else. Do not generalize too much, try to determine the specific cause of the problem, try to find or invent a suitable remedy, and patiently teach.

SELECTED BIBLIOGRAPHY

Axelrod, Joseph et al., *Teaching by Discussion in the College Program.* Chicago: University of Chicago Press, 1949. 68 p.

Cantor, Nathaniel F., *The Teaching-Learning Process.* New York: Dryden Press, 1953.350 pp.

——, *Dynamics of Learning,* Second edition. Buffalo, N.Y.: Foster and Steward, 1950. 296 pp

Cronkhite, Bernice B., ed., *A Handbook for College Teachers,* Chapters V-VII, "Varoetoes pf Teaching Method." Cambridge: Harvard University Press, 1950.272 pp.

Dale, Edgar, *Audio-Visual Methods in Teaching,* Revised edition. New York: Dryden Press, 1954,534 pp.

de Kiefer, Robert and Cochran, L.W., *Manual of Audio-Visual Techniques.* New York: Prentice-Hall, Inc., 1955.220 pp.

Eisenhart, Luther P., The Educational Process, Chapter IV, "*Methods of Instruction,*" Princeton: University of Princeton Press, 1945. 87 pp.

French, Sidney B., ed., *Accent on Teaching.* New York: Harper & Brothers, 1954. 34 pp.

Haas, Kenneth B. and Packer, Hary Q., *Preparation and Use of Audio-visual Aids.* New York: Prentice-Hall, Inc., Second edition, 1950. 327 pp.

Highet, Gilbert, *The Art of Teaching.* New York: Alfred A. Knopf, 1951. 291 pp.

Lynd, Helen M., *Field Work in College Education,* Sarah Laorence College Publication, No.5. New York: Columbia University Press, 1945, 302 pp.

Marshall, Max S., *Two Sides to a Teacher's Desk,* pp. 13-143. New

York: The Macmillan Company, 1953. 284 pp.

Millett, fred B., The Rebirth of Liberal Education, Chapter III, *"Experimentation in Techniques of Teaching."* New York: Harcourt, Brace and company, 1945, 179 pp.

National Society of College Teachers of Education, Twenty-Seventh Yearbook, *The Study of College Instruction.* Chicago: University of Chicago Press, 1939. 314 pp.

Peterson, Houston, ed., *Great Teachers.* New brunswick, N.J.: Rutgers University press, 1946. 351 pp.

Reed, Anna Y. et al., *The Effective and the Ineffective College Teacher. New* York: American Book Company, 1935, 344 pp.

Russell, John Dale, ed., *New Frontiers in Collegiate Instruction,* volume 13 of the Proceedings of the Institute of Administrative Officers of Higher Institutions. (Specifically Chapter VII, "Techniques of Handling Large Classes;" Chapter XI, "Audio-Visual Materials;" and Chapter XOO, "Laboratory Demonstration Methods.") Chicago: University of Chicago Press, 1931. 248 pp.

Schueler, Herbert, "The Madness of Method in Higher Education," *Journal of Higher Education,* 22: 90-97, February 1951.

Severinghaus, A. E., Carman, H.J., and Cadbury W.E., Jr., editors, *Preparation for Medical Education in the Liberal Arts College,* Chapter 9, "The Teacher and His Methods." New York: McGraw Hill Book Company, 1953. 400 p.

"The Discussion Method in Teaching: A Symposium," *Journal of General Education*, Vol. 8, No. 1, October 1954.

Valentine, P. F., ed., The American College, Chapter 7, "Experimenting in College Instruction." Bew York: Philosophical Library, 1949. 575 pp.

Ward, F. Champion et al., *The Idea and Practice of General Educat*ion, Chapter 10, "Teaching." Chicago: University of Chicago Press, 1950. 333 pp.

Weaver, Gilbert C. And Bollinger, Elroy W., *Visual Aids, Their Construction and Use.* New York: D. Van Nostrand Company, Inc., 1949. 388 pp.

6(I)
THE ART OF LECTURING

The nature and purposes of lectures

THE Hale Committee's Report defines the lecture as 'a teaching period occupied wholly or mainly with *continuous exposition by a lecturer.* Students attending it may be given some opportunity for questions or a little discussion, but in the main they have nothing to do except listen and take notes.'[1]

The word 'lecture' itself, as I.A. Richards points out, is an unhappy one, because 'it suggests something designed to be read and read aloud, when most often any merit the thing might have would turn on its seeming to be given without notes and to be an exhibition of thinking, or, at least, of composition in progress. There are few matters concerning his craft which the teacher should study more than these differences. They are its very elements. Speech and reading come to the ear and to the attention with different gaits. They are apt for different ends. They are vehicles which should have different cargoes. In spite of the many styles of each, what rides well in one commonly goes to bits in the other. It is odd, therefore, that so many teachers—and some eminent people are among them—will without compunction read out to their classes papers written for print—as though they had never been in an audience themselves. Odder still, how many, when they speak off the cuff, do their level best to sound like a slowed-down book. Talk of "teacher's Relation to the Student!" Nothing wrecks it more than these mismanagements.'[2]

It is, I think, useful to classify university lectures into three broad categories: *(a) inspirational, (b) didactic, (c) didactic and inspirational.* Some lectures, e.g. in literature, philosophy and fine art, are designed to generate or increase enthusiasm for a subject, provoke thinking or guide taste. The communication of knowledge is a secondary aim. The bulk of university lectures are didactic or instructional.

Their primary aim is to convey knowledge. This may be done badly or it may be done well. For instance, it is not being done well if the lecture is merely a rehash of a standard textbook on the subject—'a textbook wired for sound'. And some university lectures have been described—not inaptly—as 'material passing from the notebook of the lecturer to the notebook of the student without seeming to pass through the head of either'. A good didactic lecture can also be inspirational: the lecturer can so present the facts and conceptual structures of his subject and the methods of tackling it that he ensures not only that the student understands it but also that he develops an enthusiasm for it and is stimulated to pursue its study on his own.

The main arguments in favour of lectures[3] are as follows:

(1) Students are immature and are therefore deemed to learn more easily from listening than by reading. (This is an assumption of many university teachers which has not been put to the test.)

(2) Lectures are a good means of opening up a subject to a student, especially a subject that would daunt the student if he approached it through unassisted reading.

(3) They are a means of enabling the student to find his way through rapidly extending fields of knowledge.

(4) Sometimes lectures are necessary because there are too many books on a subject, sometimes because there are too few.

(5) The lecturer can provide a more balanced and up-to-date survey of his particular field than any textbook has to offer.

(6) Lectures may be valuable, especially in science, in presenting material which would be too complex to understand without oral explanation or too wasteful of time to acquire otherwise.

(7) They provide an opportunity for undergraduates to listen to, and be inspired by, men and women who are advancing the frontiers of knowledge in their own subject. (The fact that a man has himself made an original contribution to knowledge is, of course, no guarantee that he will be able to communicate an understanding of, and enthusiasm for his subject to undergraduates.)

(8) Though inferior to tutorials, seminars, and laboratory work in initiating the student into the discipline of his subject, they do provide,

as Professor P.J. Fitzgerald[4] points out, a means for the lecturer to exemplify that discipline in action. He particularly stresses how the lecturer can make an argument live orally far better than the printed word.

(9) Professor Fitzgerald also draws attention to the value of the lecture as a means of 'providing variety and a welcome change from solitary study' and as 'a corporate activity': a means of bringing together students of the same or different disciplines. Many tutors would argue that, as a corporate activity, it has less value than tutorials, seminars, laboratory work or field activities.

(10) Lectures are economical of staff time.

The disadvantages of the lecture as a method of teaching

The main disadvantages of the lecture is that it provides little opportunity for feedback from student to teacher. In American university and colleges there is some opportunity for feedback through periodic tests, but in British universities, unless the lecture class is small, and there is some two-way traffic between lecturer and students, or unless some means of follow-up is devised, e.g. tutorials, seminar, essay work, laboratory work or problem-solving, the lecturer frequently has no means of assessing the effectiveness of his teaching until he marks examination papers. Research in learning does suggest that feedback is likely to be most effective when the learner knows whether his answer is right or wrong as soon as possible after he has made it. 'Delay in feedback, however, may not be a major factor in acquiring knowledge if the learner is motivated and the material is not too difficult.'[5] Some of our students are not highly motivated and often find material in lectures beyond their comprehension. Research in the U.S.A. tends to show that when the lecturer's goal is to get his students to master concepts or acquire problem-solving skills, lectures are less effective methods of teaching than methods which demand the active participation of the learner, e.g. discussion groups. If the lecturer's goal is merely the transmission of information, then the lecture *may be* superior to the discussion group.[6]

Lecturing to large and small classes

This paper concerns itself chiefly with lecturing to large audiences. It is worth noting that the Robbins Committee[7] saw little virtue in formal lectures delivered to small audiences and suggests that time spent in preparing courses of lectures for small audiences would be better spent in giving more classes and in regular and systematic correction of students' own work. Someone has described the formal lecture given by a poor teacher to a small audience as 'mediocrity purveyed in an intimate atmosphere'.

There needs to be a marked difference in method of presentation between lecturing to a large audience and lecturing to a small group. The lecture to the small group can be much more of a co-operative effort between lecturer and students. It has to be prepared as thoroughly as the lecture to the large class, but the method of presentation can be much more elastic. If he wants to, the lecturer can do far more teaching than is possible in a formal lecture to a large audience. He may organise the lecture as a discussion. At least he can make provision for students to ask questions or quote their own examples or illustrations of a generalisation he has made or advance arguments or counter arguments of their own.

Some general considerations, mainly but not entirely psychological

Before considering the preparation, organisation, and delivery of a lecture, there are a number of basic points which the lecturer should bear in mind.

(1) *Conveying an attitude to a subject.* One cannot teach a subject without at same time, by virtue of being the sort of person one is and by virtue of the way in which one presents that subject also conveying an attitude, either favourable or unfavourable, to that subject. An unfavourable attitude to part of a subject may spread to the whole subject. It is even possible it may spread to the whole of university education.

A student audience is quick to detect whether a lecturer is interested in his subject, interested in them, confident or diffident, sympathetic or authoritarian, supercilious in his attitude to them and his attitude to teaching.

(2) *Organisation of material as an aid to remembering.* The most important fact that emerges from a century of experiments on remembering is that unless facts are organised into a structured pattern they are unlikely to be remembered. A lecture is much more likely to be remembered if the ideas in it are organised into a logical or systematic structure. A course of lectures should provide the student with a conceptual framework in a subject: the sort of framework into which he can fit new knowledge as he acquires it or which he can modify in the light of new knowledge. The value of a particular lecture is much more likely to be appreciated if the student sees it in the context of the syllabus for the year and in its relation to the reading he has to do.

(3) *Making an effort to see the student's point of view.* If the class one is lecturing to is not an honours class, few of its members are going to become specialists in one's own subject. Indeed, many lectures have to give courses in their subject to large classes of students of widely varying abilities and interests and from a variety of disciplines. Too many university teachers are so convinced of the value of their special subject that they make no concession to the student who is a novice in it and is not going to specialise in it. The preservation and advancement of knowledge in one's own subject is one thing; educating undergraduates is another. Hence there needs to be some separation between these two activities of a university teacher's life, though it is quite often true that one does fertilise the other.

Lecturers also need to remember that, if a student has to attend a succession of three or four lectures in a day, he has no opportunity to make an effort at recall which is the first step in the process of assimilation. This brings up the function of notes and the need for counselling students to go through their own notes of lectures, fill in and amplify them as soon as possible after they have heard the lectures.[8]

(4) *Motivation.* Lecturer cannot assume that all his students have a strong desire to learn his subject. He should, however, realise that motivating a class to learn depends upon a variety of factors, some internal to the student and some external to him. The latter are at least

partially within his control. The internal factors are the student's own motives. Every student will have some desire for success. Most students want to be liked, if not by their teachers, at least by their fellows. Some will have a strong, some a mild, others a negligible, interest in one's subject. We need to find out a lot more about the dependable motives of the students—those that we might use to help them learn more effectively. Among the external factors contributing to motivation are: (a) the personality of the teacher, (b) the methods of presentation he uses, (c) the textbooks and books on his subject he recommends and (d) incentives. (Perhaps the only incentive used by a university teacher may be the examination and that may seem to the student, at any rate early in the session, so remote that it has little effect as a stimulus to his learning.) A lecturer can certainly make use of factors (a), (b) and (c) to stimulate his students to learn.

Every university teacher has from time to time to face a motivational problem that teachers at all levels of education have to tackle—generating an interest in the student in a subject or part of a subject that does not immediately interest him. The solution of this problem (not always easy to achieve) is to find some means of relating the subject that does not initially interest him to something that already does. If, for instance, geologist has to give a course of lectures on geology to civil engineers, he needs to show them how a knowledge of geology is relevant to civil engineering. In teaching physics to engineers, the lecturer needs to utilise their interest in mathematics and in the application of physics to engineering.

Formulation of the objectives of one's teaching; the prelude to preparation of a course of lectures

Frequently the aim of university education are stated at so high a level of abstraction that they are of little use when it comes to decisions about what to teach, how to teach it and how to evaluate the effectiveness of one's teaching. A university has several main aims. The weights which individual university teachers attach to these aims vary considerably. Some give primacy of place to research, some to teaching, some to professional education, some to the provision of 'a liberal education', a concept defined in a wide variety of different ways, and so on. University teachers do need to think about what the aims of a university in a society such as ours are, and should be, but once these aims have been formulated at a high level of generality, it is necessary to find answers to questions about more specific objectives, e.g. What do I expect a graduate in my subject to know at the end of his three-year course? What conceptual framework in the subject should he have acquired? What methods of thinking about the subject? What attitudes and values? One needs, however, to be still more specific about the outcomes one wants one's teaching to achieve. Here one will find Bloom's *Taxonomy of Educational Objectives*,[9] an American effort at the classification of educational goals, helpful. Lectures, of course, have to be considered in the whole context of the teaching of a Department or School, and decisions made as to what parts of the teaching can be most effectively done by means of lectures, having regard to the nature of the subject, numbers of the students, availability of staff, etc.

SOME OF THE QUESTIONS TO WHICH THE LECTURER WILL FIND IT PROFITABLE TO SEEK ANSWERS

What do I want to get across to my students?

(1) What knowledge of my subject?

(a) What basic facts, i.e. what elements for building up more complex and abstract forms of knowledge?

(b) What terminology?

(c) What knowledge of trends and sequences?

(d) What classifications and categories?

(e) What criteria, e.g. criteria by which facts, principles, opinions are to be judged?

(f) What knowledge of the method of inquiry or experiment and the technique and procedure in my special subject?

(g) What knowledge of generalisations, principles, theories?

(2) What intellectual skills and abilities do I want to foster?

(a) Is my aim simply to get my students to comprehend what I have said without necessarily being able to relate it to other material or see its wider applications?

(b) How far am I expecting them to extrapolate in their thinking beyond what I have given them—to determine implications, consequences, corollaries, effects?

(c) How far am I expecting them to apply the generalisations I have given them (ideas, rules of procedure, theories, etc.) to the solution of problems?

(d) What criteria for evaluating the subject and the methods of the subject do I expect them to have by the end of the course?

(e) In What ways can I use lectures to initiate students into the discipline of my subject?

(3) What attitudes and values do I want to induce in my students?

What attitude to the subject and to learning in general? Tolerance, humility, open-mindedness, recognition that the last word has not been said on many, if not all, parts of the subject? 'The capacity continually to enrich and enliven his conceptual frameworks' (Michael Polanyi's definition of the hallmark of the educated man)?[10]

On how one answers these and other related questions is going to depend not only the selection of the content and methods of one's teaching but also the means one devises to test its effectiveness. Above all, questions such as these need to be answered before one decides which aspect of a subject can best be presented by means of lectures.

The preparation and organisation of a lecture

What I have said in the previous section about formulating the objectives of a course of lectures applies also to the preparation of an individual lecture. One needs to be clear about what one is trying to do in the lecture. To generalise about the preparation and organisation of a lecture, is however, a difficult task, since there are so many different subjects in a university, so many different ways of putting a lecture together and so many different ways of delivering it. The following 'do's and don't's', though presented somewhat imperatively for the sake of brevity, are offered simply as a basis for discussion.

(1) Know your subject thoroughly. It has been said that there is no better way of getting to know a subject than having to lecture on it. Clarity of exposition is not possible if you are not yourself clear about

your subject. Moreover, thorough knowledge of subject-matter ensures that you can devote most of your mental energies to so organising it that your listeners will not only grasp it but be stimulated to further thought.

Don't come to your lecture with a pot-pourri of ill-digested material hastily put together the night before or of material mugged up from textbooks which you know the students themselves are unlikely to possess.

(2) All the time you are preparing your lecture have in mind the sort of audience you will have in front of you. Difficult though it may be, try to think of the aspects of your theme that are most likely to engage their interest. Above all, remember that you are expecting them to follow you and that there is a limit to what they can digest in fifty minutes.

(3) A good lecture will have a beginning, a middle and an end. The introduction might, for instance, link up with the previous lecture, give the bibliography or other auxiliary data and define the problem which is to be discussed in the lecture. It often helps students if one follows the technique of the Scottish minister of my boyhood days and indicates that the development of the theme is to be divided into three (or more) parts and what the headings of these parts are to be. To pose a problem at the outset of a lecture is often a good way of beginning. I might, for instance, begin a lecture on 'Memory' by posing the question, 'Why do we forget?' To say that a lecture has an 'end' does not mean bringing it abruptly to stop at whatever point one has reached at five minutes to the hour. Ideally, it means that in the last few minutes one attempts a summing up of what one has said and prepares the way for what one is going to discuss in the next lecture.

(4) Planning a lecture and giving it a structure is aided if you begin by first of all putting down the main points you wish to put across. The order in which you first put them down may not be the most logical or systematic order, but, after cogitation, you settle on the best order. How you build up connective tissue of the lecture will, of course, depends on your subject-matter and the purpose of your lecture. You

will aid your students' assimilation of your lecture if you can build up a blackboard summary of the main points and sub-headings of your lecture as it proceeds.

(5) Should you write out your lecture in full and deliver it from the manuscript, or speak from notes? The opinion of most experts on lecturing is that the lecture should be delivered from notes.

(6) If it is so delivered, then there is more likelihood that it will be the spoken word and not the written word. And, as I.A. Richards has emphasised (see p.18), the essence of the lecture is the spoken word. This means using shorter and less complex sentences than would be used in a paper designed to be read; and loose, not periodic, sentences. The thought-units presented to students must be of such length that they can be grasped easily.

(7) Timing a lecture is a problem for most university teachers, especially at the outset of their careers. Most beginners tend to overestimate the amount of ground that can be covered in fifty minutes. Only experience can tell you how much ground you can cover in a lecture-period. You have to be prepared to omit, abridge and summarise and not be perturbed if you have to omit what you deem a pearl of wisdom from one of your lectures.

Beginners will find it useful to remember that a fifty-minute lecture consists of about 5,000 words. This means, allowing for inevitable pauses, e.g. writing on the blackboard and repetition of important points, a rate delivery of about 110 words per minute.

(8) 'What visual aids do I need to help me in getting my message across?' This is a question many lecturers in Arts subjects often fail to ask. The scientists, technologist, medical man and language teacher will almost certainly make frequent use of the blackboard and other aids. All of us should consider where we can reinforce the spoken word by use of the one visual aid which is always to hand. The question of more complex aids I leave for discussion in the chapter on that subject.

See *Audio-visual Aids in Higher Scientific Education.*[11]

(9) Above all remember, in preparing your lecture, that if your material bores you it will certainly bore your audience. Bear in mind the

comment of the student on the professor who yawned during his own lecture: 'The professor confirms our judgment but usurps our prerogative.'

Delivering the lecture

It is worth noting that Peter Marris in his study of undergraduates at Leeds, Southampton, Cambridge, and Northampton College of Advanced Technology[12] found that students' comments on lectures relate more to technique of presentation than to content. Of the qualities of a good lecture those that received the most frequent mentions among Arts students were: Delivery, Clarity, Interest, Originality and Guidance. Among the Science students the qualities most frequently mentioned were: Delivery, Notes, Clarity, Interest and Guidance.

(1) The impact of the personality of the teacher

> 'Personality is what everyone has got, only some have got more of it than others.' (A schoolgirl's essay)
>
> 'Personality is the effect upon others of a living being's appearance, behaviour, etc., in so far as they are interpreted as distinctive signs of that being.'
>
> (T.H.Pear[13])

I have already stated that teaching is not purely an intellectual affair. The teacher cannot teach a subject without at the same time also inducing some sort of attitude towards that subject. Woe betide him if he is a person who uses the kind of method that produces antipathy to his subject! Personality reveals itself in a diversity of ways—through facial expression and expressive movements, e.g. dress, gait, carriage, speech and writing, through the attitude one displays to one's work, to other people, through one's emotional reactions to different situations and so on. Teachers, especially university teachers, are not as alive as they ought to be to how much they reveal of themselves to their students in these different ways.

Hence the following suggestions:

(a) Don't come into the lecture-room looking like a deep depression centred over Iceland and continue to look like that through the whole of your lecture course. A dull, uninteresting personality induces boredom and inattention in his audience.

(b) The inaudibility and monotony of voice of many lecturers is frequently commented upon by students. Clarity of articulation, variety of pitch, pace, and emphasis are important features of good delivery. Speak to the four corners of the room. Before bringing out an important point pause slightly so as to ensure that you have the attention of your audience and then say it more slowly than you would the bulk of your lecture. If it is very important, repeat it or write it on the blackboard.

(c) Gesture can be helpful in holding attention and reinforcing a point, provided it is meaningful. All of us, however, need to beware of the gesture which becomes mechanical—the mannerism. Bergson suggested that a main cause of laughter was 'the mechanical encrusted upon the living'. A mannerism transforms the living being into something of an automation and becomes a distraction from what he is saying.

(2) *Look at your audience.* Cultivate a roving eye. Let your eye rove round the lecture room fixating a different individual as it moves so as to give the members of your class the feeling that you know they are there. One of the reasons for the compelling power of a speaker on television is that he seems to be looking at, and talking to us individually.

(3) *Watch the emotional reactions of your audience.* Are they getting bored, restless, somnolent? Are they really following You? What cues indicate that you have them with you?

(4) *Never make your audience feel inferior.* Remember the professor who failed to stop lecturing at five minutes to the hour. His audience of undergraduates grew restive and stamped their feet on the floor. 'Ladies and Gentlemen', shouted the professor, 'I have one more pearl to cast before you'. But before he could cast it his audience had made the door in pandemonium.

(5) *Don't get angry with your audience.* Never rouse your audience against you.

(6) *Don't perambulate about the classroom while you are lecturing.*

It is true that some university teachers find such perambulations conducive to the stimulation of their thinking, but it often means that many of their words are lost to their audience.

(7) *Don't read your lectures*. This point has already been made twice, but I make it a third time because it is basic to successful lecturing technique, and it will underline a maxim the lecturer will find it profitable to bear in mind. To use the homespun American version: 'First I tells 'em what I have to tell 'em, then I tells 'em it, and then I tell 'em what I've told 'em.'

(8) *A sense of humour is an asset in a lecture,* especially if it includes the capacity to laugh at himself. Laughter not only has an exhilarating effect upon a class, especially when attention is waning, but also contributes to the build up of a bond between teacher and class. If, however, you introduce a humorous story into a lecture it is desirable that it should be opposite: it should not be introduced simply for the sake of making a joke.

The teacher who can laugh at himself can survey his successes and failures as a lecturer with some degree of objectivity and some sense of proportion.

How are we to evaluate the results of lecture courses?

I have already stressed that we must give deep consideration to the goals we want to achieve as a result of our teaching before we decide on the best means of evaluating its effectiveness. At present, the main means of evaluating the results of many lecture courses in university is examinations, and these examination usually come long after many of the lectures have been delivered. In some Departments tutorials and discussion groups provide follow-ups of lectures and enable a lecturer to get some sort of feedback from his class, but if he has lectured to classes of 150 to 300 students, this sort of follow-up is impracticable. Personally I often wish that after lecturing to about 200 students in the Department of Education I could meet ten groups of twenty in small classroom. I do put on a voluntary seminar after each formal lecture and this provides a valuable means of interchange between students and myself.

In science and technology I take it that the laboratory work and the problem-solving exercises students are set to do provide some indication of what they have got out of lectures. When it comes to examinations, what are we really testing? Knowledge acquired? If so, what sort of knowledge? The ability to apply knowledge acquired? The capacity to use the methods of thinking, of experiment, of appreciation of a particular discipline?

What remains after the student has forgotten most of what he swotted up for examinations? How far has he got an adequate conceptual framework in his special subject or subjects? How far has he mastered its methods of inquiry? How far is he capable of transferring what he has acquired at university to further study of his subject, to the study of other fields of to life itself?

Research into the effectiveness of lectures as a method of instruction

Practically all the research on comparison of the effectiveness of different methods of teaching in higher education has been done in the U.S.A. Useful summaries are given by McKechie[14] and Powell[15].

Such comparative studies are difficult to undertake not only because of the difficulty of determining all the variables that enter into the two teaching situations but also because of the criterion problem, i.e. the problem of deciding what particular outcomes of teaching are to be measured. The fact, for instance, that one particular method is shown to be superior when the criterion is the recall of factual knowledge does not prove its superiority as far as other outcomes are concerned.

I do not think we can come to any positive conclusions about the effectiveness of the lecture as a method of teaching from the American researches. Many of them were carried out with college students working at more elementary levels than our students and in institutions where periodic testing by means of both objective tests and essay-type examinations is the common practice. Relatively few have studied the long-term effects of a particular method of teaching.

Summarising the American research on the lecture, McKeachie[16] says: 'Lectures of large size are not generally inferior to smaller lecture classes if one uses traditional achievement tests. When other objectives are used (e.g. developing concepts, problem solving skills, favourable attitudes to a subject) large lectures are on shakier ground but are not consistently inferior. However, both students and faculty members feel that teaching is more effective in small classes. Probably of more significance than class size *per se* is its relation to the teaching method used. For example, one would expect class size to be of minimal relevance in television teaching, of slight importance in lecturing, but of considerable significance in discussion teaching.'

One problem that confronts many a lecturer—the choice between expounding broad principles and building up detailed knowledge on which these principles are based—has been explored by Erskine and O'Morchoe[17] in a well-designed experiment on the teaching of anatomy.

Powell[18] summarises the findings of this experiment as follows: 'One class was taught a course which stressed principles and omitted detail while another class was taught both. Each had three lecture-demonstrations per week for three weeks and identical factual recall tests were administered to each group one at the end of the first week, another at the end of the course and the same test one month later for the details group and four months later for the principles group. The principle class scored higher on the first two tests and results were about the same (therefore an improvement for the principles group) on the third. Too much detailed information tends to confuse and dismay the weaker students while at the same time overwhelming the conscientious ones who are determined to master everything that is placed before them; both groups end by doing themselves less than justice.'

One can learn how to lecture

> 'The technique of imparting knowledge in the special way called lecturing can be learned and improved upon.' (T.H.Pear[19])

I am absolutely certain that it can, and in the above paper I have tried to suggest some of the ways in which it can. These include:

(1) Deepening one's knowledge of the psychology of learning.

(2) Learning as much as possible about the abilities, interests and

motives of one's students, and taking them into account in planning one's lectures.

(3) Clarifying one's mind as to the outcomes one wants to achieve by one's teaching.

(4) Adequate preparation and arrangement of one's material in the sort of structure that is most likely to enable one to achieve the desired aims.

(5) Mastery of the art of oral communication.

(6) Study of how best to evaluate the results of one's teaching. I further suggest that one can improve one's own technique by watching good lecturers in action in the university, on a public platform or on television. In the long run each of us has to evolve his own style of lecturing. As Kitson Clark says (quoting Kipling) at the end of his booklet, *The Art of Lecturing*[20]:

> 'There are nine and sixty ways of constructing tribal lays
> And—every— single—one—of—them—is—right.'

REFERENCES

1. University Grants Committee. *Report of the Committee on University Teaching Methods*. London: H.M.S.O., 1964, p. 170
2. CRONKHITE, B.B. (Ed). *A Handbook for College Teachers*. Cambridge: Harvard U.P., 1950, p.2.
3. University Grants Committee. *Report of the committee on University Teaching Methods*. London: H.M.S.O., 1964, pp.52-53, and LAING, A. *The Art of Study*. Leeds: University of Leeds, 1964, p22.
4. FITZGERALD, P. J. 'The Lecture: an Arts View.' This volume, p.11.
5. SANDFORD, N.(Ed.). *The American College: a Psychological and Social Interpretation of the Higher Learning*. New York: Wiley, 1962, p. 320.
6. ibid. p. 321.
7. Committee on Higher Education. *Higher Education Report*. London: H.M.S.O., 1963, para. 569.
8. LAING, A. *The Art of Study*. Leeds: University of Leeds, 1964, pp. 22-23.

9. BLOOM, B.S. (Ed.). *Taxonomy of Educational Objectives. Hand book 1. Cognitive Domain.* New York: Longmans, Green, 1956.

10. POLANYI, M. *Personal Knowledge: Towards a Post-Critical Philosophy.* London: Routledge and Kegan Paul, 1958, p.103.

11. University Grants Committee. *Audio-visual Aids in Higher Scientific Education* London: H.M.S.O., 1965.

12. MARRIS, P. *The Experience of Higher Education.* London: Routledge and Kegan Paul, 1965.

13. PEAR, T.H. Personality, Appearance and Speech. London: Allen & Unwin, 1957, p.14.

14. MCKEACHIE, W. J. 'Procedures and Techniques of Teaching: a Survey of Experimental Studies.' In Sandford, N. (Ed.). *The American College.* New York : Wiley, 1962.

15. POWELL, J.P. 'Experimentation in Teaching in Higher Education.' *Educational Research,* 1964, 6, 179-191.

16. MCKEACHIE, W.J. *Op. cit.* p. 325.

17. ERSKINE, C.A. and O'MORCHOE, C.C.C. 'Research on Teaching Methods: its Significance for the Curriculum.' *Lancet,* (ii), 709-711, 23 September, 1961.

18. POWELL, J.P. *Op.cit,* p. 182.

19. PEAR, T.H. *The Psychology of Effective Speaking.* London: Kegan Paul, 1933, pp. 145.

20. KITSON CLARK, G. and BIDDER CLARK, E. *The Art of Lecturing.* Cambridge: Heffer, 1959, p. 30.

For further references consult:

POWELL, J.P. *Universities and University Education: A select Bibliography.* National Foundation for Educational Research in England & Wales, 1966.

6(II)

THE LECTURE METHOD

Is there any point in the lecture as a form of university teaching? After all, if information is what the student wants, then surely a well-stocked library is the answer. Unlike our medieval predecessors we have lots of books and their advantage is that each student can study the book at his own speed and convenience. On the other hand, if the emphasis is to be on participation and the dialogue with the instructor, then the one-way communication system of the lecture is out. Seminars and tutorials are the obvious mode for this. So the justification for including courses of lectures in a university syllabus depends on the objectives of university teaching.

Ideally I should begin by defining these objectives and continue by inquiring how far, if at all, the lecture is a useful method of achieving them. This I do not propose to do for the following reason: agreement about these objectives—whether we mean those that teachers actually have or those they ought to have—is hard to come by. Different teachers have different aims. Nor should we deplore this; on the contrary we should welcome it, because unanimity would suggest ossification. As for ideal aims, these pose questions of value, and here again a measure of disagreement is to be both expected and welcomed. This being so, I do not propose to being by postulating some particular set of objectives which others may completely reject.

What I propose to do instead is to compare the way of the subject is taught typically at a university with the way it is normally taught at a college of commerce. The comparison will, I hope, highlight those special features absent from college teaching but commonly to be found in university tuition, features which, I suggest, university teacher feel should characterise their teaching.

A good subject for this comparison is my own subject, law, since it is widely taught in both type of institution. (Other possibilities are accounting and languages.)

Now a college of commerce student of law is taught—often extremely well—the various rules of English law; he learns to thread his way through precedents and statutes, to solve legal problem and to grapple with legal argument. But commonly this is as far as he goes. The rules are never questioned: they are taken as given. Little attempt is made to rationalise and synthesise the mass of apparently inconsistent and unrelated regulation that makes up the jungle of our law. No time is devoted to questioning, criticising or evaluating either the law or the modes of legal reasoning. And never a hint is given to the student that the English law on a point is but one possible way of solving a problem that face other societies and that the legal systems of these other societies may have given other—perhaps even better—answers to the problem.

By contrast, a university law student is taken beyond the actual rules on a search for the underlying logic and principles, if any. He is taught to analyse and criticise judicial decisions and the reasoning on which they are based. And if he is lucky, he is made to relate the law to the underlying social problems with which the law is concerned, and is forced to compare his own law with that of other countries with similar social structure. If the college student is concerned with the law as it is, the university student is concerned not only with this, but with the law as it might be and as it ought to be.

In all this I fully realise that I am being less than fair to many college of commerce lecturers, some of whom I have heard deliver lecture which any university teacher would have felt proud to give. I am also being more than fair to university teachers, many of whom give far from adequate lectures. Nevertheless, I believe that what I have outlined above is, broadly speaking, a true picture of the difference of approach between the two institutions.

What this suggests is that there are roughly three aspects of teaching a subject, and that it is the third aspect that is a particular importance to a university. These aspect are exposition, methodology and criticism. First the student must be given a factual account of the basic data; he must learn the most important rules of a particular branch of law, the key events of a historical period, the fundamental geographical features of an area and so on. Next comes instruction in the technique of the subject: the law student must learn to argue the way lawyers do, the history student to evaluate evidence as a historian does. And finally the student must be shown that the latest point of development is not necessarily the final one, that the frontiers of his subject are *only* frontiers. He has to discover that the answers themselves raise further questions; and he must to learn to realise that it is not enough to concentrate on the question already answered; as he advances, he must begin to query how far his discipline is asking the right questions or the most fruitful questions.

Having elaborated on these different aspects, let me now ask how far the lecture has any value that can be related to them. How good a means is the lecture of expounding factual data? How useful is it for instruction in technique? And how valuable is it for approaching a subject critically? But first let me consider briefly the lecture in general and quite apart from these three aspects.

The lecture generally

Though books and libraries makes lectures no longer essential, they have, nevertheless, one feature which earns them a permanent place in a university time-table. Taking a university course is not a solitary activity; it is and ought to be joint corporate venture. Entering a university course, therefore, is something more than embarking on a programme of private study in a library or by correspondence course. It means enrolling in a group activity, and the student becomes not just a person taking a course but a member of the course, which now consists not merely of the subjects to be studied but of all the students on the course. To appreciate this he must come into contact with his fellow-students and attend classes with them. He can do this of course by attending tutorials and seminars, but the lecture has a particular value here, because it is only at lectures that he can come into contact with the whole spread of students on the course. And if he is fortunate, he may find the lecture attended by other students pursing other but related disciplines, and this can reinforce the fact that the law (or classics) student is a part of an even wider entity—the university itself.

Secondly, and equally important, even if the student could get all the material of the lecture from a book, the lecture itself will still provide a welcome change from solitary reading, essential though this may be. Some students learn better from oral instruction, and many benefit from learning through the ear as well as through the eye.

Thirdly, there is the personality of the lecturer. Where the teacher is actively engaged in advancing the frontiers of his discipline, live contact through medium of the lecture can provide a stimulus that no book can give. This can be true, even though the student hardly understands a word that is said. In my first term of philosophy I had the great good fortune to hear Wittegenstein chair a discussion, which not unnaturally turned into a monologue by the master himself, and though I had little inkling of what he was talking about, the intensity of the performance has remained with me for ever. Those of us who listened to Mario Borelli speaking in Leeds admitted that his English was so execrable that we grasped not a word, yet such was his personality that in a curious way his general message got through. It is this sort of feature that leads me to value the lecture despite the abundance of books that exist.

And fourthly, there is another way in which a lecture can bring a subject to life in a way that no book can. In some subjects like law or politics the good lecturer will relate his materials to topical problems. In discussing liability for the escape of noxious objects, the law lecturer can stimulate his students by referring to Aberfan or the *Torrey Canyon.* By the time the books and journals have got round to such problems, they are no longer topical. But even in subjects lacking this kind of immediate link, with current affairs, there is one particular way in which a lecturer can make his subject live in a way that is denied to the writer. Most university teachers have a number of ideas buzzing round in their heads, idea which they hope to get to work on in due course—in the long vacation or during sabbatical leave—but which at the moment are tentative. Perhaps a law teacher has a whole number of minor criticisms of the orthodox theory of mistake in contract, or whatever it may be. For the moment he has no intention of going into print. He will wait until they add up together to a major attack on the theory. Meanwhile, how ever, he will air his ideas in his lectures, suggesting small points on which other have gone wrong or demonstrating his own theory in its infancy. And this is something students cannot get from printed material—the flavour progress in the making.

So far I have considered the lecture in general and argued for its retention on certain general grounds. Lets me now turn to examine how far it servers the students with regard to the three different aspects of teaching to which I referred.

The lecture as a mode of exposition of factual data

As a medium of basic exposition, the lecture is obviously superior to small group teaching, which is uneconomical in teaching time. On the other hand it has little superiority over introductory textbooks, and may well in some respects be inferior. For one thing it is slower: a good student can absorb a textbook in fewer hours than a course of lectures takes. For another, reduplication of material that can easily be found in the books is a waste of time.

All the same there is a place for the introductory course of the lectures, even though they may be mainly concerned with factual exposition. Some subjects confront the student with a bewildering excess of literature. Jurisprudence is a case in point. At this stage the lecturer can help the student to get his bearings and map out for him a survey of the subject and its bibliography. Other subjects suffer from just the opposite defect. There is no book—or in the teacher's view no satisfactory book—at an introductory level and the lecturer himself must make good the lack. Consider by way of proof how first—rate introductory textbooks have resulted from just such an introductory course of lectures—E. J. Lemmon's *Beginning Logic,* for example, or Lipsey's *Positive Economics*.

But even where there are good introductory works, the lecturer can help the student by showing him how to separate the wood from the trees. This is especially true of new subjects, which the student is beginning for the first time at university. The role of distinguishing principle from detail is more suited to the lecture than to the tutorials or seminar, again because it would be uneconomical of time and effort to provide this for numerous small groups.

The lecture as instruction in technique

In this the lecture is clearly inferior to the seminar and the tutorial. Being doers and not hearers of the word only applies as much to mathematics, philosophy, law and so on as it does to religion; and no amount of seeing another person argue, reason or calculate is a substitute for the student doing it himself. And this he cannot do in a lecture class; he can only hope to do it in a group small enough for every member to participate. Best of all he can do it in tutorials where the tutor can challenge the student's opinions and force him against the ropes to defend his views.

American law schools try to get over this problem in lecture classes by using the case-book method. The students prepare a number of cases in a case-book and are subsequently called upon in class to expound them and criticise the decisions. At best it proves an extremely stimulating and rewarding form of instruction. It can, however, degenerate into a mere quiz to ensure that the students have done their homework. In addition there is always the danger that the size of the audience may inhibit the easy flow of informal discourse necessary for useful discussion.

Nevertheless, though inferior to the seminar or tutorial as means of instruction on technique, the lecture is still superior here to the printed word. Arguments live better orally than on paper if the lecture marshalls the arguments and counter arguments skilfully at each step. No book or essay can quite put across the excitement or intensity of this kind of arguing with oneself that is to be seen in lectures by an eminent philosopher such as Miss Anscombe.

Moreover the lecturer enjoys an advantage over the writer in that he can simultaneously discuss a problem and illustrate it by reference to an extract, from the material under discussion. It is far easier, for instance, to lecture on the interpretation of a statutory section, pointing at words of the section on a blackboard while talking, than it is to write about it; far easier for students to listen to a lecture about a graph or a piece of literature while looking at it, than to read about it so that the eye has to switch from the graph to the commentary and back again continually. And of course, when it comes to lectures on art, the illustrated lecture has it every time over the written commentary.

The lecture as a critical approach to the subject

It is here that the lecturer reigns supreme. His approach, if he is a good lecture, is bound to be personal. It is here that the good teacher teaches not only his subject but himself. Frank-furter's *Reminiscences* relate that when Dean Pound was chary of letting the left-wing Frankfurter loose to lecture at Harvard on the constitution, Justice Holme remarked: 'Doesn't he realise that a good teacher will teach himself even if he's only lecturing on Bills and notes? '

Caution, however, is necessary. Most subjects contain a bedrock of the that cannot be disregarded. A law lecture must take care that his students can distinguish between what the law actually is and what the lecturer argue it ought to be. Otherwise they may run away with the idea that the Larceny Acts means not what the House of Lords has said it means but what Professor X thinks it ought to mean.

Conclusion

I have suggested that the lecture is in many ways inferior to the seminar, the tutorials and to private reading. All the same I have argued that it still has a useful part to play within a university syllabus. It can help to impress upon the student the corporate nature of his activity, it can serve to stimulate him and interest him in the subject, it can show him an example of a practitioner of the subject advancing the subject if only in a small degree, and it can be used to raise fundamental questions about the subject itself and the direction it is taking. How far any particular lecture does all or any of these things and in what proportion, will depend of course on the lecture himself. It will also depend on how far the lecturer and other university teachers consider the lecture to have a role in our universities. What I have said will, I hope, convince some them that it has.

6(III)
LECTURING TO LARGE GROUPS

Let us accept that, as university teaching exists at the moment, a considerable amount of the teacher's time is spent in talking to large groups of students and in preparing for such talking. Whether in such a situation we can communicate successfully what we wish to communicate, depends almost entirely on our personal background and on what we may have gleaned from experience. It does not depend on the kind of Speech Education process that a lecture has been through, because no such process exists for the university teacher.

The personal backgrounds of teachers in universities vary as much as in any other professional group. Some teachers are the products of highly articulate homes and will tend to be highly articulate themselves in consequence. But some are the products of backgrounds in which speech is minimal, where to be 'seen and not heard' is the premise on which family life is conducted. In such cases it would be unreasonable to expect more than a minimal speech skill. This family background would not be of such importance if the formal education process through which the university teacher had passed given him regular opportunities to experiment in the use of speech in a wide range of situations. But this is not the case in British education at the moment. Most children leave school and university without ever being required to show an ability to handle oral situations.

So, although some university teachers have considerable skill in handling such a complicated speech situation as the lecture, we cannot assume that this will necessarily be so in every case. Indeed, there is no reason to suppose that the new university teacher will be any more competent in lecturing than would be the butcher, the baker or the candlestick maker. We can only guarantee lecturing competence by some deliberate educational intervention, some process that sets out to develop the speech skill of a person who will spend much of his professional life trying to impart information and attitudes in oral terms.

Speech as behaviour

But before we consider the nature of *successful* speech and the educational process by which it might be produced, we need to look at speech—at the raw material available to the lecturer. To twist Aristotle's pronouncement about the Drama, we can say that speech is 'character totally in action'. It is a total psychophysical process, a total piece of behaviour. And it is behaviour that has had to be learned. Granted, the ability to produce *voice* is inborn. The child at the birth can bring together its vocal cords, pass breath between them and produce sound. But no child is born with the ability to mould that general sound into the specific sounds of a given language. The child learns to speak by imitating the speech that surrounds him. It is a laborious process, and involves far more than simple imitation of speech sounds. It involves making sense of those sounds and learning to use them in a meaningful way. It involves learning when to speak and when not to—the volume at which to speak, the amount of accompanying movement permissible, in fact a total pattern of behaviour.

When we use speech to talk to large groups of students, we are using it to communicate. But this is not the only use of the speech, nor is it necessarily the most important. It can be argued that the role of speech in the development of mental process is very much more important, for example[1]. Speech is used for the solution of problems; the man talking to himself in the privacy of his bathroom is using speech in this way. Research conducted in the University of Stockholm[2] has shown the connection between speech and silent reading. All these are important uses of speech. None is a *communicative* use in the sense that we would use the word to describe a lecturer's speech.

Speech as communication[3]

To restrict our view of speech to its communicative aspects, which is our principal concern in considering university teaching methods, raise new issues. Communication, for example, presupposes another person besides the speaker. This other person has agreed to receive the communicative act of the speaker, and to respond to it. He has agreed to go through that form of behaviour that we know as 'listening'.

What makes him a listener is the establishment of a special relationship between himself and the speaker, and this relationship is crucial to any true communicative act.

Then again, in considering speech as communication, we can ask the question: What is it about a speaker's behaviour that carries meaning? What has significance for the listener? As products of an educational process almost exclusively geared to the written word, we might be forgiven for thinking that the words a speaker is using are the factors that carry meaning to us. This is not so. Words are in a somewhat insecure position in oral language. They can be undermined by the pitch of the voice, by voice quality, by volume and by a dozen other factors. In oral languages these other factors seem to carry more authority than the words that a speaker is using. When the meaning they convey is in conflict with the meaning carried by the words, it is the meaning of the words that the listener disregards. Any ardent young lover know that 'No' can very well mean 'Maybe' or even 'Yes'. If in preparing for a lecture we consider only the words we are proposing to use, we can very well find that the reaction of our students to that lecture will be quite different from the one we had expected. The listener listens to far more than the words.

Certainly, one factor with which the words may be in conflict is *voice quality.* Sound made in association with hollow spaces has a particular quality. In the case of the voice, the arrangement of such hollow space as the pharynx, the mouth and cavities of the nose reinforce the sound made at the level of the vocal cords. This reinforcement gives a unique quality to the voice of each individual. This quality has significance for the listener. It gives him information. It allows him to build up a general picture of what the speaker is like as a person. This is important to the listener. He does not listen to isolated pronouncements, he listens to them in relation to the human being who makes them. In the case of a voice that is markedly 'nasal' the listener will draw certain conclusions from this nasality concerning the kind of person behind the voice. His reading of the personality as suggested to him by general voice quality, will of course affect the importance the listener attaches to the pronouncements of such a person. We shall see the problem more clearly if we take that not uncommon phenomenon, the male voice that is described as 'very high pitched'. In Britain an we are taught to associate such a voice with effeminacy and lack of masculine prowess. Let us imagine such a voice speaking these words:

'I have been a professional wrestler for fifteen years.'

We are faced, not with a statement of truth, but with a music hall joke. We cannot reconcile the two conflicting statements, the one reaching us in terms of specific words and the other in terms of the voice quality. We do not believe that such a man can have been a professional wrestler. We laugh because we know that he is pulling our leg. We have come down on the side of voice quality representing truth, and thrown the words out of the window.

And we cannot confine our view of speech simply to the *sounds* that a speaker makes. If the we are concerned with a communicative act, then we must consider all aspects of a speaker's behaviour that have significance for the listener. A student in a lecture does not simply sit and listen. He watches too. The speech behaviour of the lecturer that reaches the student's eye, has significance for him. It tells him things about the lecturer that he regards as important. More specifically, particular movements of hands and face can illuminate for him a statement, that is being made in words. But equally it can destroy that statement, for it seems again that where a conflict exists for the listener between what the words are saying and the information he is receiving visually, then it is the words that he rejects.

Finally, in considering speech as communication, we must remind ourselves that such speech take place in a particular situation. That situation qualifies that speech. Speech which is successful in one situation can be useless in another. The speech of the lecture theatre is totally inappropriate to the tutorial situation. To be successful, speech behaviour must be adjusted to the terms of reference of the situation in which it is being used.

Let us summarise at this point. If we are concerned with speech as communication, then we must take into consideration at least six things:

(1) The total psychological activity out of which speech arises.

(2) The organization of this activity.

(3) The relationship that must exist between speaker and listener.

(4) The fact that far more of the sound complex than simply the words, have significance for a listener.

(5) The fact that the visual aspects of speech have significance for the listener.

(6) The situation in which speech is taking place.

The narrowest view that we can take of speech then, is as a complicated piece of human behaviour that requires the organisation of mental life and its communication to someone else in terms of aural and visual signals, through a relationship.

Successful speech

We can define the end product at which we are aiming quite simply as that form of behaviour that gives precisely to a listener the information that a speaker intends. But this is not very helpful. It might be more helpful to imagine ourselves able to look in upon the behaviour of a lecturer whom we agree is skilled in his job. Here are some of the points that we would notice:

(1) His speech is geared to the psychological and physical facts of the situation. He understands the acoustic problems of the room and the educational needs of the group he is addressing.

(2) His speech reveals an organised mental life.

(3) There is a firm speaker-listener relationship, that allows the lecturer to appreciate the way in which what he is saying is being received. This appreciation allows him to adjust his behaviour so that it more effectively communicates.

(4) Technically the lecturer is well equipped. The mechanism will produce sufficient volume to fill the room. Movements of articulatory organs are sufficiently precise to make clear distinctions between one sound group and the next. There is a technical flexibility about the way in which the mechanism is being used that allows it to respond automatically to any subtle nuance of meaning that the lecturer wishes to communicate.

(5) There is a regard for vocal health. The lecturer is aware that the living tissue he is using for the production of sound, has its limitations. He is aware that if he disregards those limitations that tissue will protest dramatically.

This description is of course by no means definitive. We might wish, for example, to draw attention to such a factor as pronunciation, although only on rare occasions does this interfere with communication. It is a working definition that draws our attention to some of the points that are significant in trying to outline the target at which we are aiming.

The education of speech

Almost everyone speaks. They do so, as we have seen, because they have been exposed to speech and imitated it in the limited situation of the family and the small group of close friends. Since there is no coherent speech education process in British education, we can assume no more on the part of a potential teacher than speech which is successful for conversational purposes. So we have to face the question: Is conversational speech sufficient for the teacher in the lecture room or the seminar? A survey carried out by the speech staff of the University of Leeds Department of Education[4] makes it clear that it is not. Some 33% of graduate teachers in training were found to have speech that was in some way unsatisfactory for classroom communication purposes. This is not surprising. Conversational speech, for example, takes place with listener and speaker some four or five feet apart. In the lecture, listener and speaker might be separated by ten or fifteen times that distance. That one physical fact makes demands on a speaker that he can never experience in conversation. Then the psychology of the two situations is quite different. A speaker in a conversational situation, for example, is free to leave when he chooses. This is not true of the lecturer. Again, participants in a conversation have an equality of status that allows all kinds of interruptions and disagreements. This is not the case in a lecture.

So some kind of educational intervention is necessary if we are to guarantee that every university teacher has competence in handling speech for communication purposes when faced with a large group of listeners. Ideally, every university should be equipped to conduct such courses for its own staff. But at the moment very few British universities have any Speech Educationist on the staff, and it would be more realistic to suggest intentive courses of the three-day crash such as have been pioneered in industry. Such courses could very profitable be on an inter-university basis. The pattern developed in management operates with a twelve student group directed by a Speech Educationist. During a three day period, the group experiments with a wide range of speech situations. The situations range from the very formal type for which considerable preparation is necessary, to the informal and impromptu.

REFERENCES

1. LURIA, A. R. and YDOVITCH, F.I. *Speech and the Development of Mental Processes in the Child.* London: Staples, 1959.
2. EDFELDT, A.W. *Silent Speech and Silent Reading.* Stockholm: Almqvist and Wiksell,1959
3. WISE, A. *Communication in Speech.* London: Longmans, 1965.
4. 'University Speech : A Survey.' *Speech and Drama,* 13, No. 1, July 1963.

APPENDIX

An Assessment Scheme for the Lecture

This scheme is intended to provide a basis for listening to and assessing some of the principle features of the lecture. It is based on a four-part breakdown:

1. The technical aspects of voice and speech.
2. The organisation of the material of the lecture.
3. The relationship between the lecturer and listeners.
4. Considerations of the vocal health.

Beside each point is a question that the listener might ask himself in trying to arrive at his assessment.

The assessment is based on the four-point scale, ABC/D, where the approximate meaning of each point is as follows:

A—Very good
B—Good
C—Satisfactory
D—Unsatisfactory

It would not be necessary for a listener to make an assessment of every point, but only of those to which his attention is particularly drawn.

THE SCHEME

1. *Technical*	*Listener's Question*	*Mark*
(a) Audibility	Can I hear him?	ABC/D
(b) Intelligibility	Is he making the movement of speech precisely enough for me to be able to understand him?	ABC/D
(c) Flexibility	Is there sufficient variation of pitch, etc., to convey exactly what he intends?	ABC/D
(d) Speed	Is this sufficiently slow for me to be able to absorb each point he is making?	ABC/D
(e) Fluency	Is there a continuity about his speech, that makes it easier for me to take in his meaning?	ABC/D
(f) General movements	Do the movements he makes, apart from those immediately concerned with speech, enhance or detract from the effectiveness of the communication?	ABC/D

Total assessment of Part 1: ABC/D

2. Organisation

(a) Aim of the lecture	Am I clear what the aim of the lecture is?	ABC/D

(b) The development	Does the lecture develop in a logical and coherent way?	ABC/D
(c) The amount of material	Does he try to cover too much or too little ground in the time?	ABC/D
(d) The examples	Do the examples given help to clarify the points he is making?	ABC/D
(e) Visual aids	Do these help me to understand the points he is making?	ABC/D
(f) Preparation	Is the amount of preparation adequate?	ABC/D

Total assessment of Part 2: ABC/D

3. Relationship

(a) Needs of the	Does he understand who we are and group what ever need are?	ABC/D
(b) Lecturer/listener	Is the he simply to us all time, or is relationship he simply talking to himself?	ABC/D

Total assessment of part 3: ABC/D

4. Vocal Health

(a) Vocal Health	Is the lecturer using the physical mechanism of voice and speech in a way that will lead inevitably to vocal ill-health?	ABC/D

7(I)

THE SMALL GROUP AS A TEACHING MEDIUM

The teaching function of a university consists largely of the communication of information and opinions from staff to students, and the assertion of logical relationships between the information and the opinions. It is also implied that these relationships are, or according to the teacher's values should be, of enduring interest and value to the student. But whether or not the student retains much of what he is taught depends most heavily on his own motivations and on the shared values of those with whom he associates. He learns, or fails to learn, not only in relation to his cognitive and intellectual skills but also in relation to his experiences in the variety of social groups to which he typically belongs. For example if he associates with others who do not value academic achievement highly, he will be influenced to share these evaluations.

An influence opportunity

In a large university many students have very little face-to-face contact with teaching staff. The greatest part of their time is passed attending large lectures, reading and interacting with other students. This paper is concerned with those few occasions in which a teacher meets with a small number of students, typically described as seminars or tutorials. These confrontations are crucial determinants of the effectiveness of teaching. They contain greater potentiality for mutual influence between teacher and student than any other university activity because of the closeness of the contact. In contrast a large lecture can rarely achieve more than the simple transmission of information; influence is a function of involvement. I shall consider in turn the student and the teacher in the small group situation.

The student is almost certainly ambivalent about his position in the university. He will have some measure of enthusiasm or interest in his subject—he chose it—but he will also have encountered numerous frustrations in his studies. In lectures it is often impossible to ask for explanations of what is not understood, at least without losing face; in the libraries he often cannot obtain the books he needs. He will concur with the widespread beliefs that the teaching staff are not typically interested him as an individual; that one should do some work but not appear too zealous; that it is up to the teaching staff to initiate and to decide what is and is not to be learned.[1] He is probably somewhat afraid of the tutorial situation since it has potentiality of making him look a fool either in the eyes of the teacher or of his fellow students. Finally in the tutorials he is normally not the only student present; the points described above will apply equally to his associates, whose presence serves to reinforce in him the belief that his opinions are not just idiosyncratic, they describe how life at the university really *is*.

The teacher on the other hand is on home ground. The meeting very likely occurs in his room, and is about topics closely linked to his professional identity. He has power in the situation, can fix the topic, require students to write essays and evaluate their contributions. He too may have some trepidation in such meetings from time to time; the limits to one's knowledge are far more easily seen in discussion than in lecture.

Reviewing the points above we can see that when a small group of students meets a teacher, the most likely thing to happen is that the students adopt a passive, receptive role, possibly contributing questions on prepared essays, while the teacher 'teaches' in a manner not very different from his lecturing style. It is important to ask whether this procedure permits optimal utilisation of the opportunity for mutual influence provided by the situation.

The teacher's power

One of the most widely replicated findings to emerge from research in social psychology has concerned the effects of participation in group.[2] In summary, if a power figure in a group exerts his power, he obtains overt compliance from those over whom he has power, but finds it necessary to devise ever more ingenious controls to regulate the behaviour of the other members when he is not present. If the power figure on the other hand does not fully exert his power and encourages others to contribute on a more equal basis the group members work more slowly and express much more confusion but they become highly committed to the achievement of their task. They internalise it and work on it with enthusiasm. What they do learn they retain. These findings with regard to the behaviour of the power figure naturally hold up only where the task environment facilitates task achievement. No amount of power equalisation will increase a student's productivity if he cannot obtain the books he requires or has an intolerable work load.

We can now apply these findings to meetings between a teacher and students. Student productivity will be low where some or all of the following obtain:

—the teacher appears very knowledgeable
—the student are ridiculed if they make mistakes
—the teacher talks a good deal
—the teacher fixes the number and titles of essays
—the teacher gives no help in findings books

Student productivity will be higher where the teacher's behaviour is more like this:

—the teacher defines problem areas, rather than solutions
—the teacher shows that he does not see himself as infallible
—the teacher talks less
—the teacher checks the appropriateness of essay titles and due dates
—the teacher encourages students who introduce creative or original ideas.
—the teacher acts as a resource in finding books

Many tutorial meetings will have characteristics drawn from both lists, but it is only rarely that it is not possible for a teacher to move some way towards the second list himself. In short, tutorials meeting *may* serve only to reinforce the existing pattern of staff-student relationships, underlining that the teacher knows and that the student's task is to assimilate what he is taught and reproduce it; but equally it is an opportunity to modify staff-student relationships and hence the nature of what is learned.

Communication patterns

In listening to lectures and in reading books, the student has very little opportunity to answer back, to express confusion, puzzlement, or even new insights. If the teacher in the small group situation does not encourage feedback from his students as to what they do and don't understand, he may well forfeit their interest in what he wishes to teach them. Likewise, if the teacher uses the situation to express his enthusiasm about whatever excites him in the subject he will achieve more impact on his students' motivation to learn than any amount of working through the factual material to be covered. Or, to put it another way if teaching is a chore, learning becomes one. The more the teacher can develop can two-way communication flow with his students the more discussion will focus on the learning problems perceived as important by the students and consequently the greater will be the learning achieved by them.

Structural variables

The nature of the relationship which develops in the tutorial situation is influenced by a number of factors not yet discussed notably the size of the tutorial group, the frequency of its meeting and the subject matter with which it is concerned.

The larger the group the greater the tendency toward passive, dependent student and active, dominant teachers. Research suggests a discontinuity between groups of about six or more and five or less.[3] In the larger groups, there are a substantial proportion of passive totally silent members; in the small groups this need not to be so. Even though the leaders are less verbally dominant in the smaller discussions, the findings are that they achieve more influence over group members than in the larger discussions. The frequency of meeting influences whether a coherent sequence of discussion develops as opposed to a series of isolated episodes. This second point may often be less important than the first, so that for example a fortnightly meeting with four students may be more valuable than a weekly one with eight students.

Little empirical data exists relevant to the question of how the subject matter of a discussion influences the emergent structure, largely for lack of an adequate classification of intellectual tasks. Clearly, however, subjects do differ in the degree to which assertions can be judged as true or false without discussion and in the nature of logical thinking employed. In a subject where widely differing viewpoints exist smaller groups would be better so as to provide opportunity for the expression of these views. In a subject where empirical test is unambiguous, on the other hand, a somewhat larger group may be an appropriate setting, in which students can develop the requisite skills of matching empirical data with problem situations. Such a group still needs to be quite small if it is to avoid the problem of students not feeling free to express confusion when they experienced it.

In the field of structural variables, there is a good deal of conventional wisdom as to what goes best in a particular subject, which may often be well founded. In almost any subject the teacher is faced with choice between what is extended in terms of his available time and what is ideal in the terms of optimising student learning.

Intergroup relations

So far teaching in a small group setting has been discussed as though it were possible to analyse a single such setting in isolation. In practice of course, both teacher and students have multiple group memberships, often concurrently. So it may be for example that when a teacher attempts to develops a two-way flow of communication in his tutorial meetings, his attempts are frustrated because the students are concurrently participating in other meetings which more prestigious teacher run in other ways.

Because of their complexity such problems, which stem from intergroup rather than intra-group relations have only lately been much studied. It is becoming clearer that it may be very fruitful[4] to conceptualise whole organisations such as firms and universities as large numbers of overlapping groups each one of which maintains its intra-group cohesion by not seeing eye-to-eye with some other relevant groups. Such intergroup competition or rivalry may be visible both within and between departments and faculties.

There are clearly no quick ways in which one can respond to conceptualisations of intergroup conflict by modifying how one teaches. But the implications are clear: the quality of smallgroup teaching will be determined not so much by the individual merit of teacher or student, but by the degree to which shared standards have been collaboratively worked out by the various teachers who contribute to a particular course of study. This problem will be most acute where students are drawing on a wide range of different teaching disciplines.

The overall organisation climate therefore limits and constrains what an individual teacher can do to improve his teaching methods; but rarely, if ever, does the climate prevent doing anything at all.

REFERENCES

1. The 'alienated' student culture of red brick universities has been vividly described by BRYAN WILSON, Threats to University values', New Society, 22 April 1965. Many similar points emerge from the more systematic researches of C.D. Orth at the Harvard Business School: ORTH, C D. *The First Year at the Harvard Business School.* Harvard U.P., 1963.
2. The classic studies of Lippitt and White and of Coch and French are both summarised in PROŠHANSKY, H. and SEIDENBERG, B. *Basic Studies in Social Psychology.* London: Holt, Rinechart, 1965. Also included is a more elegant recent formulation which substantially modifies earlier positions: FIERDLER, F.E. *A Contingency Model of Leadership Effectiveness* .
3. These studies are well summarised in a Chapter 8 of HARE, A.P. Handbook of Small Group Research. New York Free Press, 1962.
4. LIKERT, R. *New Patterns of Management.* London : McGraw Hill, 1961 and CYERT, R.M. and MARCH, J.G. *A Behavioural Theory of the Firm.* Englewood Cliffs, New Jersey: Prentice Hall, 1963 explore these areas.

Further reading

For a more detailed introduction to the study of small groups see Part III of SECORD, P. F. and BACKMAN, C. W. *Social Psychology.* London: McGraw Hill, International Student Edition, 1964.

For discussion of teaching method in the light of small group research see MILES, M. B. *Innovation in Education.* New York : Teachers college, Columbia University, 1964.

7(II)

TEACHING SMALL GROUPS

In university teaching some confusion still remains over the distinction between the 'tutorials' and the 'seminar'. The Hale Committee defined the tutorial as a discussion period for up to four students, and which was 'student-centred'; and a seminar as the same for larger numbers and which was 'subject-centred'. These distinctions are not easy to maintain in actual practice, and in the modern university a small discussion class may be known either as a tutorial group or as a seminar discussion. How far such a group is 'subject-centred, would seem to depend on the type of preparation (written work in advance, for example), and the degree of limitation of discussion to the subject matter, rather than on the size of the group. The term 'student-centred' is taken to imply a high degree of participation by the students, and this again would seem to depend on the method by which the seminar is conducted.

This paper is concerned with the nature of teacher-student relationships in small groups, whatever the groups are called. The optimum size is taken to be between seven and twelve members and possibly up to fifteen. Larger classes may also be called seminars, but the type of discussion is obviously limited by the size of the class, and large seminars are not the concern of this paper because they are not covered by the definition of a 'small-group'.

The advocacy of teaching in small groups must not be seen as an attack upon the lecture method, whether by live or televised performers. The Hale Committee defend the lecture as 'a continuous exposition, free from interruptions', and this is its great merit because of the care and thought which can be taken in its preparation and presentation. But from another point of view 'freedom from interruptions' is also the lecture's greatest weakness as a teaching method. This is why small group work is essential in addition to lectures and complementary to them.

The lecturer cannot assume a full understanding of all he has said, and he does not know what the students have been thinking while he was talking—unless they interrupt him which they do not normally do in a formal lecture. Nor does the lecturer know what *more* the students want to know—unless they ask questions, which is rare *unless* the group is small.

The value of meeting students in small groups depends on at least two general factors.

(1) The opportunity for a free discussion with full participation by all the members of the group.

(2) The development of a special type of relationship between the tutor and his students.

The advantages to the students and to the tutor are:

(1) That they all have an equal right of participation, and any one of them may initiate discussion or offer criticism.

(2) That each student is expected to give his own judgment or opinion, or to show his own method of reasoning. This is in accordance with a major aim of university education, namely to help the student to think for himself and work on his own.

(3) That the students are enabled to learn from each other, and not to rely only upon the nominal 'expert' in the form of the tutor. In many subjects peer group opinion may be more provocative of thought than the views of authority. At the same time the special knowledge of the tutor can become more acceptable when given in the atmosphere of a permissive discussion.

(4) That the tutor can 'abdicate' (temporarily) his status as an authority, and take on the role of an interpreter and clarifier of what is going on in the group. His superior knowledge and experience enables him, with luck, to ask the right questions, but he resists the temptation to pontificate on the answers. The advantage to the tutor is that he can observe the students beginning to think for themselves, and revealing the weaknesses in their knowledge or understanding which may need correction. Let us suppose that the session is based on the presentation of some information either in written or spoken form. The tutor then tries to pass on the tasks of evaluation, criticism and

judgment from himself to his students, and can learn from the resulting discussion the way their approach to the subject is developing.

(5) The tutor is able to encourage a 'feedback' of the students' responses to the output of information which has been fed to them through the lecture series. Thus he is able to gain a greater understanding of the students' difficulties in learning. This is the occasion when the thoughts and questions which arose during the lecture can be verbalised put before the group. The clarification of subject matter, and the discussion of alternative solutions to problems, would seem to be a specially valuable aspect of group work in the sciences and mathematics.

(6) Also the teacher does not *always* 'abdicate'. There are occasion when his skill in thinking, or experimental techniques, is best communicated by a close interaction between the scholar or research worker and a small group of promising students.

(7) An advantage of another kind is that the tutor is enabled to establish a personal relationships by face-to-face contact with the students. With large classes contact between staff and student is normally remote, and some students never get within talking distance of their teachers.

The non-directive tutorials group

More radical experiments in group work have been tried[1-3] and are worth consideration for use in various special circumstances. In essence the non-directive type of tutorial means a move towards a more spontaneous discussion, and less supervision from the staff member. Under the present system nearly all tutors talk too much. The climate in the group should be informal and as permissive as possible, so that members may feel free to say what they like. Anything that is said may be of importance to the group so that everything that is said should be considered and attended to, even when on first hearing it appears irrelevant. Though acting as a leader the tutor does not attempt to dominate or to follow an agenda. When the group becomes, to a greater or less degree, independent of the leader then the members begin to share ideas more freely and genuine communication begins. The principal function of the leader is to draw attention to what is going on in the group. He carries out this task by re-stating, or explaining, or analysing the content, process, behaviour or relationships of the group in action.

It might be thought that freer discussion is more suitable to arts subjects, but Abercrombie[4] has shown that medical students can be helped to work in discussion groups. The discussions were based both on different interpretations of the same experimental data, on the evaluation of evidence, and on the understanding of scientific method.

The pursuit of independent truth is one of the aims of a university education, and students need practice in coming to examine their own prejudices. Certain patterns of thinking are built up from past experiences and may distort our perception of the facts in a new situation. For new thinking one has to question basic assumptions previously held. By following this point of view a high degree of freedom of expression can be justified on intellectual grounds. By free discussion we may be able to get more independent thought and a creative approach to learning, with less dependence on the lecture and the textbook, necessary though these are as basic sources of knowledge.

Another interpretation of 'free discussion' is to allow the talk to go where it will in pursuit of clearer understanding, even though it appears to be wandering off the track. Sometimes good ideas come from wild hypotheses, and this is the theory behind the 'brain storming' type of session. There is a sense in which a person does not know what he wants to express until he expresses it in words before an audience. It is by hearing himself speak that he comes to understand what he is trying to say. Thus meaning is understood by the putting of ideas together whether it be in logic for the sciences or the expression of emotions in the arts. The effect of the group is that the verbal expression of one member may enable someone else in the group to discover that he has thought or felt in a similar or related manner.

Finally, by the staff member holding a looser rein in the discussion the students may express some of their attitudes towards their work and their life in the university. An exchange of views over their own difficulties at work may increase self-confidence and help to improve group morale. The quality of a student's work is often related to the degree of satisfaction he gets from it, and it is as important for him to get an insight into his motives, ambitions and expectation as it is to make progress in his academic studies. He thus comes to see himself as a developing person, growing both mentally and emotionally towards maturity. The small group should, ideally, provide a protected and friendly environment within which students can grow and realise their potential abilities. The primary difficulty in understanding human behaviour is to understand one's own feelings and thoughts in relation to those of others. It is by seeing how they resemble and differ from each other, by comparing experiences, that the members of a group can gain a better understanding of themselves.

It may well prove more difficult in some subject areas than in others to mix discussion of academic studies with the expression of attitudes and motives, but this need not invalidate the claim that both aspects can be legitimate functions of a tutorials group.

REFERENCES

1. MILES, MATTHEW B. *Learning to Work in group.* New York : Teachers College, Columbia University, 1959.
2. OTTAWAY, A.K.C. *Learning through Group Experience.* London: Routledge and Kegan Paul, 1966. (See also the full bibliography for further references)
3. WHITAKER, G. (Ed.). *T-Group Training: group dynamics in management education.* Oxford: Blackwell, 1965.
4. ABERCROMBIE, M.L. JOHNSON. *The Anatomy of Judgment.* London. Hutchinson, 1960

8
THE TUTORIAL SYSTEM

Reason why tutorials are important

By a tutorial I mean a meeting for an hour or so between a teacher and a group of students small enough for individual conversation and discussion to be possible. The group can cannot therefore be larger than six, and two is possibly the best number. Some reasons why this type of teaching is important in university education are as follows.

Personal teaching is essential because a student, like an apprentice, learn his trade best by direct contact with a practitioner. From their school training, many students derive habits that are suited only to the absorption of information accepted on authority, at the university they need to develop an understanding of how their particular discipline is constructed, what problem lie before it and how these can be investi-gated. Otherwise their education will cease when they take their de-gree. In this process of widening their horizons, guidance is essential, both for their choice of reading and for their intellectual develop-ment. It can only be done in tutorials; contact between staff and stu-dents at other times is not close enough, especially when classes are large. For many a student, his tutor is the only member of staff whom he knows well enough to engage in conversation. Personal teaching is also of great importance as a support to the student's morale. A student's life is at best a difficult one, and he may be unprepared for the hard work, loneliness and other stresses that it imposes. This is especially true in a university made up of large departments with rela-tively few halls of residence. A tutor can do a good deal to give con-fidence by explaining to his pupils what is happening to them. The tutorial is moreover an important stimulus to work. No one likes to appear a fool in front of other people.

Reading, writing and discussion are at least as important as lecture attendance in a university training. 'Reading maketh a full man, conference a ready man, writing an exact man.' A tutorial should normally be a discussion of written work based on special reading. This basis of written work is essential. Reading is seen to be relevant and important when it is done under the stimulus of having to write a piece which will be read and commented upon. Writing is a training in thinking; at the least it involves selection from sources, or arrangement of material, and at most a critical and original treatment of a subject. To have constant practice in drafting orderly and connected prose is more over an invaluable training in expression. Probably the most important contribution of the tutor here is to select the right reading for the student. The assignment should be manageable as regards bulk and difficulty; it should be interesting and look forward to further study.

A useful feature of the tutorial is that it is flexible. Students can be treated according to their ability, their individual difficulties considered, and their load adjusted to their pace of working. Special, topics can be handled without holding up a whole lecture class.

The conduct of tutorials

Great variety is passible in the conduct of tutorials. Some tutors ask for the written work to be handed in beforehand, so that they can read it in advance and devote the tutorial hour to a discussion; but skill in persuading students to engage in discussion does not belong to all university teacher. Some tutors talk mainly about the next week's topic, devoting little of the hour to the written work, which they read separately and return with pencilled comments. But there is no need to read the written work outside the tutorial hour; the method adopted by many tutors is to read (or listen to) the students' work during the tutorial hour, and make comments, either during or after the perusal. This is an elastic technique, which leads itself well to tutorials with two students sitting beside the tutor; one student can be asked to comment on the work of another, and discussion is stimulated by the written text on the table in front. Some tutors in scientific subjects prefer to gather the group round a blackboard, at which one of the students expounds the subject; this method can be used with groups larger than two. These self-contained tutorials save the tutor's time, and encourage spontaneity of comment; on the other hand, some time is lost in going over those parts of the students' work that requires no comment.

The extent to which a tutor should analyse student's work, or comment or enlarge upon it, or try to elicit discussion from the student, is a matter of personal choice, to be exercised according to the temperaments and abilities of the persons concerned. Some tutors successfully make use of 'quiz' sessions in which they question students about a prepared topic.

The tutors' objectives are to see that the student has produced a properly-organised account of the subject, and make sure that he understands what he has written down, and has written only what he believes and can support with reason; to elucidate obscurities; to encourage enterprise in reading, thought and writing; to correct or expand the student's information; to relate the subject, to its general field and to give clues about the next week's subject, as well as a reading list, with critical comments. Help should be given with difficulties, but for a lazy student the best help may take the form of a reference which he should look up. Tutoring, which is sometimes confused with spoon-feeding, in fact has the opposite aim, namely to enable the student to work on his own, to think for himself, and to construct his own account of his subject.

A form of the tutorial system is sometimes operated in which a student is passed from one member of staff to another, doing one piece of written work for each lecturer, who tutors only in his speciality. This is an inferior method. Continuity is more important for the student than specialist expertise, at least until the final year. The staff should regard themselves as general practitioners, very willing to call in a second opinion, but responsible for the general development of their pupils. This is how confidence is generated and the student's interest maintained. The staff may at first have to revise their knowledge of parts of their subject, but they can collaborate to bring each other up-to-date and the time required is then not excessive. It is, however, arguable that in the final year some (or all) of the tutorials should give place to seminars, given by specialist to classes of ten or twelve, both because the frontiers of knowledge are being approached and specialist teaching is required, and because the student should be weaned away from any tendency to depend on an individual tutor.

The content of tutorial work

The main question here is how tutorials should be related to lectures. This is a matter for departments. In many courses, it would seem, there is a 'backbone' of information which is best conveyed by lectures. The tutorials may be designed to drive home this information, to extend it, to solve problems based on it, or to interpret it.

Within departmental policies, there is scope for very considerable devolution of responsibility to the individual tutor. This responsibility is very important to the tutor; he must be given it if he is to discharge his obligation to treat his pupils individually. It is also a clear indication that the tutor is a collaborator in the university community and not merely an employee.

The wider tutorials functions

It is natural that those who give tutorials in term-time should also advise students on their reading in vacations, especially in the long vacation, on the importance of which the university (following the Hale committee) insist. Students should not be simply handed their reading lists; each should have a personal talk with his tutor, who will relate the departmental recommendations to the student's ability and the state of his knowledge.

Because of the confidence built up by regular teaching and conversation, it is also natural that those who give tutorials should also do at least part of the general advising and encouraging of students. This is essential to their morale, and is therefore rightly regarded as a mark of a good department (and is ultimately rewarded by an entry of high quality). The extent of informal contact between pupils and tutor, apart from their official relations, is a matter for individuals, depending as it does on temperament, age, and adaptability.

At the end of each term's tutoring, the tutor should write a brief report on each of his pupils, to be sent to the head of the department and also made available to any other tutor who may be concerned.

The report is then available when degrees are decided and when recommendations for jobs have to be written. This practice is helpful to all the staff concerned.

The organisation of tutorials

Arrangements which appear to work well are as follows. Each student is allotted to one tutor, who acts as general adviser and takes responsibility for that student's personal teaching; the actual tutorial work may be shared with other members of the staff. No attempt need be made to give each member of staff a cross-section of intelligence; this could only be done initially on A-level marks, which are not reliable indices of university performance; and in any case the bright and the dull average out over the years. A method as satisfactory as any is to allot the students alphabetically.

Taking the ratio of students to available tutors in the university as a whole about 12:1, each tutor will have on the average four new pupils each year (though in some departments the ratio is much less favourable). If he takes them all weekly in Paris, he will have six tutorials a week. However, this load is not essential and can be much reduced. A great deal of a good can be done by tutoring each student for one term only in each session, which reduces the load to two hours a week. This solution is all the more attractive if the students are taught personally by other people in the intervening periods, thus in some science departments they go to examples classes taken by research students. (Conscientious research students can be a great help to undergraduates; they make contact more easily than their elders.) The load therefore need not be excessive.

Work can also be saved if summaries of lectures, solutions of problems, references, and notes on topic for tutorials, are exchanged between members of staff. An annual meeting on matters affecting tutors is useful. New tutors should be properly briefed.

Finally, it is desirable that tutoring should be voluntary and carried out by people who believe it to be important. This might be borne in mind when staff are recruited. Occasional relief for a term should be arranged, especially for those who have unusually heavy departmental duties.

9
THE SEMINAR METHOD

In a paper on 'The Seminar' Professor Ian Watt shows that the idea of the seminar as a 'teaching method' is rooted in the oldest traditions of the medieval universities of continental Europe, although its practice in current university teaching is a relative innovation, derived from Germany via the U.S.A. at the turn of the present century. Its remote history does not concern us, but it may be useful to point out the features which currently differentiate the seminar from the lecture or tutorial. In essence these are as follows.

(1) Free discussion; i.e. not formally limited by the 'teacher'.
(2) Equal right of participation of all members.
(3) The focus of discussion on prepared written work.

It might be thought that the seminar represents in pure form the ideal of the university as a community of fellow-scholars, rather than as an organisation of professional instructors and the instructed. For those whose view of the university emphasises teaching efficiency, this may be a weakness rather than a strength. The discussion which follows is largely concerned with the seminar as a teaching method for undergraduates, a different matter indeed from the seminar as experienced by the scholar who brings his research findings to his peers for judgment.

Technique

Seminar classes for undergraduates should be small enough for realistic joint discussion in which everyone can find opportunity to take part, certainly not more than twenty. If the class is much larger it becomes a 'panel' discussion with an audience either pleasantly satisfied with the light effort of listening,or unhappily frustrated by failureto exploit fleeting gaps in discussion. Ideally the class should be small enough to allow each member the chance to present a paper during a series of meetings. On the other hand the class must not be too small; six or eight members are probably the minimum for useful open discussion.

A seminar is not effective unless there is some common degree of expert knowledge enjoyed by its members. In a research seminar this is the *sine qua non* of effective participation. In a teaching seminar this is on an *ad hoc* basis and rests on previously prepared work, a paper by a class member, and a reading programme in relation to this paper, undertaken by other class members. The consequent discussion has a substantial information content shared round the table. If, as might be expected, the students are less expert or experienced in discussion technique than he is, the teacher will presumably wish to guide discussion into the most profitable channels. In so doing the teacher abnegates his status as 'teacher' and acts out the role of chairman, a special kind of *primus inter pares* which accords well with the historic notion of equality in the seminar. This allows of a comfortable degree of formality of procedure, which is vital if a group of students are to get good value out of discussion of something which interests them and which they have taken some trouble to investigate. There is a further small practical point of importance. A reasonable time limit to discussion should be set at the outset. If a discussion hangs fire it should not be prolonged by an anxious tutor strenuously trying to strike a spark. A good discussion among students loses nothing by being closed at a level of some energy and intensity of interest, provided that the time limit set is known beforehand to all members of the class and reasonable discretion is exercised about exceeding it.

There are clearly two forms of 'teaching seminar': the one a regular meeting of the same group of students working with one teacher on a group of topics as a continuing syllabus, and the other a less frequent meeting bringing students together with senior scholars and researchers for particular occasions. This latter offers to undergraduates a demonstration of the possibility of disagreement between experts, and also one hopes, of the sophisticated level of discourse to be employed in resolving such disagreements. No one would deny that this could be an important experience for the undergraduate, but if so it is unlikely that the inexpert student would be a participant. In any case this is too costly in staff time to be made a regular part of the teaching programme, even if it could be established that it is an efficient 'teaching method'.

Objectives

Whilst it may seem irrational to consider 'objectives' after 'technique' it is not really so. We have inherited the techniques to a large extent, but the questions of objectives are our own affair, and are related to contemporary university situation, although not necessarily at variance with ancient tradition. The teacher who conscientiously tries to decide about teaching methods for himself is faced with increasingly sharp contradictions in the modern university. Is the first degree an intensive training in a skill which is to be used professionally, or is the first degree primarily an experience in ' higher education' with the implication that real professional training should be postponed to a fourth year or to learning on the job? Is the university able to give must the university teacher try to define for himself what that something is so that he may make his own contribution to it? These simple questions and others more subtle deriving from them are very germane to a consideration of the place of the seminar in university teaching. For at some time the teacher must make his mind up (even if he does not declare his decision) whether he uses seminars because he is satisfied they are the most efficient method of instructing students in a particular skill, or because he believes the seminar to be at the heart of the university tradition and consequently to be used for the general benefit of his students.

The clearest statement to be made about the 'objectives' of the teaching seminar seems to me to relate to acquiring skill in learning, talking and thinking rather than to the transmission of information of professional skills; accordingly the seminar should provide for the following.

(1) Practice in preparing written work for discussion. This necessarily implies practice in using the tools of inquiry special to the particular discipline being taught.

(2) Practice in discussion. This involves facility in testing relevance and in following arguments, as well as some gain of fluency and good sense.

(3) Practice in intelligent and unprejudiced scepticism. This I take to be the hall-mark of the university trained mind, and the seminar should be its chief class room.

(4) Exercise in the use of purposeful discussion to assess new information and theories.

(5) The establishment of confidence between teacher and student that we are engaged in the principal function of the university—the pursuit of independent truth.

Problems

What has been said so far about techniques and objectives is in large measure simple and practical, but in any teaching situation the problems which arise from simple and practical premises may be anything but simple; such problems are a testing measure of the teaching method. It will be useful to refer to three groups of problems arising from

(1) quality of students,

(2) quality of teachers,

(3) library and ancillary services.

(1) Quality of students

There is great variety in student ability not least in respect of quickness of wits and powers of expression. If a seminar is being dominated by two or three brilliant students out of a class of fifteen, what are the other twelve getting out of it? If on the other hand discussion labours along while two or three ill-informed and hesitant students try to make their points, does the teacher wasting their time? What happens to the theory of equal graduates can we structure an equal participation situation? A further question is one common to all aspects of teaching at this level. Is the first duty of the teacher to his potential 'firsts', or can we comfortably assume that these fortunate souls will teach themselves, while we labour as missionaries among those who need us?

In practice 'free' discussion among students in a seminar must be guided so as to involve as many as possible at as high and serious a level as possible, partly because of the high cost of student and staff time, and partly because it is of the essence of group teaching that this should happen.

(2) Quality of teachers

It is agreeable to see ourselves in a vision of a university in which men women of great intellectual distinction devote themselves to small groups of gifted young people in a rich harmony of wisdom, sparkle, and shared humility before the shrine of 'scholarship'. A more realistic view might be that whilst few of us are outstanding teachers, and few are really incompetent, almost all of us try very hard to be good at our work and many succeed by standards currently and traditionally accepted. This is not simply a matter of learning a few tricks of the trade. It must be remembered that seminar teaching can be strenuous and disturbing. Teachers must put themselves at risk of exposure as 'pedants', mere channels of information with only a limited range of imagination and originality to bring to discussion. The screens of age and status which protect us in the lecture room and to a lesser degree in the tutorial are taken down, and the student can see us as we are. Perhaps a strong component in student concern about 'staff-student' relations is a real anxiety to have complete confidence in one's teachers. As the maturing undergraduate improves his own skills and critical capacity, such confidence can see us best be established in the near-equal exchange of free discussion. Any teacher who is sensitive about thin patches in his own knowledge may be harassed by a self-conscious fear of failure to establish such confidence. The teacher needs nerve as well as knowledge to maintain his place as *primus inter pares* if he is fortunate enough to have able students. On the other hand we ought to be at least as intelligent as those we teach, and certainly we should know more; it is also comforting that students are more ready to warm to honest intellectual modesty than to formidable brilliance.

(3) Library and ancillary services

Twenty undergraduates in a laboratory will need twenty sets of apparatus (or perhaps ten, but certainly multiple sets), and this is accepted as expensive in space and finance. The seminar is conventionally the laboratory of the humanities and calls for multiple sets of analogous tools, i.e. books, statistics, maps, research reports, photocopies of manuscripts etc. Here is the barely concealed rock on which the whole ideal system may founder. All university libraries have finite budgets which at any one time are inadequate. The problem of duplicate copies of vital books to service lecture classes of a hundred or more is now a familiar one. The provision of multiple copies of government report, for example, to be used perhaps once or twice in a seminar discussion is a luxury indeed and can hardly be met in the present context. The alternative is the hasty and competitive scramble after a necessary text which takes most of the pleasure of reading out of many students' lives. New techniques of photocopying are making a useful difference but these are expensive; the cost in a big university can be considerable and will need justifying. There are also difficulties in connection with copyright.

Evaluation

The problems add up very simply to an expensive way of teaching (and not the easiest) focused on small groups at a time when the universities are moving into a 'mass-communication' phase of higher education. What are the benefits to be gained by seminar teaching?

First and foremost is the practice of an educational technique which is at the heart of the university tradition; informed analytical discussion which, practised by experts, illuminates problems and clears the way to solutions. Undergraduates, however are not experts in this sense. It can be argued that students who do not have this experience are missing an important, even essential, part of their university education. Can this view be sustained? If a graduate can be *trained* without this particular component can its expense be justified because it is a desirable element in a tradition of teaching? If one regards first degrees as essentially training in particular skills, then seminars are a luxury and indeed many scientists and technologists take this view. In the humanities on the other hand there is a stronger feeling for the first degree as being 'educational' rather than 'training', and indeed it is easier in this context to see the seminar as part of 'training' in logical discussion and criticism of ideas and attitudes. Qualitative judgments of human situations need some awareness of the complexity of assumptions and pressures to be comprehended once one progresses beyond immediate knowledge of superficial facts. This level of understanding is more appropriately worked out in the seminar than in any other teaching system. Such teaching is by precept and example rather than by textbook and rostrum dogma.

Secondly, the seminar brings students and tutors close together as a working group. There is a view widely held among many teachers and students that university teaching ought to involve close personal relations between the teacher and the taught. This may be a great unfounded assumption but it has been absorbed to the extent that there is student dissatisfaction made very articulate indeed if the taught feel themselves deprived of expected personal contact with their teachers. Whether strictly educationally necessary or not, this ideal set of relationships can be easily established in the seminar as part of a 'work' situation. This is surely preferable to a series of artificially contrived 'social' contacts; it would seem right that social links, if desired, should grow naturally out of working links.

If we were to apply 'cost-benefit' analysis to seminar teaching (and in the present climate of university financing this is by no means a far-fetched supposition), it would be necessary to assess such cost items as the following:

(1) *Cost of student time:* seminars customarily take longer than a normal lecture period and are probably analogous to a laboratory session. Compared with the latter there is no certainty that each student is fully employed in actual work. Nor can it be said that the student is becoming familiar with professional techniques which he will exercise on his own responsibility at a later stage. How far can it be shown that the student is fully and strenuously engaged? The same question can fairly be put in respect of a lecture class, but here more depends on the effort put into his task by the teacher, and in any case there is the conventional sanction of the examination system.

(2) *Cost of staff time:* it is probably true that seminar teaching is as demanding and effective a teaching method as any other, from the teacher's point of view. It has its attractions: many prefer seminar work because of its general informality, its feeling of close face to face contact, and its high 'feedback' component (again an analogy with laboratory work). As an alternative to formal lecturing it is less

time-consuming in preparation, in spite of the supervision of reading, and of papers to be prepared. It is also much less of a personal effort than lecturing. But it is not usually an alternative; it is more often a supplement to formal teaching at the undergraduate level, with added complications of timetabling and accommodation. Above all for the teacher it represents a concentration of effort on a handful of students, whereas a carefully prepared and effectively delivered lecture will serve for a hundred or more, all of whom should learn something from it. No one knows how far seminars actually benefit undergraduates or indeed how to measure benefits gained.

The dominant factor in fudging the utility of seminar work for undergraduates is likely to be the exigencies of a deteriorating staff-student ratio in the foreseeable future. It is ironic that at about the time at which the great modern universities have established small group teaching as a normal convention for thousands of undergraduates, the next series of demands on the universities are likely to check this very considerable achievement.

At postgraduate level the seminar falls into its rightful place as the leading teaching method without question. Recent developments of graduate schools have been towards the extension of the award of higher degrees for more advanced knowledge of the field rather than for research claiming to add new matter. One-year advanced study courses have brought together classes which are small, well informed and in the nature of their recruitment academically strong. Here is the ideal seminar situation at postgraduate level. The emerging difficulty if the general staff-student ratio worsens is that teachers who want to lead such postgraduate work must add it to their expanding commitments among large classes of first degree students.

10(I)

BOOKS IN UNIVERSITY TEACHING

Introduction

A university is not primarily a place of teaching but a place of learning, and our *essential* function as teachers is *not* to give endless lectures, or to multiply tutorials, or to place Greek letters at the foot of students' essays, or to conduct examination, let alone to appear on the television or the radio. Our essential function as teacher is to assist our pupils to learn for themselves. This guidance can undoubtedly be given partly in stimulating, well constructed lectures, or in rigorous tutorials arguments or in informal conversation in the sort of relaxed surroundings which every university should have . But above all students can best be helped to work by themselves and to learn by the careful use of books and booklists.

The importance of reading

By precept and example students must be convinced of the need to read widely and thoroughly. Students have also to be taught to read critically, not to accept everything 'because it's in the book', not always to reproduce the views of others. The teacher should, therefore, always be careful to keep the literature of his subject before his pupils. Indeed some of the most effective lectures are purely bibliographical; in them the lecturer will simply discuss a number of books or articles, showing how successive contributions have added to knowledge of a particular topic, where the controversies have arisen, which the main unresolved questions are. Such lectures can be invaluable; so too can articles and pamphlets constructed in the same way, and these have an obvious use for teacher as well as for the student.

Again, a don must not only do all he can to ensure that students read, he must clearly read widely himself, keeping up with the literature in his own limited field, and reading the most important work in the subject as a whole; a modernist should do some reading in the medieval period and a medievalist in the modern, for example, and any academic who reads nothing outside the subject he professes will soon become something of a bore to himself as well as to others. It may seem an impertinence to exhort senior members of a university to read widely, but experience shows that many find it difficult to do so far a variety of reasons, not all of them good ones. A teacher who quickly shows his pupils that he not only has read a lot but continues to do so, reading and discussing the main new material as it appears, will be a powerful stimulus to those pupil—as well as to some of his colleagues.

Another aspect of the importance of books in university teaching is the use which can and should be made of original materials in print. An undergraduate often begins to get to grips with his subject, and to enjoy it to the full, when he lays aside the commentaries of professional scholars and critics and turns to original material. Some years ago in a public lecture at Leeds Mr. Noel (now Lord) Annan urged his audience not to be content with reading Asa Briggs on the Victorians, but to read the Victorians themselves. A student of any of the world's literature or philosophies must be brought to the writings of the novelists, poets, dramatists and the thinkers and be advised and helped to soak himself in them. This is far more effective and enjoyable than merely trying to commit the main views of the commentators to memory for reproduction in the examination.

Stress on reading *original* material in print applies to all the other traditional Arts subjects. In history, students should be asked to read original source in the first year as well as subsequently; in economics, surely the writing of the Adam Smith and Keynes, not just what other people have said about them. In fine art, paintings, sculpture and work of architecture demand attention, either the originals or (where that is impossible) printed reproductions: the detailed work of the critics can come later.

Moreover, students should be given every encouragement to read books in foreign languages. French is the most popular European language: this is splendid because many French textbooks and standard works are supremely helpful to students, lucid and well-arranged. There is surely a case for non-language departments having a strict language entrance requirement are probably applying a language test in the first-year examination.

The ends, then, are clear: the student must learn to work by himself; he must learn to read widely; he must pay more attention to original materials and to works of great scholars, less to second-hand commentaries and re-hashed material. Fortunately an effective university teacher has at his disposal three means of helping an undergraduate to achieve these desirable ends: advice on a reading programme; production of bibliographies; advice on book-ownership.

Advice on a reading programme

Choice, and as far a possible free choice, is at the heart of a university education. No student can master all the literature which will be recommended in his three years, but it takes many students too long to realise that such mastery is not expected of them, with the result that they worry, flounder and grumble. 'How can we possibly read all this?' is an all too familiar question. Teachers may therefore generally agree that the first advice given to a pupil should be an emphasis on his need to select those subjects which will read about as fully as time permits and those books which he will endeavour to know and to understand.

What advice can then be given to an undergraduate faced with a wide—possibly a daunting—choice of reading? A university teacher in an Arts subject can both advise on the choice and to some extent direct it.

(1) Advice on choice

(a) Introductory books. It is very helpful for a student to be given the titles of one or two introductory books at the outset of each course, books which will provide 'a birds-eye view', to enable him to see the main outline before he gets into detail. Publications in the Home University Library and Hutchinson's University Library series as well as Pelicans may be found useful here. But the wise teacher will issue a

strong warning that such works are only introductory, appetisers rather than the main diet.

(b) Textbooks. For many aspects some subjects there is no satisfactory textbook, but where there is the student should be urged to read and to possess a copy for later reference. Some teachers will share my belief that students should be discouraged from spending hours making notes on a textbook; a student with his own copy can readily refer to it.

(c) Standard works, commentaries, biographies. Here a tutor should emphasise that the student has a great deal of choice the exercise of which will depend on his own interests. Two warning may be opposite: (i) against over-concentration on one topic, a short period of time, a single person etc., (ii) against dispersal of reading effort to such an extent that knowledge remains superficial.

(d) Articles in periodicals. Judicious recommendation of these is essential, if a student is to see for himself the fruits of the most recent research. Articles show scholars at work in a particular way, and a student can thus be kept aware of the importance of advances in knowledge through research and reassessment. Articles may well be found more useful after the first year.

(e) Original source, texts, great works. The student who relies entirely on commentaries and secondary works is missing most of the purpose, interest and enjoyment. The sooner a teacher can gets his pupils behind the secondary works to the originals the better.

(f) Potted books, "nutshells", Problems series etc. When these exist a teacher should give advice on their use rather than ignore them and thereby allow his students to court eternal prediction by misusing them (usually by over-reliance on them).

Problems series (e.g. *problem in European Civilisation)* in which books and articles are summarised, opposing views given in juxtaposition and synthesis attempted, can help a student to get his bearings in a mass of literature i.e. as signposts to detailed work, not as substitutes for it. But such potted books have two other chief values: (i) for student's revision—a point which should be stressed; (ii) for teachers in trouble, unprepared and short of material—a point which can be treated with discretion.

(g) Parts of books. It is not spoon—feeding to help students to find valuable chapters in books of otherwise doubtful quality or relevance. Similarly one should help them to find their way in very large books.

(h) Reference books. Students should quickly be introduced to the main sorts of reference books·available for a particular subject: dictionaries of all kinds, bibliographies, atlases, guides and handbooks.

(2) Guided and set reading

In setting essays tutors guide the reading of their pupils by recommending appropriate books and articles. Care is often needed to ensure that the student reads what is recommended and does not fall back on the bland excuse, 'I could not get hold of it '. This is so often the excuse of the weaker brethren. When noting literature for essays a student can be reminded that some books, often the best, are 'tough going' and that academic life is not just a bed of Pengiun books or TV screens.

There are two possible ways of guiding the choice of books, and it is probably desirable to combine them: (a) to allow the student to select his own essay topic, and, by implication, the literature; (b) to encourage a student to tackle a topic which he did not choose, for his own good and in the interests of breadth.

Some teachers prefer to use a method of set reading popular in American universities, that a allocating certain chapters or pages in a book to different students who attend subsequently to summarise and discuss what they have read. Some will feel that such methods are not quite respectable but it can be argued that it may be useful to alternate this method with the more traditional one of an essay based on solid reading .

Three main point stand out. First, that a university teacher must be willing to give his pupils plenty of advice on reading, or the pupil will be submerged by the amount of literature published. Secondly, that a teacher can and should guide reading, to the point of suggesting specific chapters or even setting pages. Thirdly, the teacher will best discharge these tasks who is himself widely read in his subject—and who does not promptly borrow from the library all the books he proposes to recommend.

Production of bibliographies

A bibliography or selected reading list for each course, accurately prepared, duplicated and distributed is essential and seems to many university teachers preferable to older method of naming a few books and articles in each lecture (though that need not be ruled out). A reading list should include under separate headings: (1) one or two introductions; (2) textbook(s) for the course; (3) lists of modern books, appropriately subdivided for the sake of clarity; (4) original materials, primary sources, texts; (5) essential works of reference (e.g. atlas, dictionary); and (6) mention of any detailed, comprehensive bibliographies of the subject.

Only the individual can determine the length of such a list, and moreover, great care must be taken in its preparation.

Accuracy is called for:

in the name and initials of author or editor;
in the full and exact title;
in the number of the edition (if not the first)
and for the date of publication.

If attention is not paid to these points hours of students' and librarians' time will be wasted. Moreover it may be helpful for books not available in the university to be marked, to encourage students to try for them when at home. Articles in periodicals can, in the interests of clarity, be listed separately. Details should be given, accurately, of the author's name and initials; the title of the article (or a short-title); the name of the periodical; the volume number and date of publication.

Finally, the teacher will no doubt wish to comment on items in the list. This can be done either by incorporating comments on the list or by commenting in (say) the first lecture or tutorial. The disadvantage of the former method is that printed comments must be brief—and must not be libellous. But comments and some guidance about tackling the list are essential. To throw an extensive reading list at a class without comment is to confuse the weak and discourage the strong.

On the other hand the production of a careful list of recommended books and articles is an important part of any course and will be a great help to the students (and in some ways to the teacher as well).

A reading list should be buttressed in two ways. A copy should be supplied to local bookshops, with an indication of books most heavily recommended and of the numbers of students involved. Above all the teacher should try to ensure that books and periodicals listed are available in the university library and in departmental libraries. Requests should be made for multiple copies, not necessarily of the textbooks (which students should buy) but of books most; likely to be heavily used in general reading and essay work. Books and journals are the tools of an academic's trade, and TV circuits and glossy brochures with coloured pictures will be as sounding brass and tinkling cymbals if teachers and students alike are denied books in the quantities which they need. This applies particularly to very expensive standard works, copies of which should automatically be multiplied in the university library.

Advice on purchase of books

A university teacher has a plain duty to encourage book-ownership by students for all educated people should own a growing library, and students in particular will find that possession of books is a great help in their work. It is in the nature of university life that precept and example are the only means open to the teacher. Both should be used to the full.

A teacher will not convince his students of the advantages of book-ownership unless he owns and regularly buys books himself: well-stocked shelves in the teacher's room will have a much greater impact on the students than any amount of simple exhortation. Indeed, some may think it advisable never to urge the purchase of books, but to take it for granted that students will buy books and content themselves with guiding the students, choice. Undoubtedly guidance is needed.

Fortunately in many subjects such advice is fairly easy to give. Clearly every student should possess the main textbooks for the syllabus, ready on the shelves when needed for reference. Many of the introductory books can be purchased in cheap editions, while recently large numbers of standard works have been issued in paperbacks (some of these, incidentally are not cheap, and not all academic paperbacks are worth having); of these a student should be advised to secure a representative collection for different parts of the syllabus. Where standard works, used especially for essay and general reading, are expensive the case for multiple copies in the libraries is unanswerable. Literary texts in various languages are often published in cheap editions but many original works, sources and journals are not readily available for purchase. When commenting on the value of, and method of tacking, his selected reading list, a don is well advised to indicate briefly which books should be purchased, perhaps suggesting some order of preference. He might also remind students that books can be sold on graduation, for some books are more worth keeping in later life than others, and that groups of friends or neighbours in hall can form syndicates to purchase books. Students who take this advice will have by them the tools of their craft and a portion of the world's accumulated learning, the desire to possess which is one characteristic of the university person.

Much of the foregoing clearly applies to postgraduate research, but here one the or two points may be emphasised. An essential part of any postgraduate teaching, especially the supervision of research, is a class (meeting more than once if necessary) on bibliographies and reference works in general; in this class care must be taken to ensure that the graduate student is familiar with all the important reference material, especially such bibliographical aids as are available in university library (or other large libraries where he is likely to be working). Again a research student should be encouraged to take as much interest in what books do not say as in what they do say; this will help him to be on the look out for gaps in knowledge.

Conclusion

The university don should keep books in the forefront of his teaching work, whatever gadgets he may decide to employ. But as books and journals are sometimes difficult to use to the best advantage, student need a good deal of guidance if they are to work effectively, especially as many of them have had little practice in working by themselves at school. Happily guidance for the students can also help the teacher. As academic teachers we have a responsibility for creating the right sort of atmosphere which will encourage students to read and to think about what they have read: 'reading for a degree' should mean exactly what it says. We have, moreover, a responsibility for ensuring the availability of books and journals and for guiding our students in their use.

True, 'You can lead a horse to water but you cannot make him drink'. But even a horse gets thirsty....

10(II)

THE PROVISION OF BOOKS FOR TEACHING

Of all the functions of the University Library, the provision of books for the curricular needs of undergraduate body is probably the least complex. The aims are comparatively clear; the methods of achieving them, if not easy, are straightforward.

It must be assumed that a basic collection is in being, that for the history student the basic sources, for the science student the runs of periodicals, for the literature student the early and various editions of texts, are already provided. These are not specifically undergraduate but research material; undergraduate teaching is however carried on against such a background, and students must at intervals be directed to or be allowed free access to this material. The more gifted student in particular will find stimulation in pursuing his studies into areas which would normally be thought of as beyond the scope of the average undergraduate. Indeed, as students reach a more advanced stage in their courses, research material becomes a more integral part of their literature.

A research collection is thus a prerequisite of adequate undergraduate instruction. The straightforward task of the librarian concerning the subject of this paper follows on from this basic provision. Students must have available all the books, periodicals, reports and pamphlets which their teachers consider necessary or desirable for their curricular reading, as well as general background material. The principle is as simple as this. Most of the material is in print or available second-hand and the only limiting factor is money.

It is when this simple principle is applied that difficulties arise. The difficulties centre mainly around the question 'how available?'. To provide only one lending copy of every book required for teaching purposes would fall short of necessary availability. One hundred students, recommended to read three chapters of one book for the next week's lecture would find one copy of the that book wholly inadequate.

A fundamental, and very difficult question is how many copies of needed books should be provided in order to give a satisfactory service, bearing in mind that, for a given library grant, the greater the duplication of copies the smaller the number of different titles that can be provided.

It should be remembered that students receiving a local education authority grant are normally allowed£ 35 a year for the purchase of books and equipment. Students are therefore expected to provide themselves with a numbers of books, and it is customary for teaching departments to recommend certain titles in this category. The library should not have to devote a part of its funds to provide multiple copies of what students could be expected to own, but should hold only one or very limited number of reference copies. Unfortunately there is evidence that student ownership of essential books is not as extensive as it should be. Bearing in mind that over the country as a whole well over the three million pounds a year involved in these book allowances, some means of ensuring that the money is properly spent is desirable. But this a problem that falls outside library administration.

Assuming that within the overall library budget a certain amount of duplication of much needed texts is possible, scaled according to their importance in teaching programmes, their individual cost, the number of students requiring them and so on, the next question concerns the disposition of the available copies. The total number of copies of a work may be placed, some in the central library and some in one or more departmental libraries. And a further question arises as to whether all should be available for loan, all for reference only, some in each category (and if the last, how many in each category) and whether,and if so for what periods, heavily used books should be temporarily confined or made available on half-day or overnight loan only. These are not trivial questions, since an adequate provision and a proper availability of books required by students is a prerequisite of their efficient use as a necessary part of the teaching of the university.

However, the library must also provide material for the teacher as well as the taught, both for his teaching and for his research. The greater the provision of duplicate copies for students the greater the staff time that must be devoted to loan procedures and concomitant operations and the greater the proportion of shelf space that must be devoted to this material despite the fact that for most of the time it will be off the shelves.

At the same time, as the university becomes larger, as its library grows faster and its resources become richer, so is the student increasingly in danger of finding himself confronted by a bewildering array of research material mixed with his assigned reading. (From a different standpoint the research reader also finds this state of affairs frustrating.)

At a certain point in the growth of the library question must arise to what extent the differing and necessary functions of the library have come into mutual conflict. While the library system should be conceived as a unit providing a service at various levels for all members of university, it is nevertheless true that if the bustle of a rapid turnover in undergraduate reading interferes with the effective use of the library for research, and if the research collections confuse the new student and slow down the efficient use of the undergraduate material, the library service is weakened.

As has been provided in the United States, for example at Harvard and Michigan where considerable undergraduate collections are maintained, a separate undergraduate library can go a long way to solving a number of the existing problems of book provision for students. Its stock can be specially chosen for undergraduate use—standard works of reference, set books, recommended reading and background material. It can make special arrangements for the provision of multiple copies of the most needed books—the Undergraduate Library planned for Leeds, for example, will provide 40,000 volumes for use in the Library only, and a further 35,000 representing an average of 10 loanable copies of 3,500 most needed titles, with provision for the eventual doubling of this loan collection. It can make generous provision for seating representing a high percentage of student numbers (Leeds, with 7,000 students, plans to provide 1,200 seats in its undergraduate library in addition to the 1,200 already existing throughout the present library system), and plan the building around such a proportion of seats to books that would be inappropriate in a research library. It can arrange the books in such a way that the emphasis would be on ease and speed of use. Above all, it can provide a staff whose sole function is to provide a service based on the needs of undergraduates, able to answer to student inquiries and to give instruction in the use of literature and libraries. That the necessary books would available to the students in greater numbers and at greater speed, that the whole problem of supplying the students with assigned reading would be reduced enormously, cannot be disputed. What must be established at the same time is the potential educative force of such a library. In the disposition of related subject collections and in the character of the background reading, there are opportunities for the student to explore a broad range of literature and exploit more fully than before the literature resources in his and related fields.

There are of course dangers in creating an undergraduate library. It would be disastrous if students came to believe that such a collection, however carefully chosen, contained that need be known. Too rigid a separation of 'research' and 'undergraduate' material would create a false impression in the minds of students concerning their place in the university. That is why the central library staff would have on frequent occasions to direct inquiring students to the relevant sections of the main library. Indeed, with greater opportunities for a reader's advisory service a more intelligent and confident use of the library system as a whole might well be expected.

I have briefly indicated the problems of book provision for students, and suggested a possible solution which is in existence in the United States (and on an inadequate scale in some universities in this country), in preparation at the right level in Leeds and contemplated elsewhere. Whether such a radical solutien is adopted (and in small universities it may well be undesirable) the ends which it is indented to serve should be seen as aims in any university library system. These may be summed up as—*an adequate number of copies of all required books, appropriately disposed throughout the system, arranged in the clearest order on the shelves, in surroundings, conducive to study as well as to the easy accessibility of all books, provided by a staff equipped and prepared to give help on all problems concerning the literature, organising an efficient loan reference service.*

The success of such provision relies on its organisation and on the calibre of the staff involved in its operation. It should also be emphasised how essential is the advice of the teaching staff concerning the bookstock. Only with their co-operation, supplying early information and recommended reading whether for long term or short term use, supplying lists of the set texts and bibliographies, and generally advising the library on the appropriateness of its stock, can the aims outlined above be achieved. Unless those directly concerned in the instruction of undergraduate are prepared to participate in these ways in the task of book provision for their students, the work of the library is made considerably more difficult and the ability of the students to profit from their instruction is significantly lessened. Given the right physical conditions and a suitable staff provision, given the co-operation of the teaching staff, an adequate book service at least, and, at best, a significantly different teaching instrument will be realised.

This should be the end of the discussion; however, it is all too true that little progress can be made along these lines while financial support for university libraries in this country remains at the present level. The money provided is seriously inadequate, both for research provision and for any attempt to meet the needs of undergraduates by a satisfactory duplication of heavily used material. A radical change in attitude is required towards undergraduate provision. To talk of generous duplication as extravagant is to be penny wise and pound foolish. The provision of books for teaching is too important to remain at a low of level priority in the university budget.

* * * * *

Since this paper was written a highly important report, containing recommendations of direct relevance to matters under discussion here, has been published. This is the 'Parry Report' or to give it its full title, *Report of the Committee on Libraries of the University Grants Committee* (London: H.M.S.O., May 1967). The most important recommendation concerning undergraduate provision are that additional funds of the order of £3 per student should be made available each year to university libraries for the provision of multiple copies of material in frequent demand, and that a voucher system with adequate safeguards should be introduced to ensure that students' individual book grants are properly spent. The report also emphasises the need for co-operation on the part of teaching staff to give the guidance to students on what books they should buy and to the library on prescribed textbooks and books of reference. It is to be hoped that the UGC and the Government will accept the evidence of the Parry Report that financial support for library provision for undergraduates as well as for university libraries in general has long been, and remains, inadequate to meet the considerable needs which exist.

Further reading

University Grants Committee. *Report of the Committee on Libraries.* London: H.M.S.O., 1967 (especially pp. 39-49 and appendices 5, 6 and 7).

BOWYER, T.H. 'Considerations on Book Provision for Undergraduates in British University Libraries'. *Journal of Documentation.* 1963,19, 151-167.

Library Provision for undergraduates: 'In England (B.S PAGE); 'In the United States' (STEPHAN A. MCCARTHY). *College and Research Libraries.* 1965,26, 219-224.

11
THE USE OF UNIVERSITY VACATIONS

Introduction

The problem of inadequate use of the vacations has been brought sharply into focus in recent years. There is no evidence to show that present day students use their vacations any less profitably than their predecessors did, but an increased public awareness of universities in general and the cost to the taxpayer in particular has produced a critical climate of opinion. The problem is the twin of another—that of inadequate use of university accommodation and capital equipment. Both problem are seen by the public under the single head of sub-optimal return on capital investment, whether it be in student grants on the one hand or university grants on the other. With a conjunction of the problems, it is tempting to apply single solution—a shortening of the vacations.

The Hale Committee on University Teaching Methods in its interim report *The Use of University Vacations* (May 1963) whilst deploring the inadequacy of their use, stressed that vacations should not be used for an extension of formal teaching. The Committee's view stemmed from their basic premise that the main function of university education was for students to be taught to work on their own; to consolidate and expand the framework provided in the formal during term.

Some comments with particular reference to science-based subjects

There is no doubt that in science-based courses the load of formal teaching is a heavy one, frequently amounting to more than 20 hours per week and in some cases reaching a figure as high as 27 hours per week and, in some cases, reaching a figure as high as 27 hours per week. With the rapid expansion of scientific knowledge the problem of compression of an adequate course into three years become more and more difficult. Many subjects too, place a heavy reliance on a competence in other subject so that the curriculum becomes highly congested. Coupled with these problems is the necessity of including sufficient time for teaching fundamental manipulative and experimental techniques through practical classes. Even when formal teaching is over, the science or applied science student is faced with working out results of experiments and acquiring practice in manipulative (usually mathematical) techniques relevant to his subject. With these demands on his time there is little left over during term for building upon the framework of theoretical knowledge gained through lectures, and, for some at least, little energy to undertake this after long periods in the laboratory.

Thus, for the science and applied science student there is a particular need to use the vacations for becoming thoroughly acquainted with the basic lecture material and to expand this by reading. This is all the more important in that most science and applied science courses are progressive, the work of one term leading on to that of the next, that of one year to the following. The use of vacations for a thorough consolidation of previous work is essential to the pattern of teaching. It is likely that the majority of students use at least some of the Christmas vacation in this way and the advent of examinations is probably a sufficient incentive to ensure that the Easter vacation is used to some advantage. On the other hand, summer examinations have the effect of a psychological fullstop to the work of the session. The die has been cast, the results of the examinations are not going to be affected by work done in the vacation and any test in October would be an anticlimax to the May-June examinations. Thus the May-June examinations have the effect of a disincentive to work in the long vacation.

The examinations also act as a disincentive in another way through their relationship with the teaching programme. The tremendously accelerating rate of expansion of scientific and technological subjects has had very serious effects upon the teaching and examining system. Lecturers have to be highly selective in choosing their material; of necessity, their main stress is upon fundamental ideas and current theories take pride of place over disproved hypotheses. For their part, students are unlikely to produce new ideas and their main task is to become familiar with experimental facts and their interpretation, to acquire a facility in handling information and to become familiar with the theoretical and practical manipulative techniques of their subject. To venture outside the syllabus delineated by their lecture course is to enter a practically limitless field. Around the basic theory of their lecture course they can cull more illustrative material but this gains little credit in an examination over the correct presentation of fundamental ideas and an ability to manipulate data. A vicious circle is established—little credit makes hardly worthwhile to read and, if a large failure rate is to be avoided, lecturers are loath to examine outside the syllabus narrowly defined by their course.

It would be unfair to leave this particular aspect of the problem at this point. There are difficulties connected with reading in vacations which stem from the technical, specialised nature of the scientific literature. In many scientific subjects, the only readily available reading matter is the textbook. These are not only often expensive but, more fundamentally, the basic facts of science are facts, and it is only in rare instances at undergraduate level that there is more than one interpretation of the facts in terms of current theory. Thus it becomes apparently irrelevant to read more than one book on a particular topic (although, of course, it may be treated more fully in one book than another). There is frequently nothing between the restricted textbook treatment of a specialised topic and the extensive (and expensive) research monographs available only in specialist libraries. (This position is changing and a number of publishers are now bringing out series of monographs suitable for undergraduate use.) A similar situation prevails with review articles which are often published by learned societies; together with original papers in the scientific journals to which students, particularly in their later years, may be referred, they are to be found only in university libraries (and a few of the larger city libraries) and are usually restricted to reference purposes.

The factors outlined above operate against the use of vacations, and in a particular the long vacation, in a particular area of study—that concerned with the theoretical aspects of the course. Considering a university education primarily as an intellectual training, these may be held to be the most important aspects; yet in any scientific subject, training in practical techniques plays a significant and important role. In general, practical work require highly specialised facilities which are not available to students in vacation and, if they were to be made available, would require formal supervision.

In some subjects, however, certain aspects of practical work are best suited to organisation in the vacation. In the field sciences (botany, zoology, geology and geography) observations under natural conditions and collection of material for laboratory examination and analysis are essential techniques in the practice of the subject and field courses are organised in at least one vacation in each session. Although such courses are highly valuable and relevant they usually occupy a relatively small part of the span of the vacations.

The close association of the applied sciences with practical problems makes vacation employment a relevant activity in which the student can gain valuable experience of his subject in the wider sphere of industry. The adoption of this practice might be considered by other science departments but it is doubtful if relevant employment could be found for more than a small minority of students. It is also questionable whether more than a portion of the vacation should be used in this way; it should not detract from the student's obligation to broaden and deepen his knowledge and understanding of his subject by private study.

The 'success' of field courses and vacation employment in a relevant industry is due to a variety of factors of which the most important are the change of environment and activity on the one hand and the directed aspects of the work on the other. Field courses provide something of the nature of a working holiday in pleasant surroundings and in the sense that they are organised by the department with members of staff in charge, represent an extension of teaching, albeit on a less formal basis, into the vacation. Employment in industry again provides a change of environment and the student is under some authority and not left to his own resources.

Some suggestions

Undoubtedly, guidance plays an important part in helping students successfully to use the vacations; not knowing where to start or how to organise the work is a hurdle of magnitude. The Hale Committee recognised this and recommended that all students should be interviewed before a vacation and given advice on how they should spend it on academic work. By themselves, however, such necessarily brief interviews are not enough.

Reference has already been made to the Hale Committee's basic premise that students should be taught to work on their own. Effective use of the vacations is dependent on a student's ability to work independently and the earlier this facility is acquired the more vacations will be used both quantitatively and qualitatively. The majority of students today enter university with little idea how to organise their studies and the first year in university is a critical one. Unfortunately, this is the year of large classes and the year when least personal attention is given to a student's needs. From this point of view, the way in which tutorials schemes usually operate is the wrong way round. Preference is given to students in the later years of a course, but by this time the student has been either made by his own efforts or broken. The good student has taught himself how to organise his studies and probably made effective use of vacations; the majority, however, have lapsed into sloppy habits of study which by now are difficult to correct and in any case, a large proportion of the vacations have slipped by unused. A well organised tutorial scheme in the first year the main object of which would be to teach students how to study, is a prime necessity. If the foundations are laid correctly, the later periods of a student's university career, term time and vacations, would be far more effectively used.

Evidence presented to the Hale Committee pointed quite definitely to a greater use of vacations if they were followed by an examination. Although the Committee did not go as far as to recommend that such examinations should be instituted as a stimulus to vacation work, they did suggest that follow-up interviews should take place after the long vacation to question students upon the use which has been made of it. It has been argued above that a test in October would be an anticlimax to the May-June examinations; with a pass in the latter already allowing progression to the following year of the course, it would be difficult to use October examinations in any punitive sense. Although interviews as suggested by the Hale Committee may be useful to some extent, their effect is likely to be strictly limited without some reinforcement during the vacation. For student to be in constant touch with their tutors during the vacation is impracticable yet if they are to be taught to organise their work, they need to be able to plan their use of vacations and to be able to see how closely they are following the programme. In this connection it would probably be helpful if students were to keep a diary of the academic work done in the vacation. This would enable them to see how they are spending (or wasting) their time and, produced at the interview after the vacation might be checked and criticised by their tutor.

Guidance from a tutor needs to be individually directed in the light of a student's performance during the year. It could be more useful if use could be made of information gained through any examination taken; the student's attention could be directed to weak areas in his knowledge revealed therein. Unfortunately, there is a tradition of great secretiveness about the detailed results of examinations and whilst this is justified in the case of finals, the design and use of intermediate examinations is worth re-evaluation. At present they represent a hurdle between the end of one session and progression into the next; they provide little information to the student (or to his tutors) on where remedial action can be taken in the vacation following.

The adverse effect of the examinations at the end of the session has already been noted, and a change in the timing of examinations may have several advantages. The beginning of the summer term seems to be an ideal time from many points of view for all but finals. Students would enter them immediately after the Easter vacation which they would thereby be encouraged to use for revision—thus the traditional period free of lectures would be saved. Sufficient time would be available after the examinations for detailed discussions with students to guide them in their long vacation studies. The period after the examination would also be available for lectures in which the work of the following session could be introduced. With this background, students could use the long vacation in preparation for the subsequent session.

The device of moving intermediate examinations to the beginning of the summer term with a period of lectures following them serve to integrate the long vacation into a session instead of it acting as a hiatus between two sessions. Effective use of the vacations would be encouraged the more vacations are seen to be the integrated with the work of the year. From this point of the view, considerably more attention could be paid to the design of courses with the vacations consciously in mind. Material which can equally as well be read in adequate and readily available books as presented in lectures could be designated by the lecturer as required vacation reading which is both examinable and credit worthy.

It may seem to many of us unfortunate that today's students come far short of the ideal, that to them study is not to a worthwhile end in itself, that their interest in their subjects is sadly deficient and that they need the reward of good examination results (or the fear of worse ones) to make them work; but we must take our students as we find them and adjust our methods accordingly. Only in this way will an awakened and critical public opinion be satisfied.

12
EXAMINATIONS AND MARKING

There is room for improvement and reform in respect of degree examinations at British universities. This paper deals only with suggested improvements in examining as it is now generally conducted and does not deal with radical changes which might well be considered. We begin by noting the alleged functions of examinations as readers may well ask at the outset why it is that students are examined at all.

Alleged functions of examinations

It is said that examinations perform some or all of the functions listed below:

(1) To prevent nepotism.

(2) To test if the student has acquired a certain amount of knowledge; also whether he understands and can relate the various aspects of the body of knowledge studied.

(3) To maintain academic standards.

(4) To prognosticate in the sense that G.C.E. 'A' level examination results are regarded as evidence of suitability for entrance to a university course (although they were not originally intended so to be), and the class of university degree is looked upon as an indication of competence in a chosen occupation.

(5) To test qualities such as intelligence, industriousness, perseverance, stability of temperament, docility to discipline, calmness under stress, etc.

(6) To provide an incentive for students and the teaching staff.

(7) To check on the understanding of students, so enabling the teacher to improve the effectiveness of his methods.

(8) To provide a means of social engineering in that examinations appear just, but can nevertheless regulate the flow of entrants into educational courses and occupations.

Criticisms of examinations

Yet in spite of the alleged usefulness of traditional examinations, numerous criticisms have been made of them. These are now given under a number of points:

(1) Examinations tend to dominate and distort the curriculum and syllabus. There is more truth in this at school than at university since for the most part degree examinations are internal to the university.

(2) They stimulate unhealthy competition. This again is more often seen in schools than in universities, but in the writer's view they certainly stimulate competition in the latter institutions.

(3) Wrong values are fostered; emotional maturity and personal integrity are as valuable as intellectual functions. There is some truth in this. But a corpus of knowledge has to be handed on and, more important, thinking skills have to be fostered.

(4) Some candidates do not do themselves justice. This may be true of some candidates but the proportion is not known.

(5) Examinations encourage cramming. This is not a criticism of examinations but rather of the method of preparing for them.

(6) They do not measure present achievement or predict future performance very accurately.

There is considerable substance in the sixth criticism and there are a number of reasons for this. Some of these are given below:

(a) The motivation of students changes with time, and perhaps new abilities emerge or old ones decline.

(b) Performance in an examination depends to some extent on the degree to which likely questions can be spotted and prepared for.

(c) The inadequate reliability of traditional examinations.

This is a serious matter for it means that the score obtained by a candidate is not stable from one occasion to another.

In respect of (c) the following facts have long been established. If one examiner sets and marks two examinations in the same subject, candidates can get very different marks on the two occasions; and the marks obtained by individual students can show wide discrepancies when a single set of examination scripts are marked by two examiners. The main causes of this poor reliability are also known:

(i) There are day to day changes in the examinees' physical and mental states which affect their performance. This effect is usually small unless the time lag is large.

(ii) An inadequate sampling of the candidates' knowledge. The longer the examination and the greater the number of questions to be answered the more reliable will be the score. After say, 27 hours of examination work, marks would be unlikely to alter to any extent if the candidates sat a further 3-hour paper. But one usually needs at least four 2-hour papers for the reliability coefficient to reach 0.90 although it does depend to some extent upon the range of ability of the candidates.

(iii) Inconsistencies in standards of marking adopted by different examiners. If a mark of, say, 75% (or a first class or a credit) means the mark obtained by a quarter of the candidates in one department or university, and the mark obtained by a twentieth of the candidates in another department or university, then the same mark means different things to different examiners or the quality of the candidates varies very greatly.

(iv) The different opinion among examiners about the relative value of the students' answers. This is the most important source of unreliability. An early and classic study in the field which brings out possible snags in this connection was that of Hartog and Rhodes[2]. Typical scripts were marked by experienced examiners in the special place, School Certificate and university honours examinations, and different subjects were investigated. Generalising from the results one may say that when six examiners independently marked a set of scripts the lowest and highest marks awarded to any one script differed, on the average, by some 10 to 12%. When the examiners had drawn up an agreed marking scheme the inconsistencies were less than when they had not. It is, however, true that the marks referred, in the main, to single 3-hour or 2-hour papers, and in some instance the candidates were somewhat homogeneous in respect of ability. Nevertheless the study must be considered seriously for it clearly indicates that less thorough examinations can be very unreliable. In a well conducted examination there will, in Vernon's view be a median disagreement between any two examiners of about 3%, although the scripts of a few examiners will show discrepancies four or five times as large. So unless the examination is carefully conducted, and average and range of marks are standardized, there can be considerable differences in the proportion of honours, credits etc., which are awarded.

The reason for the differences in opinion among examiners regarding the value of answers results from the fact that different examiners look for different things. For example they may value comprehensive knowledge of facts; grasp of general principles ; originality of ideas regardless of expression; clarity of expression candidate support the set ideas of the examiner. Even in, say, mathematics the weightings which can be given to various analysable features, and the penalties, can vary between examiners.

It should, however, be noted that whereas a highly reliable examination may or may not have high validity (in that it measures what it is supposed to measure), an examination of low reliability must have low validity.

Objective-type examinations

To get round some of the difficulties in using traditional or essay - type questions use can be made of objective type examinations. These have been used to measure achievements in the U.S.A. for many years, but only in recent years has any use of them been made in this country in spite of Ballard's advocacy of them in 1923. The essential features of this type of question is that there is only one correct answer to each question or subsection of each question. Examples of questions in objective - type examinations taken from university examination papers in chemistry can be found in Education in Chemistry can be found in Education in Chemistry 2, (6), November 1965, pp. 284-286.

Advantages of objective -type examinations

The advantages of objective-type examinations are listed below.

(1) Marking is objective and takes little time. Papers can be scored by machine.

(2) A thorough coverage can be made of the syllabus since large numbers of questions can be set and 100 or more per hour may be

answered. This wide sampling of the candidate's knowledge makes for high reliability.

(3) Candidates spend their time thinking and not writing.

(4) If the question cover all levels of difficulty evenly then the mark distribution will approximate to a normal one and it can easily be converted to any other scale.

Disadvantages of objective-type examinations

But there are also objections to this type of examination and these are now stated.

(1) Setting the paper is a skilled job and needs considerable experience. If the test is badly constructed it will not bring out the capacity to interpret or apply principles. A well constructed test can do this.

(2) The examination papers take a long time to set. Moreover, the examiner's opinion as to what is to be examined in detail enters into the setting of the questions. In this sense they are subjective.

(3) A considerable amount of reading is required from the candidate.

(4) Unless care is taken they can be somewhat artificial in their phrasing.

(5) Certain irrelevant factors such as the examinee's previous acquaintance with this type of test affects performance. Thus experience in manipulating one's knowledge to the requirement of the medium is an advantage.

(6) No account is taken of candidate's capacity for lucidity of expression . If this to be examined separate papers can be set for this purpose.

Comment on objective -type examinations

There has been opposition to this type of examination in Britain in the past although the Schools Council is now trying hard to get teachers familiar with its use for the purpose of Certificate Of Secondary Education.

This opposition has been based on a number of uninformed criticism such as : an objective-type examination must be easier than an essay-type examination; the objective-type examination involves only a test of memory and so ability to think coherently and present evidence clearly is not tested ; and the objective-type examination has an undesirable effect upon study. These criticism are true of poorly constructed tests.

It should be noted that British candidate must have skill in the written medium and in writing answers in a way examiners want. British and European candidates do well in traditional essay-type examinations if they can express themselves on paper; their American counterparts do well in objective-type tests if they are sophisticated in them. But it is wrong to assume that the objective examination is necessarily a more satisfactory instrument. It may be a more convenient method of examining with large groups and it may be highly reliable. The reason that some objective tests are better than some traditional ones is that the latter are often set in an unsystematic manner and subject chancy moderation by a second examiner. An objective-type examination must be well designed or it will be a less satisfactory tool than a conventional paper drawn up by an experienced panel and marked on a systematic schedule. Both kinds of examination can be used with profit in order to improve the efficiency of the examination system.

Some suggestions for improving examinations

As was said at the outset there is, without doubt, a case for a radical revision of the present degree examination system. However, this paper deals only with improvements which might be made within the present broad framework of examining. One suggestion is that examiners might try to formulate more clearly what it is they are trying to measure. This necessitates a clear view of the objectives to which the education of the student should be directed. One taxonomy of educational objectives has been put forward by Bloom[3] and is given below.

(1) Knowledge of specific facts, of terminologies, of conventions, of trends, of classifications and categories, of criteria, of methodology, of principles and generalisations, of theories and structures.

(2) Comprehension of presented material including its translation into a more meaningful form, together with its interpretation and extrapolation.

(3) Application of the principles of the physical and social sciences to concrete problems.

(4) Analysis of the elements of the presented material, together with the recognition of their relations and organisation.

(5) Synthesis of the elements of the elements and parts to form a whole so as to produce a new communication as for example in the case of an essay, or a plan for an investigation.

(6) Evaluation in terms of either internal or external criteria.

To examine (5) an essay-type question is set, but all the other aims may be tested by means of objective-type questions. It is obvious that the intellectual skill involved in attaining these objectives overlap considerably.

An examiner need not rely on Bloom's list of objectives. He can, and should, draw up his own. But he should think of these objectives in terms of behaviour rather than in terms of vague mental qualities. For example he should ask himself such questions as: what should the student be able to do in each field of study? What are the exact elements in our teaching which are supposed to confer on the students these capacities? However, a small group of examiners functions more effectively than an individual since members of the group can criticise each other.

When the examiners have decided on the skills that are to be measured, they must decide on the kind of examination appropriate to measure each; e.g. essay-type, objective-type, a mixture of both, or a practical examination. They must also take into consideration the number of students to be examiners are particularly interested in such qualities as literary style, imagination, the examinees own thinking on the subject, etc., as in this case the amount and accuracy of the information given by the student will not, in themselves, procure high marks.

If only essay-type questions are to be used, examiners should ask themselves which parts of the field of study are most important. It is better to avoid setting questions on the less essential parts of the field and also to avoid overlapping among questions. Moreover, the most reliable essay-type questions are those that pose a definite problem and give the candidate scope for marshalling and organising his material. The rather vague open type of question may give the candidates greater freedom in respect of the ground they cover and in their approach, but it makes comparisons between them very difficult. Most university and college teachers can, as a result of talking with their students, seeing their course work, and through previous experience of examining, foresee the kinds of answers they will get. In these circumstances questions are likely to be free from ambiguities, at about the right level of difficulty, worded so that different candidates can be compared and marked consistently, while at the same time they will further the abilities and knowledge the examiner is attempting to assess.

Marking

Marking is the process whereby a differentiation is made between the various levels of performance among the various scripts before the examiner. It is done by awarding qualitative or numerical grades or by placing the scripts in rank order. After the marking has been carried out and not before, value judgements can be made regarding whether the scripts are 'good' or 'bad' or whether they should 'pass' or 'fail'.

A detailed marking scheme should be drawn up for essay-type question when the answers are largely factual in nature. If more general qualities said to be brought out by the essay are being assessed then the quality scale method can be used. The examiner should continually check that he is marking the scripts in terms of the criteria he set himself beforehand.

A number of methods of marking are available and four are now listed

(1) *Enumeration or count scoring.* This can only be used when each piece of information or fact for which a mark is awarded can be assessed as correct or incorrect quite independently of the examiner's opinion. Objective-type tests can be marked in this way.

(2) *Ranking.* Ranking means listing a group of students in order of performance, i.e. 1st, 2nd, etc., down to the bottom. The method can be used with any forms of academic work including, of course, essay-

type examinations not amenable to count scoring. There are, however, difficulties in using ranking. For example, it can be used only with small groups, for even in a group of 20 ranking uncertain near the middle of the list; the frequency distribution is rectangular and the ranks can be converted into a normally distributed set of scores; further, the significance of a rank is relative to the set of persons who have been ranked, so that, say, 20th out of 22 is poorer than 20th out of 40.

(3) *Qualitative grading.* In this method the examination scripts, or the answers to individual questions are classified into, say, five grades, A, B, C, D, E, or a seven or ten grade system. This gives a relative standard based on the performance of average groups of students rather than on supposedly absolute standards, but studies have shown that variability between examiners is sometimes reduced using this method. Once again is a form of ranking a grave defect is that one script is not usually compared directly with the scripts of other students before the grading is made; as the experience of what one examiner considers to be A differs from the experience of another their standards will continue to vary; and grading is relative to the group of students examined. Even if one grades on a 'normal curve' so that a grade of A is that obtained by the top 7 per cent, grade B by the next 23 per cent., the grading is still relative to the group of students.

Table 1

	Low				Average			High	
Stanine scores	1	2	3	4	5	6	7	8	9
True proportions	4%	7%	12%	17%	20%	17%	12%	7%	4%
Rounded proportions	4%	8%	12%	16%	20%	16%	12%	8%	4%
Relative numbers	1	2	3	4	5	4	3	2	1

If there are a large number of candidates, say 50 or more, it is convenient to use a scale of 9 points or grades ('stanine' scores—a contraction of standard nine) in which each point covers half a standard deviation. When the distribution of performance is 'normal' each stanine includes the percentage of scores as shown in Table 1 on previous page.

Thus the examiner should read 50 papers, selected at random, and sort into three piles; roughly the top quarter, the middle half and the bottom quarter (say 12, 26, 12,). From the bottom quarter of 12 the two worst scripts are sèlected, the four scripts next in quality, and the best six. This process is continued those in the piles, but the examiner must frequently check (say, after each 25 scripts) to make sure he is not straying too far from the intended proportions. The grouping as though somewhat coarse is refined enough for many practical purposes.

(4) *Numerical evaluation or a mixture of numerical evaluation and count scoring*. In this, answers are given absolute numerical marks on a numerical scale or given a percentage mark. Such marks and percentages are alleged to relate the students' performance to the degree of mastery of what was set out to be learned; also to provide fixed standards of assessment. There are considerable difficulties in using this method. For example: the examiner has obtained his marking does remain relative; it is difficult to distinguish between 14/20 and 13/20 and impossible to distinguish 70/100 from 69/100; numerical evaluation and count scoring become mixed when one mark is given for each correct fact and a few marks for style or general merit; and it is not possible to say that 16/20 for an answer to a mathematics question is equivalent to the same mark for an essay-type answer, in say, history.

Comparing or combining mark distributions

Marks on different examination papers in the same subject sometimes need to be combined to give a total score; or marks in several subjects need to be compared; or it is necessary to know if marks awarded by several examiners are comparable when each examiner marks a proportion of the scripts. Marks can differ in their means, for example, when one examiner is more lenient than another or one paper more difficult than another; or, in their 'spread' or standard deviations as whin one examiner spreads out the marks more than another, or one subject or paper differentiates between the candidates more than another does; or in the shape of their distributions.

When the marks obtained by candidates on several papers have the same means and standard deviations, the marks may be added to give an overall mark, or the marks on the individual paper may be compared directly. Thus marks to individual questions can often be added directly to give a total mark for the paper since each question may be marked out of 20, yielding a mean of around 11 and a standard deviation of about 2. But if some questions are marked out of 20 and some out of 10, or the marks on one paper differ from that on another in respect of their means and standard deviations, certain action has to be taken before the marks may be added or compared directly. Likewise certain procedures have to be followed before the marks on paper A can be made to give double the weighting of paper B. In these instances the position is somewhat complicated and interested readers should consult a psychometric text which deals with these issues, also a paper by Thyne[4].

REFERENCES

1. VERNON, P.E. *The Measurement of Abilities*. London: U.L.P., 1956.
2. HARTOG, P. and RHODES, E.C. *An Examination of Examinations*. London: Macmillan, 1935.
3. BLOOM B.S. (Ed.).A *Taxonomy of Educational Objectives. Handbook 1. Cognitive Domain*. New York: Longmans, Green, 1956.
4. THYNE, J.M. What is the weight of an examination paper?, *Brit. J. Educ. Psychl.* 1066, 36, 321-326.

Further reading

CRONBACH, L.J. *Essentials of Psychological Testing*. New York: Harper, 1960.

HUBBARD, J.P. and CLEMENS, W.V. *Multiple Choice Examinations in Medicine*. London: Kimpton, 1961.

JOYCE, C.R.B. 'The examination as an instrument in research in medical education.' *Educ. Research*, 1962, 5, 29-36.

13

PROFESSIONAL TRAINING FOR COLLEGE TEACHING

Were this chapter to be a discussion of schemes of training, now in operation, that had been devised to prepare teachers for colleges, it could not be written, for there are no such schemes. Many elementary and secondly teachers have undergone training for their life work, as investigators have, by a different regimen, of course, for theirs. But if college and university teachers do their work well, it is because they are born with competence for their calling, or were self-taught, or happened to grow into competence accidentally, as a by -product of training for other and partly alien ends, or learned to teach by teaching.

There are able college men, presidents and others, who view this situation with equanimity, if not with satisfaction. Teachers are born, not made, it is said. Can pedagogy furnish better teachers than specialized scholarly training? it is asked. If we train definitely for teaching, we shall diminish scholarship, cramp and warp native teaching faculty, and mechanize our class procedure, it is objected.

Had the subject of the training for college teaching been discussed, no doubt other objections would have been advanced. But it has not been discussed, as will be seen from the very scant bibliography at the end of the chapter. No plan of training for college teaching is in operation, and no discussion of such a plan can be found. Each of a half-dozen men has argued his individual views, and elicited no reply.

This state of facts notwithstanding, the subject is well worth discussing, and one may even venture to prophesy that in a decade, or at latest two, the subject will have a respectable literature, and enough training plans will be in operation to permit fruitful comparisons.

When specific training is first urged for specialized work, there always is opposition. The outgoing generation remembers the opposition to specialized training for law, medicine, and engineering, to say nothing for farming, school teaching and business. But in spite of obstructive and retarding objections, specialized types of training for specialized types of work have grown in number and favor, and today we are being shown convincingly that nations which have declined to set up the fundamental types of special training find themselves able to make effective only a fraction of their resources. The majority of the personnel in every higher calling has about average native aptitude for it, and it is just the average man who can be improved in competence for any work by training directed to that end rather than to another. This is, of course, true of college teaching.

In early days in this country the great majority of the college teachers were clergymen, trained in most cases aboard. Later bookish graduates came to be the chief source of supply, their appointment in their own colleges, and infrequently in others, following close upon their graduation. Well into the third quarter of last century college faculties were selected almost exclusively from these two types, representatives of the former decreasing and of the latter increasing in relative number. Neither type was specifically trained for teaching in college or elsewhere.

With the founding and developing of Johns Hopkins University a new era in higher education opened in this country. The paucity of exact scholarship came to be known, and the country's need of scholarship to be appreciated. In colleges grown from English seedlings we sought to implant graft from German universities. Independent colleges and colleges within universities, while still called upon by American traditions and needs to prepare their students for enlightened living by means of a broadening and liberating training, came to be manned preponderatingly by narrowly specialized investigators, withdrawn from everyday life, with concentrated interests focused upon subjects or parts of subjects, rather than upon students. Little thought was, or is yet, given to the preparation of college teachers for their duties as teachers and that little rested, and still in large measure rests, satisfied with the assumption that by some unexplained and it may be inexplicable transfer of competence a man closeted and intensively trained to search for truth in books and laboratories emerges after three or more years well equipped for divining and developing the mental processes and interests of freshmen.

Once fairly examined, this assumption lacks plausibility. "We consider the Ph.D. a scholar's degree and not a teacher's degree," says the dean of one of our leading graduate schools, and yet preparation for this scholar's degree has been and is practically the only formal preparation open to college teachers in this country.

It goes without saying that scholarship is one of the basal needs of college teachers, a scholarship that keeps alive, and is human and contagious. But it should be remembered that there are several kinds of scholarship, and it is pertinent to ask what kind college teachers need. Should they, for instance, model themselves on the broad shrewdness and alluring scholarly mellowness of James Russell Lowell or on the untiring encyclopedic exactitude and minuteness of Von Helmholz? Or is there an even better ideal or ideals *for them*? I would suggest that the teacher's knowledge of his subject should, essentially, be of a kind that would keep him in intellectual sympathy with the developed minds of his students, and this means chiefly two things. The more points of contact of his knowledge with the past experience and future plans of his students the teacher has at his command, the better teacher he will be; for he can use them, not as resting places, but as points of departure for the development of phases of his subject outside the student's experience. And secondly, the teacher should see his subject entire, with its parts as rich in number and detail as possible, each in its proper place within the whole. For the students' knowledge of the subject is vague and general; he is trying to place it, and many other new things, in some kind of a coherent setting; in fact, he is in college largely for the very propose of working out some sort of rudimentary scheme of things. The duty of the college teacher is to help him in this quite as much as to teach him a particular subject. And, besides, each particular subject can be best taught if advantage is taken of every opportunity to attach it to the only knowledge of it the student has, vague and general though it be. Highly specialized and dehumanized knowledge is not as useful for the college teacher as broad and vital knowledge, which is, of course, much harder to acquire. Even in the case of "disciplinary" subject, there is no gain in concealing the human bearings. The teacher should be trained to seize opportunity in the classroom and out to help the student, through his subject and his maturer life experience, to see the bearing of what he is learning on the life about him and on the life he is to lead. This is the college teacher's richest opportunity and the opportunity that tries him most shrewdly. If he to rise to it, his entire equipment, native and acquired, must come into play.

What else does the teacher need? So that he may select the best and continue to improve them, he needs a knowledge of the different methods and aims in the teaching of his subject, and so far as possible, of the results attained by each. Too much of college teaching is blind groping, chartless and without compass. Instead of expecting each inexperienced teacher to start afresh, he should set out armed with the epitomized and digested teaching experience of those that have gone before him.

Finally, the teacher needs a sympathetic and expert understanding of the thinking and feeling of college students. This should be his controlling interest. The teacher, his interest in his subjects, and in all else except the student, should be instrumental, not final. Every available strand of continuity between studenthood and teacherhood should thereafter be preserved.

This need suggest a capital weakness of the training for the doctorate in philosophy as a preparation for teaching. As it proceeds it shifts the interest from undergraduate student to scholarly speciality, and steadily snaps the ties that bound the budding investigator to his college days. It also explains the greatness of some college teachers and personalities before the eighties. Their degrees in arts were their licenses to teach. They suffered no drastic loss of touch with undergraduate thought and life. In the early years of their teaching this sympathetic and kindly understanding was fresh and strong, and they used it in their classroom and wove it into the tissue of their tutorial activities. A discerning observer of college faculties can even today discover in them men and women who entered them by the same door as these great ones of old, irregularly as we would say now,—without the hall mark, and whose good teaching is a surprise to their doctored colleagues. In one institution I know of, the best five teachers some years ago were all of this type. The training of college teachers might well, it therefore seems include an apprenticeship, beginning with, or in exceptional cases before, graduation from college.

But the duties and opportunities of the collage teacher do not stop at the door leading from his classroom. In addition to dealing directly with students, individually and in groups, and even, if possible, with their families, as he grows in service he becomes, as faculty member and committeeman, a college legislator and administrator. In exercising these important functions he needs the equipment that would aid him to take the central point of view, a background of scholarly knowledge of what education in general and college education in particular are in their methods and in their social functions and purposes. There is too much departmental logrolling as well as too much beating of the air in faculty meetings, and too many excursions into the blue in faculty legislation and administration arrangements. The educational views of faculty members greatly need to be steadied, ordered, and appreciably broadened and deepened by a developed and trained habit of thinking educationally under the safeguards scientific method and on the basis of an adequate supply of facts. That pedagogy has made but the smallest beginning of gathering and ordering such facts and developing a scientific method in this field is not a valid objection. These tasks are no more difficult than others that have been compared, as they will be, the sooner for being imposed.

It is significant that coincident with sharp and widespread criticism of the American college (justified in part by what college teachers have been made into by their training), appear demands on the part of faculties for more power. In this connection it may be remembered that autocracy is the simplest and easiest form of government, and that history shows that it can at least be made to work with less brains and training than are required for the working of democracy. As American colleges and universities have grown in complexity and responsibility, their faculties have lost power because they did not acquire the larger competence that was the indispensable condition of even reasonably successful democratic control. It is highly desirable that the power of the faculties should increase to the point of preponderance. But the added power they will probably acquire will not retained unless faculty members learn their business much better than they now know it in most institutions. Thomas Jefferson, when asked come which would come to dominate, the states or the federal government, replied that in the long run each of the opposed pair would prevail in the functions in which it proved the more competent.

To outline a scheme of such importance without any experience to examine as a basis is a very bold undertaking, and one that examine as a basis is a very bold undertąking, and one that can hope for but partial success. What I shall propose, however, is similar to the proposals of Pitkin (5), Horne (11), and Wolfe (14), my only predecessor in this rash enterprise. The general spirit and purpose of our proposals are the same. But we disagree more or less in details—which is fortunate, as it may encourage discussion of the subject, which is the thing most needed. Indeed, a lively sense of this need has led me to venture some unpopular assertions. It may also be admitted that the desiderata for teachers mentioned above are not likely to be all insured by any system of training.

The proposal submitted for discussion is that three year graduate course be established, its spirit and purpose being to train young men to become *college* teachers. This course should lead a doctorate; e.g., to the degree of Doctor of Philosophy in Teaching, or of Decendi Doctor. What degree is selected is, in the long run, relatively unimportant, provided the course is soundly conducive to its end.

The course might well be divided into three parts, having the approximate relative, value in time and effort of two fifths, two fifths and one fifth. These parts should proceed simultaneously throughout the three years the first being an apprenticeship—under supervision, of course—i in the functions of the college teacher, the second a broad course of study and investigation of the subject to be taught, and the third a course of pedagogical study and investigation. Let me suggest a minimum of detail with in these outline.

The apprentice teacher would, naturally, do the least classroom teaching during his first year, and the most during his last. He would also each year "advise " a group of freshman in studies and in life, or cooperate with students in the conduct of athletics, dramatics, publication work, or other "activities" On all this apprentice work he would report, and in all he would be guided and supervised appropriately by the department whose subject he was teaching, by the department of education, and by other departments concerned. This and other parts of the training would attract others in addition to narrowly bookish graduates, something much to be desired (other parts would eliminate those not bookish enough), and would tend to keep alive in all apprentices an interest in students, especially in student character, and to prevent them from thinking of student as disembodies minds.

The course of study and investigation in the subject to be taught should be based on adequate undergraduate work in the same and allied fields, and should be something like the honor course in Oxford or Cambridge (or our *old* M.A. course) in its conduct and purpose; it should hark back to our collegiate origin in England. The work should be in charge of a don, a widely and wisely read and a very human guide, philosopher, and friend. Stated class meetings and precise count of hours of attendance should receive little emphasis. But wide reading of the subject, in spirit that breeds contagion, running off into a study, in books, laboratories, and meetings, of the human and practical bearings of the subject, should be required and enough conference with the don should be had to enable him to judge and criticize the student's plan and amount of work, to test his mettle in handling the subject, and to aid him to grasp it as a whole and in its chief subdivisions, and to get glimpses of its bearings on and place in human life. This part of the training should lead up to and culminate in a thesis dealing with some major phase of the subject comprehendingly in its setting and connection. Naturally this program could be carried out most successfully with the social subjects, which lend themselves easily to culture, like history or philosophy, and less completely with the exact subjects, which are better fitted for precise discipline, like mathematics. But if treated, as far as possible, after the manner indicated, even the latter could be made better instruments for the training of college teachers than they are now in narrow specialization for the Ph. D degree. Among returning Rhodes scholars some excellent material for dons could be found.

The fifth of the course directed to pedagogy should include a very brief study of the methods of teaching the chosen subject, with glimpses into teaching methods in general; and courses in the history and philosophy of education, with emphasis on, but by no means exclusive dealing with, the educational and social functions of the college. It might include an intensive investigation of some relatively simple college problem in preparation for future faculty membership. All this should, of course, be intimately articulated with the student's apprenticeship work. Such a course of pedagogical study should furnish a basis for better teaching methods and for helpful self-criticism therein; should encourage the formation of the habit of thinking and working out educational problems scientifically with eyes open to the purpose of the college as a whole; and should discourage departmental selfishness in legislation and administration.

The college would, under this plan, have some of its teaching done at minimum cost by student teachers, who should receive only the graduate scholarship or fellowship now customary for Ph.D. candidates. Care would be necessary to prevent the assignment to them of mere routine hackwork without training value. It is safe to say that though slightly less mature, their services, being supervised would be more valuable than those rendered during their first few years of teaching by most better-paid winners of the doctorate of philosophy, who, if they do so at all, grope their way to usefulness as teachers, with little aid from others more experienced.

With good teaching prepared for, required, and adequately rewarded (a point to be developed later) somewhat longer schedules could properly be assigned and further economy effected. Schedules would, of course, have to be kept short enough to allow ample time for reading, for some writing and for faculty and committee work in later years. But time would not be required by *college* teachers for specialized research, and the freedom from such tasks resulting for them would be a blessed relief to many who are now compelled to assume a virtue they have not, and to conceal the love of teaching they have. And when we bear in mind the heavy mass of uninspired and unimportant hackwork that is now dumped on the scholarly world, we shall welcome the prospect of a lightened burden for ourselves.

The need of students, especially of freshmen, for advisers is widely recognized. They come into a new freedom exercised in a new environment. This makes for bewilderment that involves loss of precious time and opportunities, and present perils which involve possible injuries to many and certain injuries to some. Efforts, many and various to constitute a body of advisers chosen from among faculty members have met with but little success. With few exceptions the task is not congenial to those who now man our faculties, and for that and other reasons they are ill fitted for it. But a greater measure of success has been attained, even under present conditions, when the cooperation of volunteers from among seniors and graduate students has been had. This suggests that the problem to be placed upon the services of apprentices. Such service would be a part of their regular work having a bearing on their future career, and would therefore be supervised and rest on sustained interest and the consciousness that it was counting.

Finally, young student teachers would, under proper encouragement and arrangement, help materially to bridge the gulf, that is broader than is wholesome, between a faculty of mature men and young students. The mixing of these different generations, so far as possible, is much to be desired, difficult as it is to accomplish.

This is not the place to discuss the details of appointment and promotion plans, interesting and important as they are. But it is evident that the scheme of training outlined, if adopted, would call for changes in present practices.

The appointing authorities of colleges looking for young teachers could ascertain their strong and weak points as they developed during their apprenticeship in classrooms and in other educational activities, as well as the quality and trend of their scholarship. They would not rest satisfied with ascertaining the minute corner of the field of philosophy, history, or physics in which a man recommended had done research. Records could be kept throwing much-needed light on the teaching ability, scholarship and personality of candidates for appointment. In selecting *college* teachers, appointing authorities would value this evidence and would come to prefer teaching power to investigating ability.

Moreover, the record keeping, and, no doubt, some of the supervision begun during the apprentice years would continue during the early instructorial years. This would render it possible to evaluate and to value effectiveness in teaching in making promotions. Ambitious teachers would no longer be practically forced, as their only resort, to neglect their students and give their best energies to publication in order to make a name and get a call, in the interest of promotion. The expert teacher would have a chance and a dignity equal to that of the skilled investigator. The individual could follow, and not be penalized for so doing, his own bent and the line of his highest capacity.

The training now given in graduate schools here and elsewhere for the doctorate in philosophy will, of course continue, and increase rather than diminish. Investigators will be preferred in research, in universities, and in some college and college departments. They will be increasingly prized in the government service and in important branches of industry. The recent terrible experiences burn into our minds the imperative need strong nations have of exact knowledge and of skill that has a scientific edge. And the specific training for these great tasks will be stronger when it is based on a college course in which highly effective and whole-hearted teaching is valued and rewarded.